A *citizen* of the world speaks his mind...

Free Speech
and
Plain Language

BY

ALBERT J. NOCK

Many discriminating readers are aware of the fact that Albert Jay Nock is one of the really great thinkers of our time. His logic is strict, his writing is pungent, his philosophy sound.

Now in *Free Speech and Plain Language* he has achieved a seven-years' garner of his best work, a significant volume from one of the few living masters of classic American prose.

There is a unity to these pages, every one of which holds the savor of fine conversation with a shrewd, humorous and free intelligence: a man of good will. Stimulating, urbane, the discussion ranges from Rooseveltism, henpecking and Utopias (new and old) on through an appraisal of the value of useless knowledge to a past-master's thoughts on the limitations of prophecy.

There is also the striking idea that women can civilize society and men cannot, set forth in "A Word to Women," and a theory about promiscuity that will engage both men and women in "Women and the Marriage Market."

We are happy to suggest that the thoughtful reader will relish Mr. Nock's ideas and will cherish this volume of his essays which are destined to find a permanent place in our literature.

FREE SPEECH
AND PLAIN LANGUAGE

BY MR. NOCK

ALBERT JAY NOCK

Free Speech
and
Plain
Language

WILLIAM MORROW & COMPANY

NEW YORK   MCMXXXVII

FREE SPEECH AND PLAIN LANGUAGE

COPYRIGHT · 1937
BY ALBERT JAY NOCK

first edition

PRINTED IN THE UNITED STATES
BY QUINN & BODEN COMPANY, INC., RAHWAY, N. J.

To my friend of many years,

R. R.

These essays are republished by the kind permission of the editors of the *Atlantic Monthly* and *Harper's Magazine*. They contain a reference or two to circumstances which no longer exist—to the regime of Prohibition, for instance—but I have let these stand. The date appended to each essay will show that such circumstances did exist at the time of the essay's composition.

Albert Jay Nock.

CONTENTS

FREE SPEECH
AND PLAIN LANGUAGE

1

A Word to Women

A LONG time ago—all of three years, perhaps longer —I saw a floating item in a periodical to the effect that forty-one per cent of our national wealth is controlled by women, and that the percentage is rising. Curiously, this bit of news did not make much of an impression on me at the time, but the recollection of it kept coming back to me afterward, and more frequently as time went on. After being pestered in this way for three years or more, I bethought myself of an acquaintance who has facilities for looking up data on such matters, and asked him to get chapter and verse for me, which he very kindly did.

It appears that a firm of investment bankers operating in Chicago and New York had made an investigation into the division of our national wealth between the sexes. They did this purely in the way of business, of course, to determine the amount of stress that could profitably be laid on female clientage. The general conclusion was that at the time the survey was made, say four years ago, nearly half our national wealth was controlled by women, and that the proportion was tending to increase steadily and rather rapidly.

Some of the incidental findings turned up by the investigation are interesting. It found that ninety-five billion dollars' worth of life-insurance policies were in force in this country, and that eighty per cent of their beneficiaries were women. This alone would considerably help along the rising proportion of female control unless there were somewhere some offset which the survey did not show. An even more interesting finding is that by wills probated in New York City, over a given period, fifty estates out of seventy were left by men to women, and forty-four out of sixty-nine were left by women to women. It found that women were taxed on three and a quarter billion dollars of income annually; men, on four and three quarters. One hundred and thirty-nine women paid taxes on incomes in excess of a half million, as against one hundred and twenty-three men; while forty-four women paid on net incomes in excess of a million, as against forty-two men. Women were found to be majority or almost majority shareholders in some of our largest corporations, for instance the Pennsylvania Railway, American Telephone and Telegraph, United States Steel, Westinghouse Air Brake and National Biscuit Company.

It should be remembered, too, that American women have a good deal more purchasing-power than this survey shows, because many of those who legally own nothing are on fairly liberal allowances from male members of their families, and many more are wage-earners who spend their wages as they please. Women's collective virtual control is thus considerably larger than their legal ownership indicates. This surplus of petty wage-earning and of what might be called delegated control is not a matter of interest to investment bankers, so the survey did not attempt to take account of it; yet its aggregate must be quite large. There seems little ground for doubt that, taking virtual control with legal control, our women now have more purchasing-power than our men have. Four years ago they were within nine per cent of equality in legal control, and quite rapidly on the rise; and surely the amount of delegated control which they exercise, plus their wage-earnings, would be enough to carry the sum of their purchasing-power well over the mark of fifty per cent.

II

In Europe one notices a general prevalence of the notion that our country is a paradise for womankind. Europeans think we operate our institutions greatly to the advantage of the female sex. Some years ago a highly placed English dignitary—I think it was the present Dean of St. Paul's—spoke of the United States as "an ice-water-drinking gynecocracy." The popular idea on the Continent appears to be that our women do as they please without let or hindrance, and that they have reduced our men to the Levitical status of hewers of wood and drawers of water, if not to that of mere skulkers upon the face of the earth. Continental women—those, at least, with whom I am acquainted—indulge this notion with interested curiosity, in which one sometimes discerns a touch of envy. A more conservative opinion is that, while our women have managed to gain an unshakable ascendancy, they have also managed to establish a roughly satisfactory relation of live-and-let-live with their male entourage, mostly by way of concession, which is not as

a rule too onerous and not perhaps utterly degrading;
a relation, however, which, with all the good will in the
world, a male European would find hard and repugnant.

The wonderment is, how the American woman has
done it. This more than anything, I think, is what has
always made our women an object of special interest to
the European mind. I never saw anything to make me
suspect that Europeans of either sex like our womenfolk or admire them especially or even much respect
them, but they have always showed great curiosity about
them, somewhat like our curiosity about the habits of
the sea-bear or the peculiarities of the lemming, or the
traits in other creatures whose main interest for us is
that they keep us wondering how they accomplish what
they do, and do it apparently with no great fuss or effort,
nor any consciousness that they are doing something
unusual and striking.

One sees Europeans regarding casual specimens of our
petticoated produce, more often than not pretty poor
specimens, and wondering what on earth they have in
them to have worked themselves into their highly privileged status, and to have got this status accepted without objection or complaint. The European would say
that such a notable collective manœuvre betokens first-
rate ability somewhere, and he can not see that they
have it; his own womenfolk, by and large, seem much
abler, wiser, more mature of mind. Cleverness will not
answer; he acknowledges that American women are very
clever, but no one can be *that* clever. Nor can such a
piece of strategy be put through nation-wide on the
strength of feminine fascinations, even granting that
American women are endowed with these beyond all

other women, which he thinks highly doubtful. All the horde of foreign "observers," novelists, dramatists, journalists, lecturers and the like, who beset our shores, usually with some sort of axe to grind, always show that this problem is in the forefront of their minds. They treat it with gingerly deftness, as a rule, and hence their observations are seldom valuable, but they always exhibit a lively curiosity about it.

The best that European opinion has done with this problem, as far as I know, amounts to saying more or less kindly that our women are shockingly spoiled and that our men spoil them. In its view the American man of family appears, by his serious side, as a kind of composite of Silas Lapham and Mr. Potiphar. By his lighter side, he appears when on parade with his frolicsome daughter (or wife or sister, as the case may be) much as he does in Mr. Georges Lauwerijns's utterly delightful ballet called *Hopjes and Hopjes,* which anyone going to Brussels should time his visit to see and hear. European opinion holds what it regards as our men's weakness, their easy-going good nature, their sense of essential inferiority, responsible for letting themselves be choused out of their natural and Scriptural rights over the women of their households.

There is something in this, of course, and there was formerly much more in it than there is now. Mr. Potiphar and Silas Lapham are real enough, but they belong to an earlier day. Mr. Lauwerijns's figures are modern and not greatly exaggerated—the simple-hearted and likable old boy who never learned how to play, out on a lark with his gay daughter who is rather fond of him in her careless fashion, is on good terms with him, and exploits him scandalously. Mr. Sinclair Lewis has perhaps a little over-vulgarized a somewhat similar pair, in his excellent portrait of Mr. Lowell Schmaltz and his daughter Delmerine. But there is no longer any point in discussing the distribution of responsibility. In citing the American man's traditional easiness with women, European opinion may have had everything on its side in the days of Daisy Miller, and may still have something on its side. What it has or has not, however, is no longer of more than academic interest, because a new factor has come into the situation since Silas Lapham's and Daisy Miller's day—the factor of economic control. It may be said, no doubt, that men were culpably short-sighted not to foresee this factor's coming in and to take measures against it; but that is little to the point now, because the mischief, if mischief it be, is done, and there is no help for it.

The thing now, I take it, is to measure the strength of this new factor, and to observe some of its bearings. I venture to suggest this because no one, as far as I know, has ever taken the American woman's proportion of ownership and her probable preponderance of pur-chasing-power into account as affecting her freedom of action, and as in consequence putting certain definite marks upon our society which do not appear on any other. I am no such hidebound disciple of the Manchester school as to pretend that the American woman's posi-tion is to be accounted for in economic terms alone. I say only that her economic status has a great deal to do with defining and establishing her social status, her social privileges and immunities, and that in this relation her economic status has never, as far as I am aware, been competently considered by any critic, native or foreign; and since one short essay will hardly go around the whole subject, it may properly devote itself to this single aspect of it, even at the risk of appearing limited and partial.

III

To-day processes the refractory raw material of yesterday's heresy into the standard tissue of orthodoxy; and to-morrow re-processes its remnants into the shoddy of commonplace. Side by side with this procedure, and apparently related to it, go odd changes of fashion concerning delicacy and indelicacy of speech. A dozen years ago, it was most indecorous to say anything suggesting the doctrine that those who own rule, and rule because they own. We all knew that the doctrine was sound, but, like a sound doctrine of certain biological functions, there was a convention against speaking of it, above all against letting anything about it appear in print. The correct thing was to say that those who vote rule, and rule because they vote—standard eighteenth-century political theory. The fashion has changed now, and everybody speaks quite freely of the relation between ownership and rulership. Even our more progressive institutions of learning no longer make any difficulties about the fact that actual rulership of a population rests finally in the control of its means of livelihood, and that this is vested in ownership.

Our government "buys," we say, an island from a foreign government. One flag is hauled down, another is hauled up; one set of officeholders decamps, another comes in. But the island is actually owned by three men, and the same three men who owned it under the foreign government continue to own it under ours. They are the actual rulers of the island's population, because they can make it do what they please,—which is the essence of rulership,—since they control the source of its livelihood. Some years ago a Greenbacker or free-silverite, I forget which, discussing private land-monopoly with Henry George, said, "Give me all the money in the world, and you may have all the land." "Very well," said George, "but suppose I told you to give me all your money or get off—what then?"

Ownership means the ability to make people obey your will under the implicit menace of shutting off their supplies, or what we call in war-time an economic block-ade. I do not suggest this as an academic definition, but we all know that it is what ownership comes to. It seems clear, therefore, that the distinctive character of a pre-ponderating ownership would be pretty faithfully re-flected by the society in which that ownership was ex-ercised. Hence, when Europeans regard our society as deeply effeminized and wonder why it should be so, the most competent answer, surely, is found in the amount of economic control that is in our women's hands. How it got there is of no present consequence; it is there, and apparently there to stay. How is it possible for a society not to be effeminized when its women have so large a power of imposing upon it their collective will, of im-pressing upon it the distinctive mark of their collective character, their criteria of intelligence, taste, and style?

I suspect that the extent to which women direct our national development in the realm of the spirit is quite imperfectly realized. Putting it bluntly, they control education, they control the church, the forum, publishing, drama, music, painting, sculpture. That is to say, in the United States the musical director, preacher, publisher, lecturer, editor, playwright, schoolmaster, always instinctively addresses himself to the quality and character of interest peculiar to the female portion of his constituency. In Europe he is under no pressure to do so. In fact, this is the most noticeable difference between the practice of these activities here and in Europe, and I think the most significant as well. It is surely more than a coincidence that the increase of women's control of our practice has gone on in a fairly direct ratio to their increase in purchasing-power. A study of woman's rise to her present position discloses too many such coincidences for us to take stock in the presumption of coincidence. Her demand for political equality, for instance, was pushed hard and earnestly for nearly a century, but one observes with interest that nothing came of it until the time, almost to the day, that she arrived at equality in purchasing-power; and then she got what she wanted with relatively little effort.

Now, in any society, the status of the pursuits I have just mentioned, the status of what goes on in the realm of the spirit, is the measure of that society's actual civilization. Exercise of the instinct of workmanship alone, no matter how energetic, is not civilizing; there must go on with it a balanced and harmonious exercise of the instinct of intellect and knowledge, of religion and morals, of beauty and poetry, of social life and manners. A society may be very rich, it may have any number of industries, railways, hygiene-establishments, sport-centres, banks, newspapers, telephones, finance-companies and the like, and remain quite uncivilized. These things are in a sense the apparatus of civilization, because under proper direction they make for a diffused material well-being, and civilization can get on better if it has this as a basis; but they do not in themselves constitute civilization or even make directly and immediately toward it.

IV

My main design in writing this essay is to address a word of exhortation to our feminists. Modern feminism has contented itself with asserting the thesis of women's ability and right to do everything that men can do. Perhaps some of our more thoughtful feminists have looked beyond this thesis, but I know of none, from the days of Fanny Wright and Susan B. Anthony on to the present, who has done so. Feminism has been content with demanding the right to vote, to practise politics and hold public office, as men do, and to enter commerce, finance, the learned professions and the trades, on equal terms with men, and to share men's social privileges and immunities on equal terms. Its contention is that women are able to do as well with all these activities as men can do, and that the opportunity to engage in them is theirs by natural right.

This thesis is wholly sound. Every objection I ever heard raised against it has impressed me as *ex parte* and specious—in a word, as disingenuous. There is no doubt whatever that women can do everything that men can do: they have always done it. In the thirteenth century, women were not only studying and practising, but also lecturing, in the Faculty of Medicine at the University

of Salerno. Joan of Arc made no special impression on
the people of France as a military figure; they were quite
used to seeing women under arms in the mediæval wars.
As late as the sixteenth century, Louise Labé got a bit
bored with the routine life of a well-to-do merchant's
daughter at Lyon, so she reached down the gun, sallied
forth in men's dress, and fought through the siege of
Perpignan. Then, having had her little fling at an active
outdoor life, she went back to Lyon, married, and made
her home the centre of a brilliant literary society, and
wrote some of the most beautiful verse ever done in the
French language, or, for that matter, in any language.
She also wrote an excellent manual of housekeeping in
a practical and sententious style rather reminding one of
Cato's treatise; which seems to show that she was quite
as handy with the broom and the rolling-pin as she was
with the pen and the smooth-bore.

Then, as a type of the first-class executive and diplomat, there was Saint Radegonde, in the sixth century.
Our feminists ought to look her up as the patron saint
of feminism, and I say no more about her in the hope
that they will do so; she will be a rich find for them. In
the realm of public affairs, the women of the French and
Italian Renaissance are too well known to need mention. Even the gun-moll, generally supposed to be a
product peculiar to our time and country, has a very
early prototype. In the sixth century two spirited hussies,
mere youngsters, princesses named Chrodhilde and Ba-
sine, pranced out of Saint Radegonde's convent at Poitiers in dudgeon against the management, gathered a
band of cutthroats around them, and shot the town to
rags. The streets of Poitiers ran red with blood, and the

forces of law and order had a frightful time putting down the riot. Indeed, the two princesses never were put down. They rode off somewhere beyond the reach of extradition—some mediæval Miami, probably—and lived to a green old age, full of ginger, and wearing the halo of popular renown. That was many centuries ago, but even to this day the Nuns' War is mentioned with uneasy respect throughout the Poitou.

At any period in hisory, I think, one may find women "living their own lives" in the feminists' sense, about as satisfactorily as men were living theirs; doing, if they chose, just what men did, and doing it just about as well. One must observe, however, that these women were relatively few, they were always exceptional, and—here is, I think, the important thing—they were all marked by one sole invariable differentiation: they were economically independent. I say "all" rather inadvisedly, perhaps, for I have not looked into the pocketbooks of all the notable women in the world, from Semiramis down; but out of curiosity I have lately examined the circumstances of a great many, here and there, and have found but one exception, Joan of Arc. She was a poor girl; but her enterprise was of a very special kind, not likely to be affected by her economic status, though if she had been well-to-do she might not, quite probably would not, have lost her life in the way she did. Given a certain amount of resolution, women who were economically independent seem never to have had much trouble about "living their own lives"; nor, apparently, do they now.

It may therefore be said, I think, that the efforts of feminism have never been, strictly speaking, in behalf

of the rights of women, but in behalf of the rights of
poor women; and all the greater honour to feminism
that this is so! Those who were not poor or dependent
seem always to have been able pretty well to do as they
liked with themselves, and, as our expressive slang goes,
"to get away with it." It must be remarked that, for our
present purposes, the wage-earning woman is not to be
classed as economically independent, for she holds her
place on sufferance of an employer. By economically independent, I mean those who are fixed quite securely in
the owning class, as were the eminent women of the
Renaissance, for instance.

It would appear, however, that feminism in America
has not many more fish to fry in the way of its historic
contention. If our women of the owning class very much
want anything, they are able to concentrate upon it an
amount of purchasing-power which constitutes an economic demand hardly to be resisted; and their getting
it would be likely to accrue to the benefit, if it were a
benefit, of the dependent members of their sex as well.
A rather trivial instance of this is seen in the latter-day
style of dress. We remember that when women took to
the wholesome fashion of wearing almost no clothes at
all, especially on our beaches in summer, all the institutional voices of our society spoke out against them.
The police and our prurient and officious local Dog-
berrys made trouble for them, and employers held a
blanket threat of dismissal over the head of girls who
would not conform to more conservative notions of pro-
priety in dress. But there was enough purchasing-power
concentrated on the style to hold it in force and to bring
all objectors to terms; and the poor and dependent

women profited accordingly. Putting it broadly, Fourteenth Street could not have held up the style, but Park Avenue could and did, and Fourteenth Street shared the benefit.

Hence feminism can no longer get up an argument on the thesis that women can do anything that men can do. All interest in that contention has died out; everybody has stopped thinking in those terms, and our militant feminists are reduced to pushing minor issues, to smoothing out relatively petty inequalities of legal status, and the like. This is important and should be done; but I suggest that while it is being done the more progressive and thoughtful spirits among our feminists should consider the thesis that women can do something which men can not do.

V

Women can civilize a society, and men can not. There is, at least, no record that men have ever succeeded in civilizing a society, or even that they have made a strong collective endeavour in this direction; and this raises a considerable presumption upon their inability to do either. They can create the apparatus of a civilization, the mechanics of that diffused material well-being upon which a civilization is founded. Men are good at that; they are first-rate at founding industries, building railways, starting banks, getting out newspapers, and all that sort of thing. But there is no record of their handiness at employing this apparatus for a distinctly civilizing purpose. Indeed, it is very doubtful whether, left strictly to themselves, they would employ the greater part of it, the part that bears on what we call the amenities of life, for any purpose; they would incline to let it drop out of use. The standard cartoons and jokes on the subject all tend to show that when the missus goes away for the summer, the gent lapses contentedly into squalor and glories in his shame; and these may be taken as an allegory reflecting matters of larger consequence.

In the greater concerns of life it is the absence of the impulse toward civilization that justifies women in their complaint that men are forever children. Men feel no more natural, unprompted sense of responsibility than children feel, for the work of civilizing the society in which they find themselves; hence in respect of all life's concerns, even its very greatest, women have been fig-uratively cuffing and coaxing this sense into their heads, figuratively overhauling them, not so much for unwashed ears and unblown noses as for the persistent *tendency* toward these, the indefeasible disposition to accept a general régime of unwashed ears as normal and con-genial, and to regard any complaint of it as exorbitant.

A while ago I took occasion to write something which bore on this point, and it elicited a very tart letter from a lady, asking me what I meant by "civilizing a society." I have no notion that the letter was written in good faith; still, the question is a fair one. Words, as Homer says, "may tend this way or that way," and nothing is ever lost by making sure that one's use of terms is al-ways perfectly clear. We have already mentioned man-kind's five fundamental social instincts—the instinct of workmanship, of intellect and knowledge, of religion and morals, of beauty and poetry, of social life and manners. A civilized society is one which organizes a full collective expression of all these instincts, and which so regulates this expression as to permit no predominance of one or more of them at the expense of the rest; in short, one which keeps this expression in continual harmony and balance.

To civilize a society, then, means that when this harmony is imperfect, when the expression of one or more of these instincts is over-stressed, the civilizing force should throw its weight in favour of the under-expressed instincts and steadily check the over-stress on the others, until a general balance is restored. Social development under these conditions is, properly speaking, a civilized development; and a civilized person is one who manages the expression of his individual five instincts in just this way, and directs himself into just this course of orderly individual development.

Men have, of course, managed this individual development in themselves; though even here, unfortunately, it is seldom clear what part a distinctly feminine influence has played in its direction. Men apparently, however, have neither the ability nor the aptitude to organize and direct a collective development of the kind; and women seem to have both. Men's collective influence has never, that I can discover, even tended significantly in this direction; women's often has. It would therefore appear as certain as any generalization can be that, while women can do everything that men can do, they can also do this one thing that men can not do: they can civilize a society.

The correspondent whom I mentioned a moment ago intimated that in my interest in this matter I was entertaining myself with a mere logomachy, and that my reflections upon it were all moonshine. In a personal

view, one does not mind this; one should be always glad
of criticism, just or unjust. But the personal view is unimportant. The important thing is to observe that in
the long course of human experience, whenever a society
has gone on the rocks, as sooner or later all have done,
it was invariably the collective over-stress on one or
more of these fundamental instincts that turned it out
of its course and wrecked it. One may look back upon
any of these societies,—England of the Commonwealth,
France of the *Grand Siècle,* any you please,—identify at
once the over-stressed and the neglected instincts, and
follow through the record of progressive over-stress and
progressive repression, running directly on to final dis-
aster. Similarly, one may work out the prospects of an
existing society with almost actuarial exactness by observation of these symptoms, as critics have often done.
Hence one is concerned with the degree of civilization
attained by the society in which one lives, not on such
grounds as my correspondent might regard as more or
less fanciful, but upon the solid ground of security. An
uncivilized society has in it the seeds of dissolution, it
is insecure; and the lower the degree of its civilization,
as measured by the means I have indicated, the greater
its insecurity. The race is always instinctively in pursuit
of perfection, always looking beyond an imperfect society, putting up with it perhaps for a long time, but
in the long run invariably becoming dissatisfied with it,
letting it disintegrate, and beginning anew with another.

Our American society, mainly on account of its wealth
and material prosperity, has always come in for an uncommon amount of observation and criticism. Every
complaint of it on the part of both native and foreign

critics, as far as I am aware, is reducible to the simple thesis that it is not a civilized society. These critics do not use this precise formula,—not all of them, at least; some of them do,—but it is the sum of what they have to say, and this is as true of our most kindly critics as well as the most unkindly. It is the sum of Mrs. Trollope's observations at one end of the long array, and of Mr. Dreiser's and Mr. Sinclair Lewis's at the other. There is a complete consensus that our society leaves the claims of too many fundamental instincts unsatisfied; in fact, that we are trying to force the whole current of our being through the narrow channel set by one instinct only, the instinct of workmanship; and hence our society exhibits an extremely imperfect type of intellect and knowledge, an extremely imperfect type of religion and morals, of beauty and poetry, of social life and manners.

I am not concerned, at the moment, to comment on the soundness of this criticism; I say only that this is the sum of every criticism that has been passed on our society. Try this formula on any observer, native or foreign, and you will find, I think, that it covers the content of his opinion.

VI

Thus one is led rather seriously to wonder whether, in encouraging our women to do only the things that men can do, our feminists have not been encouraging them to take quite the wrong way with themselves. For my own part, I suspect it may be so. One may easily see how our society, if it had to, might get on without women lawyers, physicians, stockbrokers, aviators, preachers, telephone-operators, hijackers, buyers, cooks, dress-

makers, bus-conductors, architects. I do not say we *should*
get on without them; that is another matter entirely. I
say only that we *could* get on. We *can not* get on, however, without woman as a civilizing force. We can not
get on—at least, I see no way whereby we can get on—
unless women apply the faculty which they have, and
which men apparently have not, to the task of civilizing
our society.

In encouraging women to do only what men can do,
our feminists have encouraged them to put still greater
stress on the instinct of workmanship, the one instinct
which all critics say is already over-stressed to the breaking point; and this virtually decreases the stress on those
which are already intolerably under-stressed. It causes a
still more violent disturbance of balance between the
claim of workmanship and the claims of intellect and
knowledge, religion and morals, beauty and poetry,
social life and manners. Considering the available in-
dexes of these several claims, it would appear that our
critics (I venture, after all, to give my opinion in the
matter) have a good deal on their side. The development of a sense of spiritual activity as *social*, as something popular and common, in which everybody may
and everyone naturally does take some sort of hand—
this development seems really not to have got very far.
There is, for example, a great deal of music in America; yet compare the development of our sense of music
as a social expression with that which you perceive at
work naturally and spontaneously in almost any German village! Similar observations may be made with regard to our literature. We all remember Mr. Duffus's
examination of the state of the book-market, and we

are all aware of the extremely exiguous and fear-ridden existence of anything like a serious periodical literature among us; well, compare this state of things with what one finds in France, or indeed in any Continental country, for I believe our rating is reckoned lower than any of them—as I remember, we stand eighteenth on the list of nations in this particular, though I am not sure of the exact figure; it is, at any rate, shockingly low. So one may go on, through the whole roster of spiritual activities. It appears, then, that further stress on the overstressed instinct, and further repression on the others, are not what will do us any good.

Here, I think, comes in the point that feminism is in a position not only to direct *interest,* but, for the first time in the world's history, to direct as much purchasing-power as men have, or perhaps somewhat more. We have already seen that, in a commercial sense, women's interest controls all our organized expressions of spiritual activity. Take the advertising matter in any newspaper or magazine, and consider the proportion of it that is aimed directly at women's purchasing-power, and you can see at once how far publishing-policy must reflect specifically feminine views of life. Consider the proportion of woman's purchasing-power represented on the boards of our orchestras, in the contributions to churches, in the maintenance of schools, forums, lectureships, and you will see at once the direction that their policies must take. It is a commonplace of the theatre that the verdict of women will instantly make or break any production, instantly establish any general mode or tendency, instantly reverse one already established. Test the question of women's commercial control of organized expression anywhere in the realm of ethics, manners, art, anywhere in the realm of general culture, and your findings will be the same.

Hence it would seem that there is here a great social force out of which our society is at present getting but little good. I believe it is a much greater force than our feminism has any idea of; and this is my justification for suggesting so directly to feminism that it should recognize and measure this force, and then do everything possible to give it a better direction. Our society can not be civilized through women's attainment of the ends that feminism has hitherto set before them, laudable and excellent as those are. It can be civilized by giving an intelligent direction to the interest and the purchasing-power of women. At present these are exercised very irresponsibly and casually in the direction of civilization, largely because women have been over-preoccupied with the idea of doing what men can do. Modern feminism has unquestionably encouraged and abetted them in this preoccupation; and hence it seems competent to suggest that feminism should henceforth concern itself with recommending a higher and much more rational ideal of social usefulness.

Brussels, August, 1931.

2

A Further Word to Women

IN the preceding essay, the gist of my observations was
that American women enjoy an unprecedented independence, chiefly on account of their preponderance
in economic control. They own nearly half of our national wealth in their own right, and in addition to this
they control a large wage-fund and a considerable allow-
ance-fund; so that they have at present, undoubtedly,
more purchasing-power than men have, and hence are
pretty well able to do as they please with themselves.
This being so, it occurred to me to consider what it is
that they are actually doing; and appearances seemed to
indicate that they mostly content themselves with doing
what men do. I then ventured to suggest a field of activity which they, and especially the feminists among
them, seem to have left unnoticed, and in which they
would meet with no competition from men—namely,
civilizing the society in which they live.

Comment on this modest proposal took a direction
that interested me, and I should like to speak of it for
a moment; not at all by way of complaint, for everything that came to my notice was encouraging and generous. It all pointed, however, towards what I suspect

to be a very pronounced social preoccupation, and I mention it only for the sake of its evidential value, whatever this may amount to. First, then, practically all the comment on my paper was taken up with the disclosure that women own nearly half of our national wealth; it treated this fact as if it were my main point. But surely the important thing is the social implications of this fact, rather than the fact itself; and I humbly hoped that my paper had made it clear that this was the important thing. Again, all this comment seemed to assume that I was somehow chiefly concerned with the question of what women are doing with their money, whereas I was but little concerned with that; indeed, for the immediate purposes of my paper, I was not at all concerned with it.

Thus, unless I greatly misjudge it, the turn of this comment intimates a greater social preoccupation with money and the distribution of money than with the quality of human character and the direction of its development. Obviously, what a person does with his money, or with any kind of social leverage under his control, must depend finally on the sort of person he is. This being known, there is not much trouble about making a pretty accurate forecast of the general lines of use or abuse on which he will distribute his money. Hence, if one is considering people who have money, one would properly, I think, first concern oneself with the kind of people they are, rather than with the directions that their outflow of money is taking.

One kindly correspondent, however, sent me a very courteous letter of interest and approval, ending with the suggestion that I should write another paper, "a little less subtle" (her amiable euphemism for my diffidence, for subtle, alas! I could never be), telling women "just what it is I think they ought to do" to civilize a society. I suspect she guessed how tempting this large order would be to one with whom the habit of scribbling had become inveterate. If so, her guess was good, and I shall now try my best to meet it.

II

But here at the very outset a simple-minded person like myself runs into dreadful trouble over the connotation of the verb *to do*. I am afraid that even this lady's request, highly as I regard it, intimates another preoccupation characteristic of our society; I mean the characteristic preference for action rather than for thought, and especially the preference for *doing* rather than for *being* or *becoming*. Critics have remarked our inveterate persuasion that all good things will come to us of their own accord if only we keep on as hard as ever we can with doing, and let thinking go more or less by the board; and it must be said that they have a large array of evidence on their side. For example, this policy has controlled our whole economic life ever since the war; everybody has been doing, nobody has been thinking. Even now, curiously, when it is evident that this policy has not worked well, that what has been needed all along is a little less hand-over-head action and a great deal more disinterested thought, there is a general clamour for somebody to do something; thought is apparently at as great a discount as ever. Our dealings with public affairs, both economic and political, are now plainly seen to have been a series of mere improvisations; yet there is no likelihood that our policy with regard to them will change. Our society demands action, it sees public affairs only in terms of action, and action only it will have.

Hence, in the face of the two master-concerns which I have mentioned,—the concern with money and the concern with action,—a person of a direct turn of mind should be circumspect about saying what he thinks women should "do" in order to civilize a society. The first preoccupation would naturally, I think, make "doing" connote the giving of money. When men set out to "do" something for a cause, that is what it usually means; they establish trusts and foundations, and set up subsidies of one kind or another. Well, then, since our women have so much money, why not suggest that they set up a Civilization Trust somewhat on the pattern of Mr. Carnegie's Peace Trust or Mr. Rockefeller's Education Trust or Mr. Bok's International Amity Trust (I am not quite sure about these names, but the reader will at once recognize the endowments I refer to) or Mr. Eastman's Music Trust? That would be the regular thing, and very simple; all one need do is to announce the purpose, designate the trustees, and make over the money.

It would perhaps be all the simpler because women appear content to employ their money quite as men do theirs, just as they are content to employ their energy in the same occupational lines that men follow. I have pored over a great many statistics, and questioned persons who have professional knowledge of such matters, and I can find no significant difference between the sexes in this respect. Women and men alike, in a word, put most of their money into productive industry, speculate with some of it, waste a great deal of it, and some of it they give away. If, therefore, women wish to promote civilization, would they not naturally use the same means that men use, and in the same way?

The second preoccupation would almost certainly make "doing" connote some activity of an exterior and ponderable sort. In this case, I think it would probably connote something like getting up an organization, with a secretary and a constitution, a programme, perhaps some by-laws, and a "public-relations counsel" to look after publicity. Meetings would be addressed by eminent persons; papers would be read and discussed, questions asked and answered. Perhaps the organization would consider taking the matter of civilization into politics, in a tentative way; it might appoint a committee to look into the matter and report.

So why not tell my correspondent that women should first organize the idea of civilization, and then give money to promote it? That would be simple and easily understood. It would meet our society's preference for action over thought; for one may be very active in an organization and do practically no thinking at all, but, on the contrary, may let one's mind remain comfortably inaccessible and inert. It would also meet our other great preference for concerning ourselves with what a person does with his money rather than with the kind of person he is; for one may give money for a good purpose, not only without being touched by a true sentiment for that purpose, but also remaining in all respects precisely the same kind of person as before.

But the trouble about any such proposal is that civilization is an affair of the spirit, and in the realm of the spirit sheer organization and sheer money count really for very little. The preoccupations of our society being what they are, this idea is probably somewhat hard to apprehend, and hence it may bear a word or two of discussion. Organization and money are absolutely the body and blood of business and politics. They will also absolutely advance the sciences; they are a hundred per cent effective in projects like Mr. Rockefeller's institute for medical research, for example. They will also absolutely advance the arts by their scientific and mechanical side; an endowment like Mr. Eastman's gives both facilities and leisure for musically-disposed persons to improve themselves in the science and mechanics of music. But in the realm that lies beyond these, the leverage of money and organization is not direct and absolute, but indirect and relative. We are all aware, for instance, of the utter incompetence of endowments for the promotion of peace, like the Carnegie Fund and the Nobel Fund. If we were not so obsessed by the idea of an absolute universal potency of money and organization that we take it as axiomatic, we should see that peace is not to be got at in that way; it is not at all that kind of affair.

Again, education was never so highly subsidized and highly organized as in this country, and the result is so generally acknowledged to be most unsatisfactory that everybody is wondering "what to do" about it. Well, education, properly speaking, like religion, like art, like music, like international peace and amity, like any other exclusive concern of the human spirit, is fundamentally not in the money-and-organization category. Education,

according to the old and sound American definition of
half a century ago, is "a student sitting on one end of
a log and Mark Hopkins on the other"; that is to say,
it is an affair of the spirit, and as such only is it com-
municable; and in our devotion to our two master-
preoccupations we have merely succeeded in organizing
and subsidizing it pretty well off the face of the earth.

Not long ago a lady, dissatisfied with our general neglect of formative studies in favour of instrumental and
vocational studies, resolved to "do" something to promote them; accordingly she gave an immense amount
of money to one of our universities to spend in their
behalf. This gift, generous as it was, obviously represents
the smallest part of the undertaking; the great part lies
in the management of what Prince de Bismarck used to
call the imponderabilia, and one can not be as sure as
one would like to be that an American university, under
the heel of our two master-preoccupations, knows how
to deal with these, or even knows how to discern them,
or perhaps so much as knows that they exist.

So if women, like my correspondent, choose to ask
what I want them to "do" in order to civilize our society,
I think I should be obliged to say that I do not want
them to do anything, that I mightily hope they will not
try to do anything. The imponderabilia are all there is
to civilization, and I know of nothing that women can
"do" out of hand by way of managing them effectively.
Stark organization decidedly will not answer; neither
will stark money; neither, even, will interest of the conventional type. In all spiritual concerns there is something which precedes these, something which alone ever

gives them the chance of being applied effectively and to good purpose. It is something a little more recondite than any of them, and far more interesting than all of them put together.

III

One of the most striking experiences of advancing age is the discovery that a great lot of formulas which our fathers foisted on us, and which we duly resented as mere disgusting cant, are true. For example, under the head of *Works before Justification,* the austere compilers of the Thirty-nine Articles declared that "for that they are not done as God willed and commanded them to be done, we doubt not but they have the nature of sin." To the ear of youth these terms sound fantastic and re- pulsive, yet the experience of mature years bears them out as symbolic of a profound truth. Apparently there is something in the order of nature that is against the fruition of good works done outside the purview of a rather special discipline. I do not know how to account for this; perhaps no one does; but there seems no doubt about the fact. Not only do they unaccountably fail to get the results they promised, but they somehow, against all expectation, work themselves out into actual harm- fulness. Instances of this are often so impressive, even spectacular, that when the theological language of the Articles is applied to them it sounds neither forced nor archaic.

How aptly, for example, may one apply the language of purely theological formula to the whole subject of disarmament and international peace. The truth about these is, simply, that all nations would be glad to abolish war, but are not willing to let go of advantages which they know they can not keep without war. Hence the indispensable condition precedent to abolishing war is that the nations should experience a change of heart and exercise repentance and seek justification by faith. It is the disinterested acceptance of a new mode of thought, and the entrance into a new spirit. Nothing else will answer; the fact is plain to anyone with any measure of common sense, and the theological language of Cranmer's day fits the fact like a plaster. Meanwhile good works like the disarmament-conferences and the Kellogg Pact are not done as God willed and commanded them to be done; that is to say, they represent no actual self-transformation on the part of the nations, nor a real desire for any. Hence they not only fail of their good intentions, but become the instruments of a peculiarly cruel deceit; they have the nature of sin.

I hope the reader will not think my Bibliolatry is excessive if I cite another incident in Christian history for the sake of developing a little further this idea of a necessary special discipline as antecedent to good works. It was never clear to me that the story told of Simon the sorcerer, in the eighth chapter of the Book of Acts, makes him out as at all a bad sort, but rather the contrary. He seems merely to have had the honest notion which we have remarked as so prevalent in our own society, that money counts for as much in the realm of the spirit as it does outside it. The Apostle's reply intimated that in Simon's case neither money nor anything else counted for much, because "his heart was not right in the sight of God," and that he had better brisk around and transform himself into the sort of creature who could see things differently; and Simon appears to have taken the suggestion in good part, as giving him an entirely new idea and one worth thinking about.

All this leads directly to a clear and positive view of woman's relation to the task of civilizing our society. What she "does" in this relation is not, logically, the first thing to be considered; the first thing is what she does with herself. In their due season it would be very profitable and interesting to discuss money and organization and many other possible modes of an exterior and ponderable "doing," but their season is as yet remote. *Porro unum est necessarium*—the thing now is to discuss the terms of a valid conversion, a change of heart, and an entrance into a new life and a new spirit, under the regenerative power of a new and high ideal. I am aware that this pulpiteering phraseology courts offense, but I use it deliberately because the two master-preoccupations of our society are so strong that one's only chance to make any headway against them is by the force of language that is downright enough to startle their votaries out of an instinctive mechanical obedience. Having done so, I may now clear myself from any imputation of priggishness by saying in all good faith that I am not urging a moral duty on our women. My mind is furthest from that; I am merely suggesting an interesting opportunity. Nor am I appealing to any altruistic motive,—none whatever,—but to one of an entirely different order, which I shall speak of just as soon as I have made my main point a little clearer.

IV

The steady approach to social, political and industrial equality of the sexes, and the steady shift of sanctions,

conventions and moralities concerning all the sex-rela-
tionships therein implied, have brought out a spiritual
phenomenon which, from the point of view of civilization, is disturbing. Women at large accommodate themselves not only to doing what men do, but also to accepting the general standard of values that men have
set. They take their views of life as a hand-me-down
from men, and model their demands on life by those
of men. Observation of women in active life, in politics,
business, the professions, leaves no room for doubt of
this; and it is as clearly observable, often more so, in
leisure-class women. They accept the motivation which
men have given our society; they fall in with it and make
it their own.

It must be understood that I am not complaining of
this, for they are bred to these spiritual acceptances; all
the social pressure that is brought to bear upon them,
from the cradle up, tends that way. The fact and its
consequences remain, however, and are to be remarked
without prejudice. Only the other day, one of our most
thoughtful and serious writers spoke of our country as
"so hard ridden and so little blessed" by its womanhood.
The observation is not new; and it is true because the
social realignment of the sexes has brought woman's
views of life, her demands on life, her ideals of society,
her aspirations, the practical direction of her intuitions,
into an increasingly close agreement with those of men.

Here, then, is the condition that impairs and enervates
the faculty which women have, and which men apparently have not, for civilizing a society. It is an *inward*
condition; that is the point I would dwell on. It is relatively nothing serious that women should acquiesce in

various formal and external adaptations to a society which men have motivated,—a society, let us say, which proposes statistics as a reasonable and satisfying substitute for philosophy, religion and romance,—but it is very serious indeed that they should acquiesce in an *inward* adaptation to it. There is no great harm done by women's sharing with men all the material comforts, assistances and gratifications available in a rich and powerful society; but there is great harm in their sharing men's inward persuasion that these are all that a properly constituted society may be asked to provide. That women join with men in giving play to the instinct of expansion is all well enough; that instinct is part of their being. But the case is far different where they join with men in a view of this instinct as the only one whose expression is to be taken seriously; and in a corresponding belief that an expression of the race's other fundamental social instincts—the instincts of intellect and knowledge, of religion and morals, of beauty and poetry, of social life and manners—is to be regarded casually and irresponsibly, as something outside the serious business of life, and in which one's participation is to be determined by fashion or by fancy.

Until this disability, which, as I have said, is now forced upon women by all kinds of social pressure—until this is removed, not much can be effectively "done" toward civilizing a society.

In my judgment this disability, resulting as it does in a decay of faculty, is the most calamitous that women have ever suffered. In my former paper I called our feminists' attention to this, though in my diffidence I did it rather playfully; still, I hoped they might penetrate to

my suggestion and take it in good part. I am myself, I
hope, too good a feminist not to be appalled by the monstrous price that women are paying for such advantages
as their approach to legal, social and industrial equality
has brought them; that price being the weakening of an
invaluable special faculty—let me say, the surrender of
an *ad hoc* superiority—through their broad general assumption of "the male psychology" toward their newer
interests and toward life at large. Though my love for
equality and justice approaches fanaticism, I can yet
understand how, with this price levied against it, woman's progress in emancipation might be thought to have
come a trifle high.

Thus the upshot of my theological language of a moment ago is that in order effectively to "do" anything
for civilization the individual woman must revive this
moribund faculty and get it into a convalescent state
by a deliberate revision of her views of life and her demands on life. It is a task for the individual only, a
straight job of self-transformation; and the freer one is
to do it, the easier, naturally, it will be.

This was all I had in mind when in my former paper
I brought up the point that our women have so much
money. The possession of it rids them of the most powerful of all social pressures—economic pressure—to shape
their spiritual nature by man's pattern. Certainly not
all our women have this freedom, certainly nothing like
a majority have it; but, as I intimated in my half-jocose
little allegory of the fashion in clothes, if those only
who have it would make it serve them in this task of
self-transformation, we should have a new world.

V

This task implies, in general terms, first, that woman should get as complete an understanding of the claims of the four neglected social instincts, and as acute and lively a sense of their validity, as she has shown herself able to get of the claims of the instinct of expansion. The lady buyer, broker, executive, politician, knows precisely what these latter claims are; she is as perspicacious about them as any male colleague; you can not fool her about them for a moment. She also has no doubt whatever about their validity. They are abundantly real to her; her assumption of "the male psychology" toward them has in fact made their reality mount up to an enormous preponderance, as practically the ultimate reality to which her being responds. Women, then, especially those who are free of economic hindrance, may carry just these powers of perspicacity, concentration and assurance over into the realm of the spirit, and employ them in just this way for bringing their inner nature into a larger conformity with the best that one finds there.

That is what the notable women of the French and Italian Renaissance did. In looking over their record with this clue in mind, I was interested to see how intelligently and perseveringly they made a business of spiritual activity; as real a business as our emancipated sisters now make of promoting bond-issues, practising law or hawking cosmetics. The realm of the spirit was as real to them, as engaging to their powers, as the realm of politics; and the discipline necessary to make them at home in it—"the intending of the mind," to borrow

Newton's phrase—was as familiar and as cogently practical to them as the discipline of arithmetic.

The task of self-transformation implies, further, a great engagement of the emotions; just such an engagement as that which now invigorates and fortifies woman in meeting so competently the claims of the instinct of expansion. She now throws an immense deal of sound affection, honourable pride, even a great deal of pseudo-romantic vision, into her stockjobbing or cosmetic-peddling; the natural forces which she confronts in the course of these pursuits are such as foster them and call them into play. The psychology of "pepping up sales" is in a sense sound; it contemplates the focusing of just these emotions by clearing and stimulating a sense of these natural forces as a challenge. Perhaps the most impressive example of its effectiveness in the service of the instinct of expansion is seen in the concentration of Russia's emotional power upon the Five-Year Plan. Well, the women of the Renaissance, while remaining in all respects women of the world, not only disciplined their intellect, but also disciplined and stimulated their emotions into just such a profound concentration upon the natural forces which they found confronting them in the realm of the spirit. They dealt with the great natural forces of mystery, the forces of beauty, the forces of love, as ably and as passionately as our well-disciplined modern woman deals with the forces of supply and demand.

Thus these women were great civilizers, probably without knowing it, and certainly with no self-conscious effort. They seem not to have laboured under the sense of a special mission to society; what they "did" appears

to have been largely occasional. But they were nobly
serious with themselves, their eye was single; and their
record makes one sometimes suspect that civilization is
perhaps—just possibly—best promoted by indirection.
One especially suspects this when one observes the very
puny results accruing from direct, self-conscious efforts
to promote it. But, however this may be, one may believe that, if the personality of our women reflected a
spiritual discipline at all commensurate with the freedom that their economic independence allows for its
undertaking, there would be no need to worry much
about any secondary means of enhancing that personality's effectiveness upon society. Its contagion would
find its own ways, and perhaps all the more easily without conscious guidance.

One can not be more specific than this without the
risk of presumption; how should I particularize to
women upon the incidence of a special faculty which
they have and I have not? If I should offer the detailed
"constructive suggestions" that are always in popular
demand, and any confiding woman undertook to follow
them, she would no doubt make a great mess of it, and
I should merely become one more example, among many
in my sex, of the futility of trying to show one's grand-
mother how to sift ashes. Taking my stand firmly on
the side of reason and prudence, I shall confine myself
to clearing away a possible slight suspicion of inconsistency.

VI

It may be asked, if I doubt that civilization is much
furthered by direct self-conscious endeavour, why I

should write an article intimating that something of the kind is called for. If women are not to transform themselves in obedience to a social motive, why should they do it at all? Well, the social motive is very noble and elevated; I have all possible reverence for it; yet I am reluctant to recommend it, feeling, like the Psalmist, that I should not be meddling in great matters which are too high for me. I prefer to leave this sort of exhortation to the sociologists and political liberals, who are handier at it than I am, and content myself with suggesting a motive that is less grandiose but quite as valid, and, if possible, perhaps a shade more congenial.

When someone asked the physicist Michelson why he worked so hard over measuring the speed of light, he replied that he did it because it was such great fun. That is the only motive that I would suggest—happiness. Apparently the women of the Renaissance had no other; quite unconscious of any exalted social mission, they seem to have worked like beavers at remaking themselves merely for the enjoyment they got out of doing it. Probably, indeed, there is no happiness like this, once the initial obstacles are got over. Even the cold and profound thought of Bishop Butler takes on a faint glow of warmth in contemplating it, for he says that, if it were not for the practical difficulties attending the process, the enjoyment of self-transformation would hardly be distinguishable from a kind of sensuality. But one need say no more on this subject; it is one on which the humblest intellects are in agreement with the philosophers and saints, for it is open to the supreme test which anyone is able to apply—the test of experience.

Happiness; only that. At the present time it is un-

commonly clear that our overindulgence of the instinct
of expansion has got us into a most unhappy pickle.
Political and economic imperialism; a great war; desperate collisions of interest in the consolidation of
gains; the reign of a purblind and truculent nationalism;
a lunatic contempt of immutable economic laws; a period of unexampled collapse, prostration, anxiety, and
wretchedness; well, there we are! For some of us—I hope
many—the worst of our tangle will begin to unwind, I
think soon; but the question is, What then?

Should it not presently occur to independent women,
even to some of those who have gone furthest with "the
male psychology," that the instinct of expansion has
been a trifle overworked, and that perhaps the male
psychology towards it was not an unqualified good thing
for women to assume? Would it not strike them as worth
while now to make a stringent revision of their whole
standard of values, to ease off some of the stress on the
claims of expansion and bring those of the other fundamental instincts into some kind of balance and harmony
with them? I do not put these questions in a general
way. I ask only whether it might not occur to these
women that they would themselves be happier if something of the sort should take place *within them*. Over
and above the immediate issues of the day, the present
period seems to me to force the question whether a life
made up, on its serious side, of an exclusive concern
with the claims of expansion, and, on its lighter side, of
an exclusive concern with the *curiosités qui ne peuvent
nous donner qu'une sensation egoïste et passagère*—
whether this life can be permanently interesting; interesting, I mean, primarily to those who are able to con-

trol its quality. Does such a life offer enough happiness
to make it worth living, even to those who dominate and
shape it?

"One is inclined," as Stendhal said of us, years ago,
"to say that the source of sensibility is dried up in this
people. They are just, they are reasonable, but they are
essentially not happy." When a journalist asked Mr.
Edison on his last birthday, I think, or next to the last,
what he thought about human happiness, he replied
simply, "I am not acquainted with anyone who is
happy." There is no need of documentary testimony on
this point; the faces that one sees and the voices that
one hears are enough to establish it. May I say also, as
discreetly as possible, that even the faces and voices of
our economically independent women are not those of
happy people? Why should they be; how *can* they be?
Our whole national history may be fairly epitomized
as a ruthless rampage of the instinct of expansion upon
a vast field of exploitable richness; and, with the claims
of the other social instincts thus continuously sacrificed
to the claims of expansion for a century and a half, how
can even the beneficiaries of this rampage be happy?
The thing is impossible, for, as we all know, every un-
used or misused or misinterpreted instinct becomes a
source of uneasiness.

I suspect that even men are now somewhat reluctantly
suggestible about the quality of the collective life which
they have created; there are some signs that this is a
season of repentance. Perhaps even we, some of us,—I
speak as a man,—are beginning to think that things
might go better if all hands were a little happier; if
there were a little less recourse to raw sensation in the

quest of happiness, and a more resolute clearing of the inner springs of joy. Possibly we might incline more favourably than heretofore toward the idea of a life that gives a little less play to the instinct that we have so horribly overdriven, and a little more to those that we have repressed and deformed; a collective life, in short, that does not flatly preclude the enjoyment of a humane and reasonable happiness. But although we may regard the idea of such a life rather thoughtfully, just now perhaps even wistfully, we have no faculty for realizing it. Women have; and if the women who are economically free would abandon "the male psychology," and so remodel their inner nature as merely to liberate this faculty, they would need give no thought to what they should "do" in order to apply it socially. It would apply itself.

Brussels, November, 1931.

3

Women and the Marriage Market

BROWSING in the voluminous literature that has grown up in the path of the feminist movement, one is struck with the very special, almost professional, quality that pervades it. In addition to the controversial character of the subject, this literature seems written mostly by people with some kind of axe to grind, some social theory to promote or personal end to gain. Thus, we get biological and anthropological views, Freudian and behaviourist views, views of women who are in some sort bearing the burden and heat of the day and hence are moved to erect philosophical defense-mechanisms for women in business, women in industry, women in the home, women here or there. We get a fine uncompromising traditional masculinity from writers like Mr. Ludovici and Mr. John Macy, and their point of view is reflected with admiration by Mme. Gina Lombroso. Special phases of the subject are worked out in pseudo-fictional form, both in books and drama, by writers whose minds appear to need a little chloride of lime dusted on them every now and then—a type of mind, by the way, which seems to have completely pre-empted these fields of literary endeavour, and to be ex-

ploiting them in a fashion which commands more wonder than admiration.

Amid so much professional discourse I have been waiting to hear a voice from the grandstand, but so far, in
vain; and now, looking over my own qualifications, it
has occurred to me that I myself might venture to speak
for the unlearned. I have no science of any kind. I never
read a line of Freud, and know not what behaviourism
is. I have no social theory to press, I am not an employer
or an industrial shareholder, and I could not earn a
penny by writing mephitic fiction if my life depended
on it. Born void of conventional moralities, I have never
been able to take to heart the divorce-statistics, the un-
dermining of the home, the vulgarities of the mismated,
or to get up steam over the supposititious depravity of
my juniors, over the grubby little curiosities attributed
to Lily May and John Henry, or over the means they
are reputed to employ either to assuage or exacerbate
them. If those concerned can stand it, I can. There are
certain sanctions of taste and manners by which I measure such matters for my own guidance, but this is a
single-standard affair and purely personal, and I have
not the faintest desire to foist those sanctions upon other
people or even to recommend them as likely to work
well for anybody but myself.

So while the industrious, the public-spirited and the
righteous could no doubt find a better representative—
I hope so, at least, though what they say on this subject,
when they speak for themselves, is not encouraging—I
think I might venture to put myself forward as a spokesman for the unlearned and the disinterested. I am heart-
ened to this modest proposal by recalling the remark

of Goethe, that a very little common sense is worth a great deal of philosophy; and indeed, common sense is notably, almost peculiarly, a property of the unlearned and the disinterested. One feels acutely the force of Goethe's remark when one is confronted with contemporary theses based upon putative sex-differentiations, or with proposals to mould the relations of men and women by various quasi-mechanical devices, such as tinkering with divorce-laws, for instance, or such as were lately suggested by Judge Lindsey and Mr. Samuel Hopkins Adams. Common sense has no proposals to make and no devices to suggest; but it can, I think, throw a good deal of light on the fundamentals of the matter which the learned are making such a fuss about, and thus perhaps exert a calming influence by showing that the matter is worth hardly any fuss at all.

II

First of these fundamentals is the fact that female companionship is the one thing, next to food, that men will have at any price. Women get on most handily without men; men can hardly turn a wheel without women. Women may like men, may want them, but do not need them. Men may dislike women, may not want them, but do need them. There are some exceptions on both sides, but very few, and I should say from my own observation, about equally divided. I have seen some half-dozen men in my life who seemed independent of women's companionship, and about as many women who could not get along indefinitely and very comfortably without men. John Adams, in his vigorous commonsense way, built his whole political philosophy on the generalization that "the first want of man is his dinner, and the second want, his girl." This is a truth of as wide application, probably, as any outside the realm of mathematics. I quite believe that if it were not for women we should soon have not even a semblance of anything which we now call civilized living. How this came to be so is a matter for the researches and speculations of the learned; the business of the unlearned is with the fact alone.

But in applying this truth, observation discounts the universal assumption that this interest in female companionship is always primarily biological. Often it is, but quite as often—I personally believe far oftener—it is not. The general run of the learned, and the whole crop of fictioneers, seem to assume that man is led to woman primarily by a raw animal interest, and that what accrues from it collaterally, if anything, is lagniappe. I believe that if Mr. Sherwood Anderson, say, or Mr. James Branch Cabell, really examined the matter, he might be surprised to find how often it is the other way around. It stands to reason; for, after all, the means of satisfying a purely biological interest in womankind is of extremely easy access. Even when this interest degenerates into a kind of collector's mania, as in the classical instance of Captain Macheath in the *Beggar's Opera*—

> I sipped each flower,
> I changed every hour,

—almost any moderately personable male individual can roll up quite a catalogue of achievement in the course of fifteen or twenty years of steady application. But those whose actual demands on womankind are primarily of this order are not found as often as our literature, both popular and scientific, would indicate.

The second fundamental fact to be remarked is that man, requiring female companionship more than anything in the world except food, and having to deal for it with beings who do not nearly so much require his companionship—who can, in fact, get on quite well without it—must deal for it on such terms as he can get. This throws woman at once into the rôle of a *merchant*, which is precisely what she now primarily is in her relations with men, both by birth in a long heredity, and by exactly the same order of social training that has made such marvellous merchants of the Quakers, Jews and Armenians. She has certain goods, certain lines of trade, any of which is susceptible of high specialization, and she can make her own terms for them in whatever market may be open to her.

The moment this is understood a number of rather obscure matters become clear. The proverbially formal attitude of women toward one another where men are concerned—to put it as gently as possible—the very special character of their criticisms and judgments on one another, are the outcome of a primary and strictly competitive commercial relationship. The parallel with Potash and Perlmutter's attitude toward Klinger and Klein, and their criticisms and judgments on the ethics of Sammet Bros., is quite exact. Again, the old question of woman's natural disposition to please men and subordinate her will to theirs becomes commonplace when one translates it into commercial terms as the disposition of a capable merchant to attract and keep customers. It is noteworthy that the higher the rise in general competition, as in countries like England, where there are more women than men, the more that disposition becomes manifest.

Other qualities that are put down by common consent as characteristic of the sex, their possessiveness, their inflexible obstinacy tempered only with guile, their inability to take any but a personal estimate of anything, their unhandiness with abstractions, their skill at compromise, their overweening devotion to expediency, are all characteristic of the born and bred trader. Even "woman's intuition," of which so much is made in poetry and drama, does not come out particularly in real life except in matters which bear directly or indirectly on her trade. It is a secondary intuition, bred of special experience, and exactly corresponds to that developed by similarly special experience in the Jew and the Armenian. What is known under the grandiose name of "sex-antagonism," upon which so many top-lofty structures of speculation have been built, is of an obviously commercial character. Certain matters of etiquette and deportment, certain reticences, dissimulations, affectations and the like, are but so many modes of merchandizing, by no means peculiar to women, but peculiar to merchants with goods to sell. Sit down to dicker with an Arab merchant in Constantinople for a shirt-tail full of glass beads, and in half an hour you will see them all. Not the most experienced lady in the land can give a more beautiful and effective exhibit of coquetry than my dear and good Armenian friend M. will improvise for you any day in a casual retail transaction involving twenty-five dollars. I have seen him do it not once but many times.

Even the baser characteristics usually ascribed to women become understandable in this view; and not only so, but when they are fairly considered their baseness largely evaporates. At least, if women are culpable on these scores, they are no more so than our most honoured merchants who employ a like procedure. These characteristics prove nothing about woman's affectional nature. Arguments about the affectional life of women in relation to men become for the most part absurd when you parallel them with arguments about the affectional life of merchants in relation to customers. A merchant is often personally fond of a customer, but in that case the customer stands before him in two distinct categories. With respect to the one, the sky may be the limit; while with respect to the other, the iron law of *caveat emptor* may be relentlessly pressed. This is a common phenomenon of business. Once when E. H. Harriman left C. P. Huntington's office, Huntington closed the door behind him, and said with a chuckle, "He's a nice little man. One of these days I'll have his railroad." My Armenian friend M., to whom I just now referred, and my Jewish friend E. are as good friends as one could have; they would do anything in the wide world for me on the score of friendship. But in a commercial transaction either one of them would take my skin off, salt it, and hang it on the fence. In point of ethics, one must think twice before passing judgment on this, for in their view it would not be an unfriendly act. They would sincerely resent—and rightly, from their point of view— any such implication. Their action would be neither

friendly nor unfriendly; it would lie entirely outside the
purview of friendship. If I chose to stack up against
their little game, it would be for me to take the consequences of a collision of skill, as one does with one's best
friends at bridge or draw-poker. When, therefore, the
behaviour of women in analogous circumstances comes
under review, it must be steadily borne in mind that
men at large do not appear before women primarily
as potential objects of affection. They appear before
them primarily as potential customers.

III

The standard terms laid down for the enjoyment of
woman's companionship have regularly been, and still
usually are, marriage. This arrangement is comparable
to an exclusive long-time contract for regular deliveries.
In her first fundamental need, woman is like man; she
needs bread, and she contracts to get it in perpetuity
by regularly exchanging some commodity that man, in
obedience to his second fundamental need, finds desirable. This is the gist of the agreement; its subordinate
terms usually are modified to the advantage of one or
the other party according to the "higgling of the market," whereby either merchant or customer proves himself the more astute. But the basic understanding on the
customer's part is one of exclusive contractual title to
whatever it is that he bargains for. It has been remarked
that man is much more conservative than woman with
reference to marriage. This is bound to be true, because
he is dealing contractually—and can only so deal—with
a person who has a natural monopoly, limited indeed,

but for immediate purposes quite effective, of what he most needs. In similar circumstances throughout the whole realm of commerce the customer's attitude corresponds precisely to his; and any fanciful differentiation in his case on the ground of sex is nonsense.

The standard terms, then, are what they always are in business, namely: what the traffic will bear. There is no disparagement in this observation, for it is sound Manchester doctrine. There are many individual exceptions in actual practice, as there are everywhere in the realm of business; for while every woman appears before man in the basic role of a merchant, not every woman is a good merchant. Women make their under-valuations, failures, bankruptcies, like other traders. Jan Steen got a ridiculous price for what is regarded by many as his masterpiece; so did Milton; so, I read the other day, did the German novelist Feuchtwanger—and he a Jew, at that! But these exceptions do not invalidate the general rule of business practice, and no more do those exceptional cases of women who either mismanage their holdings or do not know their value. Men, too, have sought to strengthen the customer's position by political means, by exactly the same order of discriminatory counterbalance which governments have put in play against other disturbing economic factors—against the Chinese on the Coast, against the Jews in Roumania, Poland, Russia, against the Quakers in England, Virginia, the Bay Colony, and so on. This has worked hardship, but on the whole women have contrived to do well under it; the best proof being that their natural monopoly always gave them the means of breaking up this counterbalance whenever they chose, yet they have not used it, but in-

stead have elected to accept the disability until they
could get rid of it by less summary methods, meanwhile
making what collateral gains they could by indirection.
But even under this handicap their economic security
was usually assured, which was the main thing. In one
way or another, too, they have generally got a great deal
besides.

In the United States, however, owing to a variety of
circumstances, the customer's position—originally none
too well stabilized—has gone rapidly from bad to worse
until at the moment it has hardly any recognized rights
at all. Women have learned the art of organization; they
have gained a sense of their collective power as an economic factor in society, not only because so many of
them have become economically independent, or because
so many avenues of economic opportunity have been
opened to them, but also—and the force of this is seldom
noticed—because so large a volume of economic patronage and administration has been left in their hands.
Women do about all the reading and play-going that
is done in America; at least they are responsible for most
of the play-going, since men mostly "go along" under
their influence. They keep up most of our music, they
maintain most of our painting and sculpture, they are
the mainstay of our churches, our educational, cultural,
and social institutions, they are the arbiters of taste and
style for both sexes and in all particulars. Consequently
production in these lines is regulated exclusively, one
may say, by their wishes and preferences. There is not
a department of spiritual activity in America that is not
substantially effeminized. It may be all the better for
that, or all the worse—that is for the learned to decide;

it is a matter, as Aristotle says, "for the determination of the judicious." The unlearned is content merely to remark the fact and to take note of its obvious consequences, one of which is that indirectly women have gained complete control of numerous and powerful economic forces and are exercising it very vigorously. He remarks again, moreover, a curious parallel in this respect between the status of woman and the status of the other great merchant race in America, the Jews. Take out the women, and there would be precious little spiritual activity left in our country, even such as it is. Take out the Jews, and the residue would disappear well-nigh bodily.

Thus there has been brought about an enormous enhancement of woman's natural monopoly, and an enormous broadening of its scope; and the inevitable effect of this has been to raise prices. It extends woman's bargaining-power over many more competitive points of stock-in-trade than heretofore. Formerly all women were equipped by nature to satisfy more or less well a demand for sex-companionship, as they still are; most of them were equipped by training to satisfy a demand for a housekeeper or "helpmate," and many still are, and even those who are not can make a pretty good fist at it with a little practice, if they are so minded, by aid of modern mechanical devices and methods. Some, formerly—quite a few—had one or another kind of accomplishment, rather limited as a rule, or a still more limited intellectual interest. But in all those lines of trade there was heavy and brisk competition; customers had a large margin for shopping around, according to the old and true proverb that there are as good fish in the sea as were ever caught. The only thing that offset this—and it did offset it effectively—was a tacit trust, or trade-agreement, to keep up prices. William, in search, say, of sexual companionship, could shop around from Elizabeth to Mary, and from Mary to Adeline, all equally well equipped and equally ready to talk business, but when it came to signing on the dotted line, he could get no better than standard terms from any of them, according to the formula "with all my worldly goods I thee endow." James, in search of a domestic paragon, and George, who was looking for someone with a sweet disposition who could play the piano, were in the same case. They were up against the trust, and they had to take trust prices or none. If any of the sisterhood black-legged on the price-fixing agreement, and was caught at it or even seriously suspected of it, she never got a second chance.

IV

It takes very little imagination to show that the recent modifications of all this—modifications just now so much complained of—are by no means irregular, but are, on the contrary, so much in order that they should surprise no one. They follow straight out of the great shift in actual economic control. Being quite in order, indeed quite inevitable, one hardly sees what can be done about them, or what parsnips are buttered by mere reiterated complaint. There is a curious fatuity, and an equally curious inconsistency and incompetence, evident in those who denounce "our modern laxity," and propose to shore it up with an artificial backbone of legalistic and institutional devices. The inconsistency is apparent when one sees that every one of these modifications easily passes muster by the ordinary ethics of trade, against which, in any other connexion, the plaintiffs never have anything to say. In point of fatuity these plaintiffs remind one of those pacifists who are taken in by the window-dressing of politicians to the point of actually believing that economic tendencies can be withstood by scraps of paper. Their incompetence comes into view when one considers the very limited purview of their objection; at bottom it hardly ever reaches beyond easy divorce and irregular sex-relations; for under these may be grouped every count relating to the "sanctity of marriage" and the "inviolability of the home." All this merely raises the previous question whether human beings are made for institutions, or institutions for human beings. Was the home made by folks for folks, or were folks made for the home? Plenty of people there no doubt are in the United States to defend the latter thesis, to judge by the volume of rabid institutionalist nonsense poured out on us ever and anon; and, therefore, it is no bad thing to have their divagations occasionally bumped up hard against the rock of fact, thus enforcing a general reëxamination of their basic logical position.

The great good in this recent broadening of the scope of female monopoly is that it enables women to push the stickers. Hitherto they have been courted for sexual companionship and its appanage of domesticity. I am careful to say "courted" for them, not desired for them. The conventional assumption—one may say the official assumption—was that these were the prime desiderata and that their quality governed the whole market; so women were bred and trained to give them first place in their inventory and in their stock-display. This was all very well; women still wish to be courted for those sterling commodities, and they always will be.

But a great many women must no doubt have been all along conscious of the purely conventional character of this rating, and must have felt something of the æsthetic and spiritual dissatisfaction that my Armenian friend M. would feel most acutely if nobody ever was supposed to have recourse to him for anything but cigarettes. His cigarettes are wonderful, he is immensely proud of them, and as careful of them as he should be—and I fear is not—of his immortal soul. But he is too artistic, too fine-grained a merchant, he has too high an idea of his vocation, to rate his cigarettes as a staple in his business. Exquisite as they are, they are a side-line, and properly ancillary to the agreeable course of real trade. One can not smoke all the time—at least, if one does, one's taste is so vitiated that one might as well smoke anything—a cigarette is gone in a moment, and then what have you? But substantial India shawls, Oriental rugs, curious tapestry, Spanish jewellery—these are staple goods, all hidden in the dark depths of his premises; and when a really appreciative customer comes mousing after them and buys them, he throws in a cigarette and a cup of coffee such as the customer never saw the like, and his face radiates the pride of the true high-grade merchant as he winds up the transaction by soaking the customer for every red cent that the traffic will bear.

Women are able, in their present circumstances, to re-appraise their merchandise more nearly to what com-

mon sense and the plain natural truth of things suggest
as a normal scale of values. It may be doubted that they
ever regarded sex-companionship as a staple, or as worth
anything like its current rate. They merely accepted the
conditions of the market, as an African trader accepts
those of a market which runs more to tin mirrors than
it does to more substantial utilities. There are many
indications that this is the case, though it does not appear, on the other hand, that they rated it at all below
its relative value—a thing which no good merchant
would do. They do not do this now. If men mostly desired that form of companionship, as it is by no means
clear that they did, or if collateral circumstances forced
it into prominence and gave it an artificial enhancement
and prestige, which was really the case, women adapted
themselves to doing business under this disability. They
accepted certain codes, segregations and restraints, as the
Jews accepted those of the pale and the ghetto; and
such is the marvellous elasticity of human nature that
they did well under them, and apparently found them
not too irksome, often even reconciling themselves to
them and taking pride in a rather elaborate conformity.
This discipline, however, sharpened their mercantile instinct to a razor-edge; and in consequence, man lost
heavily in the long run through its enforcement.

All this time, too, I repeat—for it is worth repeating—
women must have been conscious that they had far more
valuable goods in stock than those which they were
pushing on the market, and they must have felt a resentment, perhaps larvated in most cases but none the
less nagging, at the subordination of their best goods
in the scale of conventional values. It is fair to suppose,

I think, that the general run of women—excluding those,
I mean, who actually specialize in that line—would reluct
at an interest which was purely or primarily biological,
much as my Armenian friend would reluct at being
known as a tobacconist. For commercial reasons they
might conceal their objections, or even pretend a corresponding interest; but their true feeling in the matter
is probably beyond doubt.

Now, the change which women, aided by circumstances, have engineered throughout all this has tended
to bring down in both sexes the estimate of purely sexual
companionship to about the relative level held by my
Armenian's cigarettes. There is no doubt about this; it
could not be otherwise. This really is the feature of the
situation which so troubles my contemporaries; and it
would indeed seem that the reduction of this estimate
is bound to bear fruit in just the phenomena which they
view with alarm. Along with this deflation, the codes
of our day, theirs and mine, have certainly been vacated,
restraints certainly broken, and segregations certainly
lifted. It is not important to determine the exact relations of priority, or of cause and effect; for all practical
purposes the fact of concomitance is enough.

This deflation, then, no doubt works havoc with my
contemporaries' institutionalism, quite as they say it
does; but it may turn out to be a very good thing, notwithstanding, and its outcome may reveal my contemporaries' dread of it as immensely exaggerated. They say
that this revaluation gives a letter-of-marque for un-
bridled sexual license, and so it really does—there is no
doubt of that—if one wishes so to use it. But their as-

sumptions beyond this point seem questionable. They
do not, apparently, realize that this revaluation affects
the estimate of both sexes alike. A Dutch naval officer
of about my own age said to me the other day that "the
young girls and boys think nothing of starting off together on their bicycles for a week at a time, no one
knows where, and no one knows what they do." Well,
in America—I have no right to an opinion about Hol-
land, though I should like to venture one that it is quite
the same there—I dare say they mostly do nothing that
he would find too reprehensible. This officer, I think,
was assuming that mere propinquity carries the same
risks as it did in our day of rather careful segregation,
whereas it seems really to carry none. Female nakedness,
even, is apparently no longer provocative; women notoriously dress—and undress—to suit their own comfort
and convenience, and no male of the species under thirty
years of age appears to notice what they do. Our literature and drama may indicate that we are "obsessed with
sex," but the aspect of naked joyousness on one of our
bathing-beaches does not indicate it; and I imagine that
those of us who are much below middle age experience
no great titillation of the senses from our pornographic
literature and drama, but find it quite unsuggestive. *A
priori* one would say such was likely to be the case, and
a posteriori one finds much evidence that it is so. The
general spread of information about birth-control is another thing that is sometimes taken as an index of wan-
tonness, but here again there may be a misapprehension.
The fear of pregnancy was one of the chief circumstances
that built up artificially in both sexes an enormous ex-

aggeration of the importance of sexual companionship;
and it would seem that the dissipation of this fear should
be a great factor in the deflation-process that I have referred to—in the reduction of sexual companionship to
what every analogy would suggest as its normal level
of significance. I have great doubt that its general tendency—its resultant line, speaking in mathematical terms
—lies in any other direction.

In France, the old order of restraint and segregation
still largely prevails. Late one afternoon not long ago
in a Paris café, I observed some students sitting with
what seemed to be borderline girls, youngsters not exactly in the professional class, but probably not averse
to profiting by eligible chance acquaintance. No doubt
there could have been sexual companionship somewhere
in the group, and possibly there was; but there was no
evidence of it in their discourse, and no evidence of any
obsession with such matters. They were content to chatter freely in great good fellowship; and I was so impressed by the number of intellectual interests covered
by the conversation that I made a point of coming back
next day to do some more eavesdropping. The particular feature that I noticed was one of manner. These boys
treated the girls precisely as our boys at home, in their
more serious moments, treat our flappers; their frank,
interested and agreeable manner carried no hint of sex-
differentiation. They could not treat girls of their own
social station like that; and the tone of the conversation
proved how much better off these girls were in being
able thus freely to show their customers the best line
of goods that they had in stock, untroubled by *arrière-
pensée* or by conventional restraint and reserve.

V

In any great social change, even though it be salutary, one must take a certain amount of fat with the lean. I suspect that in their despondent view of this great change my contemporaries do not always correctly measure the proportion of lean which we are getting. I also suspect them very strongly of an obstructionist attitude which interferes with our getting a great deal more lean than we do. I can address them thus freely because they are my contemporaries; we were all brought up together in the times of ignorance which, I hope, God winked at, though a survey of our social inheritance from that period makes me doubt that He did. In the matter of divorce, for instance, their ground of complaint is far from clear. In the days when marriage represented the most that the traffic would bear, the case was different; but now that the conditions of trade have changed, many women feel that the price-fixing agreement on marriage could in all justice to everybody be allowed to lapse, and that allowing it to lapse would facilitate business in many instances, and be a considerable convenience. But the attitude of my contemporaries is mostly what makes this impossible. They powerfully reinforce the unintelligent pressure of public opinion against the habitual association of a man and a woman in any form or mode of companionship unless they are married. Hence, in such cases as do not correspond to those in the general run of former days—and they are many—the inevitable tendency is to vacate marriage of any actual significance and reduce it to a mere *pro forma*

affair. Those who complain of this evasion should re-
fresh their memories of the Sherman Act; they are complaining of something that has had its counterpart in
American business-practice so long that the memory of
man runneth not to the contrary.

Women at large would cordially agree, I think, that
marriage is as good an arrangement as has yet been devised for a companionship contemplating certain definite desires and purposes; and those are still common
enough to insure for a long time—much longer than we
need yet worry about—the safety of the institution. But
many of them appear to feel the need of social arrangements that would accommodate other modes of companionship on terms more convenient to both merchant
and customer. Suppose, for example, a man living in
one of our small cities or towns desired a companionship
like that of Joubert with Mme. de Beaumont, and there
are thousands who would give their eyeteeth for it, and
whose social value would be enhanced by it many-fold.
The woman might be ready to trade, she might be carrying a stock as valuable as Mme. de Beaumont's, and willing to close it out on Mme. de Beaumont's terms; but
without serious inconvenience she could trade only on
terms of marriage, terms which would be in that case
purely nominal, and any idea of investing them with
a serious meaning would at once show them to be pre-
posterously inappropriate and impracticable. This state
of things is increasingly felt by many women to be onerous; and the mere liability to a casual and gratuitous
implication of sexual companionship in the premises is
increasingly felt to be immaterial. A sexual companionship might grow up fortuitously in such a case, or it

might not; with Joubert and Mme. de Beaumont, as with many others, there is every reason to believe it did not. But whether it did, or whether it did not, they ask, what of it?

My own impression is that the current "laxity" is tending definitely, and without the least impairment of wedlock's true and proper values, to the establishment of just such social arrangements. Moreover, this tendency seems to me irresistible. It must never be forgotten—and my contemporaries above all should weigh the fact well—that woman is, and as far as we can see will always be in her primary basic relations with men, a *merchant,* a merchant with a limited natural monopoly of certain goods which men will get on the best terms they can make, but which they will have at any price. In a situation like this any artificial interference with the course of trade has always worked disastrously when it has worked at all, and has always cost more, directly or indirectly, than it brought in. The most that it has ever done is to put a premium on skilful circumvention, and this is the most that it is doing now.

The prevailing "laxity," I believe, in short, is the outward and visible sign of a demand for social acknowledgment of the individual woman's competence to regulate such matters pertaining to her trade as she has already the economic power to regulate. Many women when courted, say, for marriage, home-making and motherhood, are now economically able to reply, "Well, I am not specializing in that line at the moment, and I hardly think I have anything in stock that would suit you. I am developing other activities, to which marriage, housekeeping, and motherhood would be a great embarrassment. If a customer comes along who is interested in my staple lines I shall make appropriate terms with him. Then if any other mode of companionship comes to seem collaterally desirable we will manage it under conditions less likely to disturb the main course of trade." These women, whatever their actual procedure, appear to be questioning why such an arrangement, which is already within their economic power to make, should not also be freely adjudged within their social competence. As long as the question remains in their minds an open one, as long as it meets only with an answer which they consider irrelevant and peremptory, so long will they use their economic power in their own way.

I may say in conclusion, however, that I am entirely with my contemporaries in the low estimate that they place on the present run of American womanhood. In their quality of merchants, and with reference to their magnificent, their unparalleled commercial opportunities, I am obliged to regard our women as mostly a very poor lot, listing a stock that is but little better than junk. This is by no means a personal estimate. It is drawn from the current exhibit of those elements in our civilization which I have enumerated as under the complete economic control of women, and which reflect the tone of specifically feminine patronage and administration. One must say, I think, that it is a very indifferent exhibit, raising extremely strong presumptions against those responsible for its production. I am ashamed of them, and think they ought to be ashamed of themselves and do better. But this is not important to the foregoing discussion. The important thing is to get clearly in mind, once for all, the basis of practical fact upon which alone those manifestations of feminism that many find so dismaying can reasonably be appraised; and that basis is found in the two fundamentals set forth at the outset of this paper.

Brussels, February, 1928.

4

The Misuses of Adversity

CONSIDERING the untold tons of garbage that are
shot daily from our presses, it would be an intrepid
person who should demand a new book on any subject.
Nay, with books no longer the symbol of light and leading that they once were, but now become only a symbol
of *was uns alle bändigt, das Gemeine,* no one with a literary conscience would ever so faintly suggest that another should be added to the list. Some years ago, I asked
one of our ablest publishers how he got books out of
his authors. He said, "I don't. On the contrary, I do
everything in my power to keep them from writing
books." I have always treasured the memory of this publisher and honoured him as a loyal friend, not only to
literature, but also to me; for while I, poor sinner, have
fallen from grace once or twice since then, his words
have kept my lapses at a minimum.

How many of us wretched addicts, indeed, should such
words put in the way of giving literature the very best
service we could possibly render! One thinks of Thiers's
profound remark to Count Walewski, who, not content
with a career in diplomacy, vainly imagined he could
write a good play. "What possessed you to do it, Count?"

said Thiers, on the first night. "It is so hard to write a play in five acts; and it is so easy not to write a play in five acts." How can temptation rear its head against this solid wisdom? Yet it does. At the present moment, for example, now that this idea has occurred to me, I am tempted to make it the subject of a long essay, in the hope of touching the flinty hearts of publishers, editors, literary agents, and above all, the deceitful and desperately wicked people who organize literary competitions. But I forbear; though the impulse is almost overpowering, I shall resist it, for in the cause of righteousness one good example is worth a thousand precepts.

Again, things being as they are, one's literary conscience would not only stay one from suggesting a new book, but would also admonish one to go very gingerly about recommending a new book to the attention of any public, large or small, general or special. With the noisy vogue of bad taste and vulgarity everywhere rampant, the public is deafened to every voice that is not pitched in the shrill falsetto of utter self-abandonment, and hence the sober appraisal of a new book may easily be taken as its proverbial damning with faint praise. Then, too, even in recommending a serious book to a very small and special public, as I have twice lately ventured to do, one is uncomfortably conscious of Emerson's sound principle of never reading any book, no matter what, that is not at least a year old. Of contemporary literature, indeed, even serious literature, one can hardly read too little—*man lese nicht die mitstrebende, mitwirkende,* said Goethe—and almost invariably the mere passage of time discloses any contemporary critical estimate of it as worthless.

But though one may not ask for a new book or even recommend one, I suppose one is still free to say what sort of new book one would most enjoy reading. I imagine one might permit oneself to do this, provided it were done on the clear understanding that one had nothing in view beyond the indulgence of a harmless whim. I hope so, at any rate, for I have long had such a book in mind, and now, having made manifest the spotless purity of my intentions, I should like to say something about it.

II

It would give me a deal of pleasure to read a historical essay that followed out two lines of speculation, one of which I am quite sure has never been explored at all, and the other only a little way. History is notoriously a chapter of accidents, and historians have often entertained themselves by speculating on the probable changes in the course of events if this-or-that accident had not happened precisely when and as it did. If, for example, an unknown soldier's bullet had not pierced the breast of James Wolfe, on the Plains of Abraham, would George Washington ever have been the leader of a successful revolution? If Napoleon had not been laid up with a bad cold in the head, would he have shown better strategy at Borodino, demolished the Russian army, and turned the campaign of 1812 into a brilliant success which might have altered the whole course of subsequent European history? Speculation on accidents of this order is common enough. There are, however, two extremely commonplace types of accident which I believe have never been properly considered in their historical aspect; that is to say, I have never seen more than a bare hint of any speculations concerning the probable course that history would have taken if in certain given instances such accidents had not intervened.

Hence I should be delighted to read an essay which considered, first, the accident of individual poverty from the historical point of view. Twenty-five or thirty years ago I applied myself to a long study of the works of Henry George, which led me in turn to look closely into the circumstances of his public career and private life, and into the fortunes of what is commonly known as the "single-tax movement," which was launched into American politics towards the turn of the last century. I wondered then, and have wondered ever since, whether George would have consented to put himself and his philosophy at the service of an Adullamite political jehad if he had not been always so miserably poor. It seems most unlikely. His instinct was strongly against doing anything of the kind, and the cast of his mind was so eminently philosophic that one might expect him to have regarded the politics of America as Socrates regarded the politics of Athens—as something, that is, for a really sound politician to keep as far as possible away from. Instead, however, of concentrating his energies on remaining a man of thought, he divided them, and became in great part a man of action. One might make out a good case for the thesis that the corrosive action of poverty inflamed a naturally ardent and nobly sympathetic temperament to the point of making him peculiarly accessible to the urgings of what Mr. H. G. Wells calls the Gawdsaker—to the point where immediate action, even ill-considered action, in behalf of those as poor as himself, seemed a paramount duty.

This being so, it is interesting to speculate upon the historical position that George and his economic philosophy might even now occupy if the determining factor of poverty had not been present. Indeed, a thoughtful person might find that the principal effect of a close survey of this remarkable man's public career is to make one wonder what his influence would amount to at the present time if he had not been so poor.

Similarly an essayist might find a first-rate exercise for his imagination in trying to estimate the force of Napoleon's dire poverty as a factor in the fate of Europe. In all that has been written about Napoleon, I doubt that this has been done. Even *War and Peace,* which sets the high mark probably forever as a masterly job of deflating and debunking a historical personage, leaves this factor out of account; yet it must have been considerable. Napoleon, as Count Tolstoy says, makes his first appearance in French history as "a man of no convictions, no habits, no traditions, no name, not even a Frenchman"; moreover, he was dead broke, unsuccessful and despondent, an adventurer, offering his sword here and there, with no takers. The irregularities of his conduct in the French service caused him to be struck off the list of general officers, September 15, 1795; he was in disgrace. Nevertheless, the most extraordinary freaks of chance—a deadlock of partisan political forces, the puerile incompetence of his colleagues, the insignificance of his opponents—opened the way for a free exercise of "his frenzy of self-adoration, his insolence in crime and his frankness in mendacity," whereby his career was made.

Now, no doubt these opportunities lay open to any adventurer who happened to find himself on the spot at the moment, and if one had not been there, another might, and the consequences to Europe might have been quite the same. Napoleon certainly had no monopoly of the very moderate amount of sagacity that was needed to perceive the prospect which these freaks of chance held out, and to profit by them. But that is not the point. The point is whether, for example, if his father, dying in 1785, had left him a good substantial income, Napoleon would have been on the spot when the moment came, or anywhere near it. One may reasonably doubt that he would. It is highly probable, almost certain, that the moment would have found him much more congenially employed elsewhere, very likely at home in Corsica; his previous history gives a distinct colour to this supposition. I imagine that if he had chosen to stick to the practical side of military affairs, as seems most likely, he would have ended his days as a first-class competent artillery officer, high in the service; and if he had gone in for the theoretical side, he might have made himself another Clausewitz or Moltke. I believe that a disinterested examination of the matter would show that the basic reason why the disgraced Corsican adventurer, Nabulione Buonaparte, found himself on that particular spot at that particular moment was that practically all his adult life he had been poor and busted and looking for a job. Very probably, too, it was the sudden reaction from this condition that enhanced all the evil qualities in his nature and made them dominant, for this is what so regularly happens in such circumstances that its regularity has given rise to the common proverb concerning the risks of putting a beggar on horseback.

The essayist might have even more fun out of examining the career of Louis-Napoléon in the light of this idea. An anonymous writer of the last century says he knew Louis-Napoléon well for twenty-five years, and was almost certain that if he had not been so poor as he was, there would have been no Second Empire. A great deal can be said for this view. Even granting that he would go back to France in 1848 and put himself up for the presidency of Lamartine's ramshackle Second Republic, one might find pretty good ground for believing that as a rich man he would have been content to stay in that position and do what he could with it, rather than incur the risks and animosities involved in disintegrating republican solidarity and honeycombing the Legislative Assembly of 1849, in preparation for a *coup d'État.* But the more one considers the state of French politics ensuing upon the fall of the July monarchy, the less reason one sees why, if Louis-Napoléon had not been poor as Job's turkey, he would have dreamed of going back to France at all.

I shall not anticipate the essayist by recounting the conditions, subjective and circumstantial, which make this seem probable. Suffice it to say that but for his hamstringing impecuniosity, Louis-Napoléon was doing extremely well where he was. Always a studious and reflective man, in spirit much more a philosopher and poet than an emperor, he might have lived on very pleasurably in London, developing his ideas on free trade in association with Richard Cobden and John Bright, and in correspondence with Enfantin, the Péreires and Michel Chevalier. He might have written his projected history of Cæsar, continued his studies on the abolition of poverty, and no doubt made quite an impressive thing of his twin schemes for an international currency and for what would seem to be a very practicable sort of United States of Europe, based on the suppression of customs-frontiers. English society had received him most favourably, putting its best resources at his disposal for the beguilement of his lighter moments; while for those still lighter, he had the devotion of the blonde Miss Howard, who appears to have made herself always entertaining and delightful; and there is some evidence that her rôle in the drama of his life in London carried several capable understudies as well. As far as one can see, the only "out" in this excellent situation was his distressing poverty.

I believe one could draw up a highly plausible argument for the thesis that but for this one factor there would have been no Second Empire, and hence doubtless no calamitous messing about in Italian, Mexican and Oriental affairs; probably a satisfactory composition with Prince de Bismarck in the middle 'sixties, such as almost any bourgeois republic, however imbecile and venal, but alive to its own interest, might easily have arranged; indeed, Louis-Napoléon himself had two capital chances to arrange one, and flubbed them both. Above all, there would have been no Mlle. de Montijo, and hence no Wissembourg, Wörth, Spicheren, Sedan; and for the probable changes ensuing in English, German and Italian history, a whole volume of speculation would hardly be enough. As it stands, that history was determined by a skilfully pumped-up revival of the "Napoleonic tradition," and the primary spring of action behind that revival may well have been Louis-Napoléon's poverty. The various stories about his unshakable faith in his "star" have very much the air of something put out after the fact; or, as the sinful would say, the air of being mostly hooey.

The anonymous author whom I mentioned a moment ago says that after witnessing two days of the revolution of 1848 he never read a word about any of the revolutionary movements that took place in France during the nineteenth century. It was enough for him, he says, to know that these movements were invariably led by men in want of five or ten thousand a year. My essayist might look into this matter a little; my notion is that he would find plenty to reward him. It was the accepted understanding among those who were "in the know" that Lamartine proclaimed the Second Republic for money. The great orator was at that time not only in his usual state of being flat broke, but he was also about $70,000 in the red, and hounded by creditors. With a republican revolution under way, and a right smart chance of himself being president of the republic, he could get his debts paid; as in fact he did. He was somewhat a Daniel Webster of his time; and it is not unreasonable to suspect that his financial disabilities may have had a great deal to do with making him the fugleman of the shouts for a revolutionary republic.

The essayist might make similarly interesting finds among men who were prominent in the other upheavals that France went through after 1789. He could probably turn up something out of the White Terror of 1815, a good deal out of 1830,—Louis-Philippe never let himself or anyone else forget how desperately poor he had been; his preoccupation amounted almost to a mania,—more out of 1851, and he could fill a long chapter with a study of the needy political adventurers of 1870-1873, Gambetta, Favre, Jules Simon, and their fellow-strivers. While on this last period, too, he might digress for a moment to note a striking example of the effect of individual wealth upon the course of history. When the National Assembly met at Bordeaux in February 1871, it is almost a certainty that if the Orléans family had bestirred themselves in their own behalf, their dynasty would have been restored; which means that if this family had not been rich enough to keep out of the unwholesome prairie-dog's nest of French politics at that period, there would have been no Third Republic.

I have cited this century of French history only because it affords so many conspicuous and consecutive examples of the kind of thing I mean, and not at all implying that my essayist could not find plenty elsewhere, for they are like the sands of the sea for multitude wherever politics exist. Plenty such he could find in our own history, without rattling any skeletons in our neighbours' closets. I have in mind one statesman who influenced the course of our political history most profoundly, whom beyond doubt poverty nudged into politics in the first instance, as the easiest way to keep his body and soul together. I would give his name, but that his memory is dear to many, and some of them might think I was going out of my way to disparage him.

III

My mention of Mlle. de Montijo, better known as the Empress Eugénie, appropriately introduces my essayist to his second line of research, which is a study of henpecking from the historical point of view. All of us who have maintained even the most formal and austere relations with the fair sex may be presumed to have a fairly clear theoretical idea of what henpecking is; some of us, unhappily, perhaps most of us, have got our knowledge of it at the hands of that harshest of pedagogues, experience. My dictionary defines henpecking as domineering by one's wife; but when one thinks of Mme. du Barry and Mme. de Montespan, when one thinks of grandmothers, mothers-in-law, maiden aunts, elder sisters and débutante daughters, *Gott soll hüten,* this seems a very limited definition. One might put it more generally, I think, that henpecking is the habitual imposing of the female's will upon the male, whereby the male's disposition towards the matter at issue is overridden, and his will nullified.

The strategical methods employed in this exercise are very various, running all the way from the hawklike possessiveness of Mme. Polosov, the tragic tears of Mme. Karenin and the freezing hauteur of Lady Dedlock, to the intransigence of Mrs. Raddle, the bickering of Mrs. Caudle and the strong-arm methods of Mrs. Proudie. Those who know more of such matters than I do tell me that by nature practically every woman has all these methods at immediate command, and is also gifted with an extremely fine tactical sense in the matter of their mobilization and deployment. I suppose I might add that my own desultory observations rather tend to bear out this view.

The anonymous friend of Louis-Napoléon, whom I mentioned a moment ago, says in the course of some observations on the Empress that no one has traced the effects of henpecking on the course of history, and he cites some instances in support of his statement. Nevertheless he is not quite right. The henpecked man has mostly been fair game for the Jerrolds and Gavarnis of the world, but the essayist and historian have also sometimes taken him quite seriously. One's real complaint is that they have not followed through on him, not given the factor of henpecking anywhere near all it is worth, not as a rule taken more than its immediate consequences into account; whereas its more remote consequences are often the most important. For example, in the cardinal instance of Jeanne Poisson's henpecking Louis XV into the Seven Years' War, they do not go beyond the immediate political consequences to France, usually stopping with the defeat at Rosbach, the loss of Canada and the extinction of French influence in India; whereas the really interesting thing about this bit of henpecking is what it did to Germany and the German spirit, and what might have befallen these if the lady's seductions had not worked.

Maria-Theresa, wishing to recover Silesia, got together a group of nations in an alliance against Frederick the Great. To make this alliance strong enough, she had to get France into it; so she sent that strange creature, Prince de Kaunitz—albeit a first-class diplomat, though one hardly sees how he could be—over to Paris to labour

with Louis XV. France had just come out of the war
of the Austrian Succession with about as much to show
for it as the United States got out of the war of 1914,
and Louis felt towards this new proposal somewhat as
Senator Johnson might feel towards a suggestion from
the French Government that we should go over to
Europe in force next summer and help exterminate
Hitler. De Kaunitz encountered a deaf ear and a marble
heart; there was nothing doing; so he took the matter
up with Louis's lady-friend, Jeanne Poisson d'Étioles,
Marquise de Pompadour, and got results. It seems that
old Frederick, who was nothing of a lady's man, regarded
Jeanne's pretensions with blunt Prussian derision, and
had lampooned her outrageously in some pretty salty
verse—he could do that sort of thing rather well when
he felt like it—and Jeanne looked upon Maria-Theresa's
project as a providential chance to get even.

This was the prelude to the Seven Years' War, which
left Prussia flat; it was only Elizabeth of Russia's death
in 1762, and the immediate withdrawal of Peter III from
the alliance, which enabled Frederick to win the war
by the skin of his teeth. This victory, coupled with those
of the two preceding wars, no doubt laid the foundation
for the Germany of 1870-1914; but the preceding wars
had also firmly consolidated the German spirit, the
superb *Ernst der ins Ganze geht* which the domestic
policies of Frederick and his father had liberated and
fostered, and which was to make the later Germany the
most highly civilized nation of Europe. As far as this consolidation was concerned, the Seven Years' War was
superfluous and useless; and as far as the development
of those policies was concerned, it was mischievous and

retarding, for all the power and resource of the German *Geist,* which might have been so fruitfully employed otherwise, had to be concentrated on the problem of sheer physical recovery from the terrible blows which had well-nigh scourged Prussia off the face of the earth.

If, then, Jeanne Poisson had not henpecked Louis XV, Frederick would have had seven clear years of comparatively easy going in the administration of Prussia's internal affairs; and the question at once arises, what would have been the effect of those years on the future of Germany, not only as a factor in international politics, but also, and of far more consequence, as a moral and intellectual force in the world? Even under the handicap of the Seven Years' War, that force, as we all know, has been very great; and the fact of its having been so great adds interest to the conjecture at what it might have been, and might now be, but for that handicap.

The line of investigation in this instance is fairly easy to follow. For one that is less so, if the essayist cared to go back as far as the year 1535, he might look into the political consequences of the henpecking of Ercole, duke of Ferrara, by three of the most unbearable Frenchwomen who ever gained a place in recorded history. Then there was Prince Menshikov's Lithuanian servant-girl who seems to have put Peter the Great up to most of the good things he did, and also some bad ones, and who habitually burned the ground around his imperial moccasins when he did not show enough alacrity about heeding her suggestions. She became Catherine I of Russia, and if Catherine II's polyandry had not preëmpted the interest of our prurient reading public, she would no doubt be quite a figure in our modern fictional biography. Again, there was Sophia-Dorothea, whose henpecking of her husband resulted in the death of her first-born son, which opened the way to the throne of Prussia for her second son, who is known in history as Frederick the Great. Again, there was Susanna Wesley, who, despite her absorbing labours as the mother of nineteen children, still found time to hold the bull-whip relentlessly over her husband and her son John, who became the founder of Wesleyan Methodism. So one might go on through a long and varied list, from the contemplation of which one arises with an enhanced respect, perhaps tempered by some little touch of uneasiness and apprehension, for the astounding qualities of generalship therein set forth and made manifest.

IV

"Why, of course that is true," cried a vivacious French friend, with whom I lately broached this topic of henpecking. "Who does the milking in Europe? The women. The American woman won't do it, so the man must, with the result that presently he is bored with it, and invents a machine to do it for him. She won't sweep; the man gets tired of living in squalor, and rather than do the sweeping himself, he invents the vacuum-cleaner. She won't cook; so for a while the man risks dyspepsia and ptomaine poisoning on the utterly uninteresting food which your public eating-places provide, and then invents automatic toasters, roasters, boilers, fryers and God knows what not, on the forlorn chance that he can get something out of them that is fit for a dog to eat. She can't think, can't read anything worth reading, can't converse intelligently, can't sit still; the man puts up with her restlessness as long as he can, and then invents the automobile, the radio, the motion-picture, in order to take her out of herself, and thereby give him a few hours of peace.

"If you looked into it, I believe you would find that henpecking is responsible for half the so-called labour-saving gadgets in the world; and I assure you, my friend, this henpecking has made considerable history already, and is making more every day. It goes against my grain to say so, for I like your people and admire the many good things they have done, but I believe they are fast taking leave of their ancient and inbred integrities, and are setting up instead the ideal of a national life which shall yield all good things to everybody at the touch of a button. My understanding is that you call it the More Abundant Life. I call it a life without any worthy purpose to guide it, without intelligence, without principle, without conscience—in a word, without character. I don't like many things that are going on at home in my own country, and still less do I like some things that our neighbours are doing; but neither they nor we are setting up any such ideal of a national life as that. Your Mr. Hopkins, the president of one of your colleges, said as much in a recent issue of that magazine which you sometimes write for, and he is right. More of you ought to be saying the same thing, and saying it straight from the shoulder, for if you persist in following after that ideal, you may take it from me that it will sink your civilization straight down to Peg Trantum's, as our old friend Panurge says, fifteen fathom below the corridor that leads to the black pit of Demigorgon."

My friend's imagination may have been a little over-wrought, though I do not imagine he meant to hold the influence of our women wholly responsible for this un-promising state of things; yet no doubt their influence must be reckoned with in casting up the sum of that responsibility. But we are not concerned with this at present, for I cite the conversation only as suggesting still another point of departure for a research which the essayist might find rewarding; and with that I bring my little flight of fancy to an end. I reiterate my belief that poverty and henpecking have never been appraised at anything like their actual importance in determining the course of history; and while, as I said at the outset, I would not dream of asking for a book on the subject or take the responsibility of recommending one, yet if such a book should by any chance appear, it would be just the book that I should like to read.

New York, September, 1936.

5

Artemus Ward's America

IN February 1923, France was in very bad shape indeed. She was at the height of the war, the real war, whereof the disturbances of 1914-1918 were only a curtain-raiser—the war which is still going on, apparently unbeknown to our futile "disarmament-conferences." Under these hard circumstances France celebrated the hundredth anniversary of the birth of Ernest Renan, scholar, philosopher, man of letters. M. Poincaré made a speech, not as a member of the government, but as a member of the French Academy. M. Barthou, the present Foreign Minister, also spoke, not as a politician (I think he was out of office at the moment, though I am not sure), but as representing one of the other constituents of the Institute of France,—if my memory serves me, it was the Academy of Sciences,—and next morning the *Temps* devoted a good four-fifths of its space to a report of the event.

To get an idea of this in American terms, we should have to imagine our country far deeper in the doldrums than it was two years ago, yet taking its mind off its troubles long enough to celebrate, say, the centenary of Ralph Waldo Emerson as a national event; with Mr.

Roosevelt representing Harvard University—and really doing it, doing it in the grand style—and ex-Secretary Adams representing the American Historical Society, also in the grand style; and the New York *Times* giving up something like twenty-two pages of its daily issue to the occasion!

America has often been reproached as doing little for its illustrious dead except for those whose memory can be profitably capitalized by politicians. This is as it may be. What has not been sufficiently remarked, I believe, is that in such cases the exigencies of exploitation lead us to glorify these worthies for qualities that they did not conspicuously possess, and to slight the qualities that really made them great. In putting out their memory for public consumption we misbrand it for partisan purposes so flagrantly that if our politicians had to face an equivalent of the Food and Drugs Act there would be close quarters in the penitentiary most of the time.

For example, we do not celebrate Lincoln as a politician, yet his actual title to fame is that he was far and away the greatest politician we ever produced, and doubtless one of the first half-dozen politicians of the world. As a politician he was candid, always ready to say, as he did say, that the way of the politician is "a long step removed from common honesty"; but many American politicians have been equally candid—think of Penrose, Quay, Cameron. He never enriched himself in office, but very few of our Presidents have done that, and many politicians below the rank of the Presidency never turned a dishonest dollar—think of Hamilton, who made so many rich, yet remained all his life quite poor. Lincoln was nationally-minded, when his mind at last became set that way—well, think of John Adams and his son, John Quincy, who were born nationally-minded. Lincoln was eminently humane, generous, affable, humorous, patient, simple-hearted—but, dear me, so was Tim Sullivan. It is this misdirection of homage, this persistent excess of adulation for the wrong thing, that throws an air of fictitiousness and unreality over our praise of Lincoln and indeed over practically the whole body of Lincolniana.

Then on the other hand we celebrate Thomas Jefferson as the master-politician who built a powerful Minerva-like political party all out of his own head, and therewith saved the country. In April of every year his name is consistently and most blasphemously invoked upon clandestine purposes which he abhorred, and for the most part by men whom he would not have let set foot on his premises. Can one imagine, for instance, Mr. Roosevelt darkening the doors of the man who said in 1800, "What an augmentation of the field for jobbing, speculating, plundering, office-building and office-hunting would be produced by an assumption of all the State powers into the hands of the general government!" and who said in 1821 that "our government is now taking so steady a course as to show by what road it will pass to destruction, to wit: by consolidation first, and then corruption, its necessary consequence"? I can not imagine it.

The fact is, if Mr. Claude Bowers will permit me to say so, that Mr. Jefferson was but an indifferent politician. His party pretty well formed itself, out of material supplied mostly by the opposition, much as in 1932. The biographer's fable of a kind of political

Svengali or Professor Moriarty makes agreeable reading
even for those who know better, but it will not wash.
To glorify Mr. Jefferson for these qualities is to misread
his greatness completely and culpably; and in proportion
as they are magnified, the qualities that really made him
great are obscured.

But why should a people consider its illustrious dead
so closely? Because its attitude toward them is an index
of the national spirit; it marks the difference between
a nation and an agglomeration. In 1882 Ernest Renan
made an address at the Sorbonne on the question, "What
is a Nation?" He showed that geography, language, race,
religion, military requirements or economic interest
does not make a nation. Some combination of them may
constitute a source from which one draws one's gains,
but, whether severally or in combination, they do not
give rise to a national life. A nation is a soul, a spiritual
principle evoked by the common possession of a rich
legacy of remembrances, and by the will to keep improving this hereditary property for the benefit of those
who shall receive it hereafter in their turn. "Man does
not improvise himself," said Renan, austerely; a nation,
like an individual, is the culmination of an age-long
spiritual tendency; and therefore the cult of ancestors
is the soundest of all cults, because it is our ancestors
who have made us what we are.

This doctrine is manifestly a little out with the temper
of our enlightened age; for the moment, at any rate, one
would say that improvisation is quite the rule, and that
a spiritual heritage is about the very last thing that our
enlightened age could be induced to take stock in. But
suppose we grant provisionally that there may be some-

thing in the idea; then the next question is, Why should a people ever remind itself of any names but the famous ones? Because its spiritual heritage is purely a quality-product, and fame, which is largely the product of accident and circumstance, is no measure of a contribution to it. To recognize and correctly appraise a sound contribution, wherever found, is an index of the national spirit's intensity, and thus the names that are great but not famous are a touchstone. We may put it that a people which has the true measure of its Bacons, Renans, Jeffersons, and feels a sense of spiritual continuity with them, is by way of being a nation; and a people which, over and above this, has the true measure of its Falklands, Jouberts, Thoreaus, and feels a sense of spiritual continuity with them, is by way of being a great nation.

II

These thoughts were brought to my mind last spring by an interesting circumstance connected with the memory of an American who was not famous. He was not famous while he lived, and he is not famous now. Charles Farrar Browne, who wrote under the pen-name of Artemus Ward, was born at Waterford, Maine, on the twenty-sixth of April, 1834. When his centenary came round, I looked through various publications for some mention of him, but found none. Probably the Cleveland *Plain Dealer* said something about its old reporter and contributor, but there was no copy of that paper handy, so I do not know. Such of our national publications as profess and call themselves literary said nothing; or rather, I should say, those that I examined said nothing—I can not pretend to have seen them all. The London *Times Literary Supplement,* however, in its issue for the week of April 26, gave him the whole of the front page and a column and a half run-over on the second.

One might suspect, of course, that the *Times's* essayist was hard up at the moment for something to write about. What with an article promised, press-day coming on, and one thing or another turning up to distract one's thoughts, this sometimes happens. Yet the essay did not read as if that were the case, but quite otherwise. Then, too, essayists have always to reckon with editors, and editors are notoriously close-fisted with their space, and inhospitable towards topics of doubtful interest. Moreover, the roster of British literary worthies is extremely long, and an essayist who is out to see what he can do with a respectable but obscure literary figure need not cross the ocean to find one. All in all, we may take it, I think, that Artemus Ward was not lugged in by the ears as a filler, but that the *Times* regarded his centenary as valid front-page matter. This raises the question why the *Times* should so regard it. The essayist says frankly that "to most English people Artemus Ward is now only a name; yet the name persists." Well, but why does it persist? Did Ward actually contribute anything to the spiritual heritage of English-speaking people that would justify the *Times* in reviving his memory? If so, what was it?

Certainly nothing in his public career; it was too short. He died in his thirty-third year, on the sixth of March, 1867. He had a first-rate reputation as a professional humorist, and as a lecturer in this field he did exceedingly well. He seems to have been successful with any kind of audience; he delighted Western silver-miners, Mormon elders and their flock, as well as the miscellaneous audiences of New York and London, where the high lights of politics, letters and society forgathered with the humbler hearers of his discourse. He edited *Vanity Fair* for a short time, in succession to Charles Godfrey Leland, but he could not brace his paper against the stress of the Civil War, and it died on his hands. One doubts, though, that he would have done much better under easier circumstances; his gifts did not lie that way.

Thus there is nothing in his career as editor and lecturer that helps us to reappraise him in terms of our own time. His personality was by all accounts most prepossessing and charming, but it is gone, and the other adventitious aids to his popularity have only an antiquarian interest for us, if any. All he has of present value —assuming that he has anything—is contained in the slim bulk of his writings; and here too the topics that he treated, and the names that appear on his pages, seem all but mythical. He wrote little and irregularly, almost scrappily, never at any length. His best work is in the odds-and-ends that he published in the *Plain Dealer* and *Vanity Fair* in the guise of letters from an itinerant showman; and in the three or four contributions that he made to *Punch*. As the writings of a professional humorist, I think one must say that they are largely dissatisfying. The *Times's* essayist loyally makes the best of them, but can not quite commit himself to the conventional apparatus of eccentric spelling, extravaganza and frontier dialect that served the popular notion of American humour seventy years ago; nor yet can we.

No doubt there is excellent humour in Ward's writings. For instance, with the current ethics of our stage in mind, one may see great humour in his account of a disagreement with a former partner whose name was Billson, over a matter of policy.

Billson and me orjanized a strollin dramatic company, & we played The Drunkard, or the Falling Saved, with a real Drunkard. The play did n't take particlarly, and says Billson to me, Let's give 'em some immoral dramy. We had a large troop onto our hands, consistin of eight tragedians and a bass drum, but I says, No, Billson; and then says I, Billson, you hain't got a well-balanced mind. Says he, Yes, I have, old hoss-fly (he was a low cuss)—yes, I have. I have a mind, says he, that balances in any direction that the public rekires. That's wot I call a well-balanced mind.

Again, remembering our purely conventional accept-ance of the death-scene on the stage,—Mimi, Violetta, Tristan, Valentine,—this incident in Billson's earlier career is delightfully amusing:

The miser'ble man once played Hamlet. There was n't any orchestry, and wishin to expire to slow moosic, he died playin onto a claironett himself, interspersed with hart-rendin groans.

But if all Ward's humour were as good as this (and by no means all of it is; his work is very uneven) we should still be obliged to say that one must look else-where for a really significant contribution to our spir-itual heritage.

Where, then, are we to look? If his quality as a hu-morist is not conspicuous, if there are others who, to say the least, perfectly stand comparison with him in this field,—as certainly there are,—did he have another quality that does conspicuously set him off against them? Is he a victim of the misbranding process which I described at length a moment ago, so that in citing him as a humorist, as we invariably do, we are citing him for the wrong thing? I think it is highly probable.

III

I suggest that Ward was the first really great critic of American society, and that in this capacity he remains to-day, as he said of his Grate Show, "ekalled by few & exceld by none." In fact, the only one who seems to me to stand with him is another victim of popular misbranding in our own time, Mr. Dooley. In our appreciation of both these men it is interesting to see how far our instinct outruns our intelligence; we think they affect us by the power of their humour, when nine times out of ten what actually affects us is the power of their criticism—and here, no doubt, we have the reason why their names persist. For instance, there is no great humour in Ward's oft-quoted observation on the fanatical extravagances of Abolitionism; what really interests us is its exact correspondence with history's verdict upon them. Nevertheless the predisposition bred by misbranding leads us to think we are interested in the humour which is not there, rather than in the criticism which is there. I quote the remark afresh to show how this is so:

Feller Sitterzens, the Afrikan may be Our Brother. Sevral hily respectyble gentlemen and sum talented females tell us so, & fur argyment's sake I mite be injooced to grant it, tho I don't beleeve it myself. But the Afrikan is n't sevral of our brothers & all our fust wife's relashuns. He is n't our grandfather and our grate-grandfather and our Aunt in the country. Scacely. & yit numeris persons would have us think so.

There is no trouble now about making a sound critical estimate of the public questions that led up to the Civil War, or of the men whom those issues brought into prominence. Making one in 1862 was another matter. Every political *démarche* has a pretext as well as a cause; and for one reason or another things are usually managed so that the lambent warmth of patriotism shall play around the pretext only—one could write a very telling treatise on the function of the pretext in practical politics. The ability to disengage the pretext, to appraise it for what it is, and to keep a clear and steady view of the cause, is a mark of the true critic; and the ability to do this amid a riot of the worst passions and the meanest prejudices is a mark of the great critic.

Ward had this ability. He was a Unionist, a friend of the Administration, yet his greatest praise of Lincoln was for remaining "unscared and unmoved by Secesh in front of you and Abbolish at the back of you, each one of which is a little wuss than the other, if possible." He had no illusions whatever about the actual place of slavery in the category of war-issues. On tour in Alabama with his Grate Show at the outbreak of the war:

I saw a nigger sittin on a fence a-playin on a banjo. "My Afrikan Brother," sed I, coting from a Tract I onct red, "you belong to a very interesting race. Your masters is going to war exclosively on your account."

"Yes, boss," he replied, "an' I wish 'em honorable graves," and he went on playin the banjo, larfin all over and openin his mouth wide enuff to drive in an old-fashioned 2-wheeled chaise.

A public movement launched under a pretext of liberation always breeds a monstrously inflated notion of the qualities of the people or class whom it is proposed to liberate. The more highly vocal and voluble element in American society idealized the Negro in Ward's day as elaborately as in our day it idealized the indigent Poles, the oppressed Armenians, the suffering Belgians, and now idealizes the proletariat. The old showman stopped at Richmond after the surrender, and a Negro bellboy showed him to his quarters:

I accompanied the Afrikan to my lodgins. "My brother," I sed, "air you aware that you 've been 'mancipated? Do you realize how glorus it is to be free? Tell me, my dear brother, does it not seem like some dreams, or do you realize the great fact in all its livin and holy magnitood?"
He sed he would take some gin.

Ward knew well the kind of men that circumstances were bringing to the fore, in both high places and low. He seems aware that great national disturbances leave a society with its *Oberhefe* and its *Unterhefe* precipitated, as in German beer—its scum at the top and its dregs at the bottom. The essential levity of certain characters who are prominent in our *Oberhefe* to-day must, I think, remind the judicious of the old showman's advice to Lincoln concerning his Secretary of War:

Tell E. Stanton that his boldness, honesty and vigger merits all prase, but to keep his undergarmints on. E. Stanton has appeerently only one weakness, which it is he can't allus keep his undergarmints from flyin up over his hed.

At the outset of Mr. Roosevelt's Administration, also, certain features of the New Deal must have brought to mind Ward's admirable suggestion for the make-up of a Brain Trust:

"How 'bout my Cabinit, Mister Ward?" sed Abe.

"Fill it up with Showmen, sir! Showmen is devoid of politics. They hain't got any principles. They know how to cater for the public. They know what the public wants, North and South. Showmen, sir, is honest men. If you doubt their literary ability, look at their posters and see small bills. If you want a Cabinit as is a Cabinit, fill it up with showmen, but don't call on me. The moral wax figger perfeshun must n't be permitted to go down while there's a drop of blood in these vains."

In the muck of the *Unterhefe,* as well, Ward's eye easily made out the unsavoury figure of the profiteer. His *Romance of William Barker, the Young Patriot,* is a brief but pungent summary of the doctrine of "business as usual." He also knew the patrioteer, whom war lets loose upon the community as a sneaking spy and inquisitor-at-large. Boarding a train in Alabama:

I had n't more'n fairly squatted afore a dark-lookin man with a swinister expression onto his countenance entered the cars, and lookin very sharp at me, he axed what was my principles.

"Secesh," I ansered. "I'm a Dissoluter. I'm in favor of Jeff Davis, Bowregard, Pickens, Capt. Kidd, Bloobeard, Munro Edards, the devil, Mrs. Cunningham, and all the rest of 'em."

"You're in favor of the war?"

"Certingly. By all means. I'm in favor of this war and

also of the next war. I've been in favor of the next war
for over sixteen years."

"War to the knive?" sed the man.

"Blud, Eargo, blud!" sed I, tho them words is n't
origgernal with me.

Ward measured the depth of routine patriotism in
North and South alike with unfailing accuracy. He wrote
several pieces showing the progress of the war-fever
among his neighbours in Baldwinsville, Indiana, and
they reflect faithfully all the ignorant ferocity, the puer-
ilities of petty self-interest, the abject hypocrisies, that
were rampant in every twopenny town in the United
States seventeen years ago, and in similar circumstances
will be rampant again. These pieces are so closely ar-
ticulated that I can not quote from them; they must
be read in their entirety. One may say as little as one
likes for their humour, but their criticism is sound and
searching. The showman was gentler with the South, as
became a visitor; yet where can better criticism be found
than this, in his letter from Richmond after General
Lee's surrender?

There is raly a great deal of Union sentiment in this
city. I can see it on every hand.

I met a man today—I am not at liberty to tell his
name, but he is a old and inflooential citizen of Richmond, and sez he, "Why, we've bin fightin agin the Old
Flag! Lor bless me, how sing'lar!" He then borrered five
dollars of me and bust into a flood of tears.

IV

It is closeness of correspondence with the verdict of
history, or with what Aristotle calls "the determination

of the judicious," that establishes the validity of criticism. Ward's pages give a remarkably complete appraisal of what our publicists call "the American psychology," whereby one may see clearly what it looks like, and what the civilization ensuing upon it looks like, when viewed *sub specie æternitatis*. There are very few aspects of our collective life which he does not illuminate and exhibit as they really are, rather than as distorted by the myopia of prepossession or the delirium of vanity. Like a good artist, he does this by indirection. The great literary artist is one who powerfully impresses a reader with an attitude of mind, a mood, a temper, a state of being, without describing it. If he describes it—if, that is, he anywhere injects himself into the process—the effect is lost. This is the literary art so manifest in the Gospel narrative; and it is this that makes Turgeniev supreme among modern artists.

Ward once said of writers like himself (and I venture to emphasize his very remarkable words) that "the truth has found more aid from them than from all the grave polemists and solid writers that have ever spoken or written. . . . They have helped the truth along *without encumbering it with themselves*." If, indeed, we approach Ward as a critic, leaving aside all thought of his humour, we may see how ably he has helped along the truth about our civilization; and how, too, he has helped it along in the way that good things are as a rule most effectively helped along—by indirection.

As Ward saw America, its god was Good Business; its monotheism was impregnable. Of man's five fundamental social instincts only one, the instinct of expansion, had free play, and its range was limitless. The instincts of intellect and knowledge, of religion and morals, of beauty and poetry, of social life and manners, were disallowed and perverted. The old showman is himself a most orthodox monotheist; when all comes to all, he worships only the god of Good Business and him only does he serve. At Oberlin College he called on Professor Peck "for the purpuss of skewerin Kolonial Hall to exhibit my wax works and beests of Pray into."

Sez Perfesser Peck, "Mister Ward, I don't know 'bout this bizness. What air your sentiments?"

Sez I, "I hain't got any."

"Good God!" cried the Perfesser. "Did I understan you to say you have no sentiments?"

"Nary a sentiment," sez I.

"Mister Ward, don't your blud bile at the thawt that three million and a half of your cullud brethren air a clankin their chains in the South?"

Sez I, "Not a bile. Let 'em clank. . . . The pint is, can I have your Hall by payin a fair price? You air full of sentiments. That's your lay, while I'm a exhibiter of startlin curiosities. What d'ye say?"

Ward understood the conventional defense-mechanisms and subterfuges that must be employed pretty regularly to lend plausibility to one's adventures in the service of the one true god. Prince de Metternich says that when he visited Paris in the days of Louis-Philippe he grew so sick of the word *fraternité* that if he had a brother he would call him cousin. For nearly twenty years the word "moral" has been so debased in the promotion of political mountebankery and scoundrelism that the sound of it affects a decent person with the utmost repugnance. Ever since 1917, when I have caught a statesman or a publicist using that word in even the most innocent connexion, it has instantly brought to my mind the letter that Ward wrote to a newspaper editor for puffs of his Grate Show.

My show at present consists of three moral Bares, a Kangaroo . . . besides several miscellanyus moral wax statoots of celebrated piruts & murderers. . . . I shall have my hanbills dun at your office. Depend upon it. . . . Also git up a tremenjus excitement in yr. paper 'bowt my onparaleld Show. We must fetch the public sumhow. We must wurk on their feelins. *Cum the moral on 'em strong.*

In all this we may see how well Ward anticipates "the determination of the judicious," how precisely his criticism agrees with the verdict of history. Likewise when one surveys the general order of civilization that he exhibits, one sees the same close correspondence. A society that gives play only to the instinct of expansion must inevitably be characterized by a low type of intellect, a grotesque type of religion, a factitious type of morals, an imperfect type of beauty, an imperfect type of social life and manners. In a word, it is uncivilized; well, just such is the society that Ward depicts. Baldwinsville's intellectual pabulum is provided by the local *Bugle-horn of Liberty,* edited by Mr. Slinkers; Ward gives us specimens of Mr. Slinker's editorial style and substance, and they afford a competent measure of his readers. Baldwinsville's religious aspirations are satisfied with what Burke calls "the dissidence of Dissent, and the protestantism of the Protestant religions," as interpreted by Parson Batkins. Its resources of sentiment and poetry are measured by the showman's courtship of Betsy Jane Peasley, and their subsequent domestic life. Its ideal of social life and manners is displayed in the merrymaking over the birth of the showman's twins. In all, Baldwinsville is perhaps not devoid of interest, yet clearly the student of civilized man would find little there to serve his purpose; and, while its citizens are doubtless not devoid of certain virtues, he would find them intolerable company.

Ward copper-rivets his criticism by his complete identification of the showman with this profoundly imperfect society. The showman carries the atmosphere of Baldwinsville with him wherever he goes; its views of life and its demands on life are his; they are sufficient to delight and satisfy him. As a guest of the Shakers, he applies to their peculiar practices the standards of a religion as grotesque and imperfect as their own, and does it with an utterly naïve unconsciousness that any other standards might be applicable. Among the Mormons and the Free Lovers he applies the standards of Baldwinsville's factitious morality in the same naïve fashion. He confronts the Woman's Rights Association with Baldwinsville's most straitest doctrine of domesticity. In the realm of æsthetics he responds cordially to the sex-attraction of Piccolomini and Patti, but wonders why Patti does not sing in English since she does so well in Italian. The male members of the troupe do not interest him, and he pronounces the immemorial judgment of Baldwinsville on the futility of their occupation.

As fur Brignoly, Ferri and Junky, they air dowtless grate, but I think sich able-boddied men would look better tillin the sile than dressin theirselves up in black close & white kid gluvs & shoutin in a furrin tung. Mister Junky is a noble-lookin old man & orter lead armies on to Battel instid of shoutin in a furrin tung.

But while wisdom, shrewdness, and penetration may make a great critic, they are not enough to make a critic of the very first order. They make a Swift or a Juvenal; they do not make a Cervantes or a Rabelais. Lucidity of mind is not enough for that; it must be balanced by largeness of temper, by an easy, urbane, unruffled superiority to the subject of its criticism. Swift was a great and sound critic, but of this temper he had all too little; his writings bristle with the *sæva indignatio* which induces in the reader a frame of mind quite alien to that which criticism of the first order brings out. Ward's contemporary, Mark Twain,—he was a year younger than Ward,—was a great critic, but the *sæva indignatio,* when not actually present in his writings, is never far off; one is conscious of it as of a thunderstorm yet distant but likely to break at any time. Ward had the true critical temper; it pervades his criticism and makes it wholly acceptable. Its influence dissolves rancour; by its aid one surveys the hardness and hideousness of Baldwinsville in a truly Socratic spirit, with no resentment, and with no evangelical desire to expostulate with the citizens of Baldwinsville upon their waste of life. To see how thoroughly pervasive Ward's critical temper is, let us notice how the old showman writes his wife from "the Athens of America."

Dear Betsy: I write you this from Boston, "the Modern Atkins," as it is denomyunated, altho I skurcely know what those air.

How insignificant the remark seems; yet, when we let it sink in, how well it manages to colour one's whole cast of thought, and to induce precisely the right frame of mind in which to approach the gentle, rather agreeable, but somewhat self-contained provincialism which characterized the Boston of 1860. Probably this is as interesting an exhibit as one could find of the medium in which criticism of the first order works. The inscription on Ward's tomb says that "his name will live as a sweet and unfading recollection"; and his name may indeed remind us that a critical equipment of the first order must include sweetness no less than light.

V

And so we come back to our text; we come back to our reason why a people should keep alive the memory of its great men, the obscure as well as the famous; and above all, why it should carefully and clearly discern the qualities that made them great. If I were asked whether France is a nation, I would not waste time over the consolidating genius of Louis XI. I would point to the celebration of the memory of Ernest Renan, and invite my questioner to consider closely the spirit that animated the speeches of M. Poincaré and M. Barthou. I would say that a nation exists where there is a sense of participation in a common spiritual heritage, and a will to improve that heritage for the benefit of those to whom it shall be in turn passed on. Where this sense and will do not exist, no nation exists. There may be an agglomeration of whatever sort, held together by adventitious ties of whatever sort, but this is not a nation.

Our histories tell us that the Civil War finally and forever established the United States as a nation, rather than as an association of sovereign states. One hesitates a little about accepting this statement. The Civil War forged out a political entity, but a political entity is not a nation; far from it—think of the old Austrian Empire. We are an economic agglomeration of importance, doing business over an enormous free-trade area; but, as Renan said, "a customs-union is not a fatherland," and there is even better authority for suspecting that a people's life consisteth not in the abundance of the things that it possesseth. The question whether the United States is actually a nation has interest, and I leave it with my readers, since I can not pretend that my own opinion in the matter is particularly valuable. I merely suggest that in the nature of things a people's regard for its spiritual ancestry would seem to be a fair measure of its right to call itself a nation, and also a fair index of its national life.

Brussels, May, 1934.

6

Thoughts from Abroad

THE currents of Chance lately washed me up on the shores of a little-visited European country which I soon found to be in some respects perhaps the most interesting in the world, at the moment. I can be more at ease in writing about it if I give it the thin disguise of a pseudonym, so let me call it Amenia. It deserves this name not only because it is a very beautiful land, but also because its inhabitants are so uncommonly amiable and gracious to strangers; I find that they have an international reputation throughout all Europe for this trait. They will take no offense, I am sure, at my masking their country under a fanciful name, for I am merely following an old-fashioned convention which has its root in delicacy, like the convention that governs the British House of Commons, where one member may pretty well say what he likes about another member, provided he do not name him.

What made Amenia so interesting to me, as a visitor fresh from America, can be summed up in a sentence. From our point of view, nearly everything in Amenia is wrong, and yet the country manages to get on remarkably well. By every rule of the game, Amenia ought not to get on at all, but it somehow does. Its politics are frightfully wrong, its economics are wrong, its views of a proper constitution of human society are practically all wrong; yet there the wretched country is, impenitently racking along, quite as if its fundamental theories of collective human life were as sound as ours.

I submit that to a student of civilization this is an interesting state of things, and doubly so at the moment. For example, Amenia is solvent, as I hear few countries are; certainly those I see and read about seem mostly busted. The *publice egestas, privatim opulentia,* which Sallust puts into the mouth of Cato as evidence of a nation's decline, is visible everywhere. I notice in a London paper to-day the statement that our own national debt now amounts to twenty-two and a quarter billion dollars; also that Britain's national debt is eleven times as much as it was in 1913. My notion is that it would take a bit of scratching to get that amount of money together in either country. Amenia has only a trifle of debt, which worries nobody, and which she could clean up on short notice without overstraining herself. Amenia, moreover, pays as she goes. Amidst the general fiscal dilapidation of the last four years, Amenia has balanced her budget each year. I was told that in the good days when our bankers were dusting money around Europe all so freely, some of them urged a loan on Amenia, but the government said no, much obliged, they thought they would try to squeeze along on their own. Again, business in Amenia is very fair—nothing startling, but probably up to Sam Weller's standard of normality—while in other countries it is apparently slack. Again, Amenia seems to have no unwieldy labour-surplus. Everyone able to work has some sort of job which perhaps will not make his everlasting fortune, but which manages to keep him going; and in this respect, too, other countries are not so well off, according to all I hear.

In drawing comparisons between Amenia and other countries, however, I have not the least idea of advertising Amenia as a happy hunting-ground for American visitors, and making it out so attractive that everyone will wish to go there. Not at all. On the contrary, I think that for many reasons the average run of our tourists would do better elsewhere; Amenia, I should say, is probably not quite their kind of thing. Still less would I suggest that we ought to copy Amenia's ways and views and ideals. Amenia did not impress me in this stark fashion, either as bait for the vagrant impulse to "go places and do things," or as an institutional model. It impressed me only as an incentive to a study of absolutes. What I saw there turned my mind back on itself, and made me reëxamine a number of matters which we tend to put down as absolute; absolutely Good, absolutely Bad, absolutely True or False, absolutely Right or Wrong. What my conclusions were, or whether I came to any, is of no importance. The only thing I wish to dwell on is the sheer pleasure of being in a situation that moves one strongly to review the *chose jugée,* to reopen questions that mere use-and-wont has led us to regard as definitively closed, and let one's consciousness play over them freely. There are few exercises more exhilarating than this, and Amenia is one of the few spots left in a highly uninteresting world that stimulate one to pursue it.

II

I shall put down my impressions at haphazard as they occur to me, with no special care for arrangement. In the first place, I found that there is a great deal of illiteracy in Amenia; and by the way, I was led to this discovery by the conspicuous and delightful absence of roadside advertising-signs. I was told that the Amenians are fifty per cent illiterate; some put it higher. Having no passion for statistics, I did not take the trouble to look up the official figures; it was enough for my purposes to know that most of the people I saw about me were unable to read or write.

In our view, this is of course wrong. It is an absolute of our social faith that illiteracy is Bad. This is one of the very few points, indeed I think the only one, at which Mr. Jefferson succeeded in striking his belief deeply into the American consciousness. He put literacy as a condition of good citizenship, and the people accepted his view; which was in itself, perhaps, an indication that the matter would stand a little sifting. No one now, I imagine, has any doubt that general literacy is a Good-in-Itself—that is to say, an absolute. This belief is a republican heirloom, passed on in complete integrity, and unexamined, from the casket of eighteenth-century political theory to its present place in Columbia's shining crown.

Just so. I noticed, however, that the capital of Amenia is remarkable for its bookstores; it has relatively more and better bookstores, I believe, than any city in the world. In fact, the only commercial exhibits there that strike a stranger's eye are the bookstores and jewellery stores; the rest are unimpressive. Leaving aside all questions of comparative quality, I tried to estimate how many bookstores New York would have in the same ratio, first, to its actual population, and second, to its proportion of literacy; but the figures were so incredibly fantastic that I did not think it worth while even to make a note of them.

These premises seemed to warrant the inference that Amenia has a small but serious reading public; one that owns its books and reads them, and that in general may be thought to regard a book as an instrument of culture rather than as a stopgap for idle time. This inference is borne out by a French authority, who says that Amenia has *une petite élite extrêmement brillante et cultivée*. My mind then went back to the immense masses of garbage shot daily from the press of more literate lands, and I wondered just what the net gain—understand me clearly, the *net* gain—of a general and indiscriminate literacy really is. Our republicanism assumes that there is a net gain, and so indeed there may be, but just what is it? With all our devotion to "research," I do not think that our institutions of learning have ever entertained this question; yet I submit that it is worth attention.

In the eighteenth century, before Western society had been penetrated by the minor commonplaces of republicanism, Bishop Butler—almost a contemporary of Mr. Jefferson—remarked that the great majority of people are far more handy at passing things through their minds than they are at thinking about them; and therefore, considering the kind of thing they usually read, very little of their time is more idly spent than the time spent in reading. This fact is more noticeable now by far than it was in Bishop Butler's day; and when set off against Amenia's condition, it is bound to make one wonder what, precisely, this particular absolute of our republicanism amounts to. What, precisely, would the civilization of Amenia gain by a more general spread of literacy? What, precisely, would ours lose by a shrinkage of literacy to Amenia's level? Does the indiscriminate spread of literacy encounter an unsuspected moral equivalent of Gresham's law, that "bad money drives out good"? Does it encounter a moral equivalent of the law of diminishing returns?

The whole question is rather a pretty one, and as far as I know, our doctrinaire republicanism has hitherto had no better answer for it than the "plain argument" which Lord Peter applies to the doubts of his brothers, in the *Tale of a Tub;* and this, while in a sense perhaps effective, is hardly satisfactory.[1]

III

One can not go to and fro among the Amenians for any length of time without perceiving that their theory of business is wrong. Their idea is that supply should

[1] Satirizing the doctrine of transubstantiation, Swift brings in Lord Peter at dinner, carving slices of bread for his brothers, Jack and Martin (i.e., Calvin and Luther), assuring them that it is mutton, and becoming very angry when they express their doubts. " 'Look ye, gentlemen,' cries Peter, in a rage: 'to convince you what a couple of blind, positive, ignorant, wilful puppies you are, I will use but this plain argument: by God, it is true, good, natural mutton as any in Leadenhall market; and God confound you both eternally if you offer to believe otherwise.' Such a thundering proof as this left no farther room for objection." *Tale of a Tub,* section 4.

follow demand, and that the purchaser should seek the vendor; whereas the Right Idea, as we all know, is that supply should precede demand, and that the vendor should hound and bedevil the purchaser with all kinds of importunities, in order to keep demand going at its maximum speed. Thus the ideal development of a nation's business is a joyous game of what in our youthful days we used to call "outrunning the constable"; and hence, to an American eye, nothing is more unnatural and shocking than the stringency with which Amenia's business is kept down to the level of solid requirement. Hardly anything is done deliberately to increase consumption. The Amenians have only the vaguest and most uncertain notion of "creating a market," or of splitting up purchasing-power among a dozen or more competing varieties of what is actually the same thing. Yet, as I said, somehow or other business manages to do very well under these conditions, and it is perhaps equally remarkable that the visiting stranger who comes here quite unaccustomed to these peculiar ideas of business soon finds that he too is doing very well, even though he sees the line pretty sharply drawn between amenities, comforts and conveniences, on the one hand, and mere gadgets on the other. Perhaps his contentment tends to show that human beings are highly adaptable and very easily corrupted. I argue nothing from it, but offer the fact merely as an object of interesting speculation.

The Amenians have not even learned the art of sophisticating their products. Their excellent staples, such as flour, olive-oil, wine, come to you pretty much, one might say, as the Lord made them. Nor have these interesting people learned to sophisticate their workmanship. Amenia reckons its money in écus or *escudos* (pronounced *scoots*), worth at the moment about four cents apiece. You can buy an excellent suit of clothes, custom-made of domestic wool, for five or six hundred scoots, and the workmanship will be as good as the fabric; that suit will stand hard wear, and thrive on it. Shoes, too, that one buys handmade for something like two hundred scoots, show no sign of the familiar devices to "make people shoe-conscious," and thereby increase consumption; and the same may be said for the workmanship put into everything one uses, as far as my observation goes.

These practices seem to spring from the root-idea that things should be made to use rather than to sell; a distinction first drawn in literature by Canning, I believe, in the rhymed fable of Hodge's razor. Moreover, the Amenians do not appear to believe that the "pursuit of happiness" contemplated by Mr. Jefferson's great document means only the accumulation and use of purchasable things. Yet, in spite of this handicap, not only does business manage to drag on, but also most of the Amenians whom I saw seemed a great deal happier than under the circumstances they should be.

For example, I spent three weeks at one of Amenia's principal health-resorts, which is in a most beautiful mountainous region, with no settlement of any size near by. I never saw a place where one was thrown more heavily on one's own resources. One could not buy anything more interesting than postage-stamps. One could take delightful walks, and enjoy the air, birds, trees and flowers, but there was no golf, tennis, squash, ping-pong, cinema, radio or gramophone; the hotel had only an utterly impracticable billiard-table and a decrepit up-right piano of French make, much out of tune. There was not even the usual job-lot of abandoned books lying about the lobby; not a book on the premises save what one brought for oneself.

The guests were a good cross-section of Amenian society. The four learned professions were there, some royal blood and hereditary high-life, some *arriviste* or Brummagem high-life, some industry and trade. The average age of the company ran unusually young, and on that account I was all the more curious to see what they would do with themselves. I soon remarked that no one was at all afraid of being left alone with his own thoughts; and this, if not absolutely Bad, is seriously irregular, for if a person is alone and thinking, he is not doing anything to increase consumption. There was no great "get-together" movement organized to insure one against the chance of a moment's solitude. No one seemed in such desperate need of company; on the contrary, the guests kept contentedly each one to himself pretty much all day, except for casual meetings. There was a very pleasant cordiality all round; if someone came along, well and good, but if not, well and good. No one was bored; with nothing whatever to "do," and no apparatus to help fight off boredom, everybody seemed quite unreasonably and perversely happy. Again, in the evenings I remarked how the whole company showed itself capable of immense enthusiasm over the simplest parlour-games, peasant-dances, peasant-songs. Royalty, high-life and all grades of bourgeois rollicked through boisterous and exhausting dances with bursts of uproarious laughter, and seemed to be having the best time in the world, up to half-past ten or so, when all hands went quietly to bed.

St. John's Eve came on while I was there, and the thing to do on St. John's Eve, apparently, is to make brush-bonfires of eucalyptus, rosemary and other aromatic twigs, and leap across them through the flames. It seems a very moderate sort of diversion; I do not know what the significance of it is, nor could anyone tell me. However, everybody went in for it with immense energy and gusto, and got no end of fun out of it, though some of the ladies singed their legs a bit, and only missed setting their skirts afire by the closest kind of shave.

Three weeks of this sort of thing is bound to set one's mind going over the assumption which, though tacit, amounts to an absolute—that happiness is built up of purchasable things. These people were not poor, yet they were not only capable of being happy as lords without a dollar's worth of apparatus to help them, but also they did not appear to care whether they had any apparatus or not. The sum of their activities for three whole weeks did not increase consumption, or assist the development of mass-demand, to the amount of a punched nickel; yet they were quite happy. I could not help recalling the contrasting observation of Stendhal, on a visit to the United States, where there is such an immense amount of the apparatus of happiness available everywhere, that "the springs of happiness seem to be dried up in this people," and the amazing statement of Edison, eighty years old, when a reporter asked him what human happiness consisted in, "I am not acquainted with anyone who is happy." Perhaps the visitor to Amenia might be a little put to it to say offhand precisely what human happiness does consist in, but the question is forced on him by such incidents as the ones I have just cited.

Indirectly, too, it is forced on him by observation of the instinct for the *ne quid nimis*, the instinct for the level of real requirement, that he sees coming out everywhere. In the matter of transportation, for instance, Amenia's railways are cheap, safe, clean and good, but that is all one can say, and all one is supposed to say; they do not pretend to lure you into taking them merely for the fun of the thing. The same is true of the motor-roads; they are excellent, plenty good enough for anybody who has to use them, but they are not a standing temptation to the canine love of joy-riding. I remember once, when my charming friend Cassandre was standing up stoutly for France, she said there was great hope that the French would remain a civilized people, for they had not yet put down any cement roads; when a nation begins to lay cement roads, she said, it is gone, past any hope of reform or redemption. There would seem to be something in this from the Amenian point of view, which regards a road primarily as a thing of use rather than of pleasure. I took a two-hour walk between four and six o'clock of a beautiful afternoon, on a main road out of one of Amenia's largest towns—her fourth in population, I believe—and in that time I saw only one motor-vehicle, a truck.

In three months, during which I covered Amenia pretty thoroughly from end to end, I did not see a single tractor, reaper or binder. I saw grain being reaped with sickles—only twice did I see scythes in use—and threshed with flails. I saw irrigation carried on in pre-Mosaic fashion by boy-power on vertical treading-wheels, and by donkey-power on horizontal pumps. By all accepted rules, these practices are wrong and bad, yet really— really, now—just how dogmatic may one be about erecting their wrongness into an absolute? They got results— there is no question about that—and as to their effect on the sum of human happiness, it is difficult, very difficult indeed, to assure oneself one way or the other. On the evidence available, I am by no means sure that the net sum of happiness in Amenia would be increased by further mechanization of these processes. It might be; I am simply not sure. On the evidence attested by Edison and Stendhal, I am not sure that the net sum of happiness in the United States would be reduced by demechanization to the level of Amenia. Again, it might be, but I am not sure; I can only say that I found the question a very powerful solvent of dogmatism, and as such I recommend it.

IV

Amenia's population is most improperly distributed, for two-thirds of it is rural. Agriculture is the country's chief industry, and it is carried on mostly by small independent holdings. In urban growth, Amenia is far behind other European countries. One notes with surprise and disapproval that the huge industrial proletarian agglomerations which are perhaps the most conspicuous characteristic of true prosperity—though William Cobbett gruffly called them *Hell-holes*—do not exist. Amenia does relatively little in the manufacturing way, and hardly any processing. Almost one might think that the Physiocrats had come to life there, and were spreading their detestable doctrine of the *produit net*. It is here, perhaps, that one sees Amenia's most egregious departure from the Right Way. Surely by this time Amenia should have learned that the chief end of man in his collective capacity is to industrialize himself as completely as possible, remove the land from competition with industry in the labour-market in order to force down wages by creating a standing labour-surplus, and then go in for a strong policy of economic nationalism; that is to say, a policy of selling everything one can to everybody, and not buying anything from anybody.

Amenia is well off for natural resources, especially in minerals and water-power, but there is unanimous testimony that the Amenians are extremely lackadaisical about exploiting them; and if anything can be absolutely Wrong, this is. The Right Way with natural resources is to turn them over wholesale to private enterprise, to be looted as rapidly and thoroughly as possible. All precedents point to this as of the essence of prosperity. Yet it would appear that the Amenians are merely pecking at their minerals, and realizing on only about eight per cent of their available hydroelectric power. A Scots engineer who has been twenty years in Amenia told me that a couple of foreign prospectors had struck gold there lately, but nobody seemed to be properly worked up about it. The general sentiment was that the gold would stay put; it would not run away, and there was no occasion to get into a great sweat over digging it out. There seemed to be enough gold around already to go on with, so why not let it lie awhile? This Scotsman told me that the Amenians had always taken this easy attitude towards "development," and hence they still have pretty nearly everything that nature gave them to start with.

This may be put down to lack of enterprise, and properly so in a sense, no doubt; it depends on what one's notion of enterprise is. But there is a little more to it than that, I think. It may be, in part at least, the outcome of a sense of moderation, for the Amenian struck me as being by nature the most consistently temperate person I ever saw. Once led to look for this trait, I kept an eye out for it continually, and saw it exhibited everywhere, whether in small matters or great. To take one instance, rather unimportant in itself, but bearing on a question that has lately been a good deal discussed in the United States, a wine-merchant who took me over his property showed me certain casks to which his workpeople were free to resort at any time, for as much as they cared to drink; and he told me that in the whole history of the firm, which ran considerably over a hundred years, there had never been a tipsy person on the premises.

With its colonial resources Amenia follows the same easy policy as with its domestic resources. Though one of the smallest countries of Europe, its colonial holdings are enormous, exceeded only by those of England and France. One is rather surprised by the fact that whereas about fifty-five million of the earth's people speak French, about seventy million speak Amenian; and the Amenian tongue is perhaps the most widely diffused language in the world, except our own. Amenia's colonies are very rich; a really capable and energetic administration, such as the English or French or old Leopold's Belgians or we ourselves know how to furnish, could get simply no end of profit out of them.

Yet Amenia bears the white man's burden very lightly. It gets some return out of its colonies, but nothing like what it might get. A young and progressive Amenian told me sadly that the colonies had for years been "virtually abandoned." Amenian colonial policy does not, in our expressive phrase, crowd the mourners. It seems to be not unlike the policy of "salutary neglect" which farsighted Englishmen advocated in the days of Pitt. It neither exploits the native peoples in an economic way, nor does it essay to moralize either their private convictions and habits or their social customs and practices; it does not tell them what they should eat or drink, or wherewithal they should be clothed. Hence the colonies are contented under Amenian rule, I am told, and are not all the time raising disturbances and insurrections. "The Amenians don't try to civilize their colonies," an Englishman said to me, with a touch of irony in his tone; "consequently they've still got them. We bossed ours around and tried to make them do our way, and so we lost them."

All this again may be put down to mere shiftlessness, but once more I suggest that the innate sense of moderation may account for something; and perhaps the extraordinary spirit of tolerance and courtesy, for which, as I have said, the Amenians are internationally noted, also accounts for something. If one gets a moderate yield out of one's colonies, well, enough is enough, and why jeopardize peace and good feeling by squeezing them? Meanwhile, if the heathen in his blindness bows down to wood and stone, why bother him about it? Why not

look the other way and let him bow? If he would rather
go naked than wear Amenian textiles, it is bad for business, no doubt, but why force him all at once to accept
a strictly cash-registral evaluation of life and its amenities, even though it be orthodox? Why not break the
glad news to him a little gently and give it a reasonable
time to sink in? If a widow sets out with pomp and cere-
mony to burn herself alive on her late husband's fu-
neral pyre, why not conclude that there is probably
something in it from her point of view, and let it go
at that?

v

Amenia's government is a simon-pure military despotism; it governs by general orders. Yet up to date it
has been extremely disinterested, able and efficient; the
best and cheapest government, I should say, that is to
be found anywhere. Doubtless it will not remain so, for
that would be contrary to all human experience with any
kind of government, but such is its record at the moment. It went through the motions of submitting itself
to a popular mandate the other day, and was approved
by a large majority. I do not know how far this election
was "on the level," or how sincere the government was
minded to be about abiding by it. One's general knowledge of government makes one skeptical; Herbert
Spencer cites with approval the generalization that
"wherever government is, there is villainy," and it seems
to be, on the whole, a sound one. Nevertheless, for all
I actually know or have heard, this election may have
been honestly undertaken and scrupulously conducted.

I suppose the sight of a military dictatorship should

have set me thinking of Spartacus, Masaniello, Jack Cade, Daniel Shays, the Whiskey Boys and all the other great liberators, until I was ready to turn my back on Amenia in disgust. What it did instead, however, was to set me thinking about some of the absolutes of eighteenth-century political theory, and wondering what basis they have in actual human experience. Representative government; the parliamentary system; universal suffrage; "checks and balances"; a responsible executive —Amenia has thrown all these overboard, and yet is governed well and cheaply. The question is not whether other countries would do well to throw them overboard, but whether the quality of government is as much a matter of systems and institutions as we think it is. Rival systems are now everywhere competing for the world's attention to the colour of their several shirts—well, just what is the necessary and inevitable effect of *any* system upon the quality of government?

America had great students of government in its early days; it is a pity that they are now so much more read about than read. One of them was William Penn. The sight of Amenia's contribution to the great current rivalry of systems brought to my mind this paragraph from the preface which Penn wrote for Pennsylvania's original "frame of government":

When all is said, there is hardly any frame of government so ill designed by its first founders that in good hands would not do well enough; and story tells us the best, in ill ones, can do nothing that is great or good. . . . Governments, like clocks, go from the motion men give them; and as governments are made and moved by men, so by them they are ruined too. Wherefore governments rather depend upon men than men upon governments.

Against its background of competing systems, moreover, Amenia's autocracy suggests what is no doubt the most pressing public question of our time, namely: whether eighteenth-century republican doctrine has not put upon the mass-man a burden greater than he can bear. Heretofore the question has not been so much with the mass-man's actual capacity as with the advisability, for purely collateral reasons, of letting him have anything like a free hand in shaping social and political institutions. The rapid spread of republicanism, however, has given us of the present day an uncommonly good chance to appraise the type of social ideal towards which the enfranchised mass-man chooses to move. Therefore, quite aside from all considerations of sincerity, integrity and good will, the question now is whether the mass-man is able, or will ever be able, to direct the development of society in accordance with his own ultimate best interest. Has he the force of intellect to perceive clearly what that interest is, and the force of character to pursue it steadfastly? Do his present performances encourage the belief that he will ever have them? Has republican doctrine, in short, any basis either in actual experience or in reasonable hope?

We have, too, an uncommonly good chance to observe the kind of leadership which at present succeeds in imposing itself on the mass-man's allegiance, and to remark its conformity to a historical type. At almost every turn of the world's affairs nowadays, one is most sharply and painfully reminded of the French revolutionist's saying, "I *must* follow the mob, because I lead them." Finally, aside from the light it throws on the possible unsoundness of republican doctrine and the possibly dubious character of republican mass-leadership, Amenia's condition makes one wonder whether political nationalism has not gone over the margin of diminishing returns. Economic nationalism seems clearly to have done so; may not its political counterpart have done so too? Amenia is small and isolated, and it is possible for a one-man government to maintain political nationalism there at something like reasonable expense. Elsewhere, however, people are uneasy about the rapidly growing cost of Statism, centralization and bureaucracy, and well they may be; in the United States, for example, people are extremely uneasy about it, and with reason. Is it not possible that political nationalism, like a business which is economically overgrown, has begun to cost more than it takes in? Or, to cite the comparison attributed to Lincoln, has it become like the tugboat that stopped running whenever the whistle blew, because it had a four-foot boiler and a six-foot whistle? Is political nationalism any longer commercially practicable (if I may so put it) over an area of much more than township size? It is an interesting question and a serious one; one which, from present appearances, the larger and more highly integrated political units will soon be obliged by circumstances to entertain.

VI

Probably Amenia will not long remain as I found it, for there are the beginnings of a lively onset towards "development" and "progress." I heard these words often; they seemed to mean a closer approach to the condition of other nations. Well, improvement is always possible, and the study of other people's ways is always useful. "They measuring themselves by themselves," the Apostle says, "and comparing themselves among themselves, are not wise." One energetic young Amenian assured me that "we shall be a civilized country in ten years." A visiting friend may not presume to give advice to his hosts, but he may perhaps be permitted to observe in a general way that when one is examining other countries one is likely to find that the most valuable testimony they bear to the nature of true civilization is often of a negative kind; and that this is particularly true of civilization's higher and finer concerns. A friend, too, may without impropriety, I think, venture in all gratitude to express the hope that the "civilized" Amenia of ten years hence will be in all respects as charming and captivating to the cultivated spirit, as interesting and thought-provoking, as the Amenia which I have had the good fortune to visit.

Brussels, August, 1933.

7

Our American Upper Class

OFFICIALLY we are a one-class country, and proud of it. The nation was founded at a time when feeling against a titled and hereditary upper class was running strong. Even God, according to one of our earlier poets, was getting a little tired of kings and was ready to take responsibility for a republican order of society. The prejudices conceived in that time are still ours, officially. In a popular way, perhaps, they have worked out somewhat more towards a collateral tradition that "in the United States one man is just as good as another, or a little better." Thus the haughty shop-assistant or beauty-specialist who patronizes her client and calls her "dearie" is more in the popular than the official tradition; while the publicist or the electioneering statesman who butters up the "great and glorious democracy of the West" and its many-headed sovereign, is more in the latter. But both traditions are based upon resentment of anything savouring of standards and sanctions specifically associated with a titled and hereditary upper class. A person who wishes to be well thought of finds it safe business to govern his public conduct, his manners and his general view of life by distinctively middle-class standards and sanctions, and to be rather ostentatious about disparaging all others.

Matthew Arnold, who divided his fellow-countrymen into Barbarians, Philistines and Populace, said that America was a country like his own, but with the Barbarians left out and the Populace nearly so; our society was almost solidly Philistine. This indeed has been our official ideal. We have never owned up to a lower class, a Populace or proletariat; what might be thought to answer to a Populace is merely so much Philistinism in the making, and hence already Philistinism by brevet. The thought of a formally-acknowledged upper class is as jealously resented as the thought of a formally-acknowledged Populace, perhaps more so.

This resentment was burned into us in the first instance by our experiences under British misrule, by the French Revolution, by the spectacle of Napoleon's tyranny and freebooting; and it was backed up by the political theory of the eighteenth century—the theory of individual right to free self-expression in politics. But when one considers the actual differentiations of our society, one is conscious of a curious anomaly. One finds that we are not actually against an upper class, because we have one and think highly of it. We are merely against the formal acknowledgment that we have one. We are not against a hierarchy set up by an association of Church and State, because we have one; we are all aware of the very close association of our government with what Burke so well styled "the dissidence of Dissent and the protestantism of the Protestant religion." We are merely against acknowledging this association to be what it actually is. We are against acknowledging that we have anything corresponding either to the "lords temporal" or the "lords spiritual." But let one take, for example, the group of persons whom Mr. Gerard lately designated as the real rulers of America, and test it by all the marks that historically differentiate an upper class, and one will find that it answers perfectly in every respect but that of formal title.

Test any such group by the mark of privilege, and it answers. No modern society ever more lavishly endowed its beneficiaries with privilege. The public-land grants to our transcontinental railways alone would make the land-holdings of the entire British nobility look like a real-estater's subdivision. It would be an interesting job for a statistician to compute as best he could the annual cash value of the purely law-made property in this country, *i.e.,* the annual revenue proceeding from the un- earned increment of land-values, from tariffs, from fran- chises and concessions—from all forms of the privileged private monopoly of what is by nature public property. Perhaps the sum would be imposing enough to encour- age him to go on and make an estimate of the sum-total of these values for the whole century and a half of our republic, just to show the actual aggregate cash subsidy that our society has bestowed gratis upon its upper class since we became a nation.

Or, again, test our upper class by its immunities and exemptions; no group in any modern society ever en- joyed more or greater. It is a common saying—and a common fact—that in this country "you can't convict a million dollars." You can't even convict it of colossal stupidity. Because Mr. Henry Ford knows how to throw a cheap automobile together and market it profitably, he gets complete immunity for any ridiculous statement he sees fit to make on any subject. Because Mr. Owen Young has come to the front as a corporation-executive, he gets immunity for whatever deplorable nonsense he chooses to talk on subjects unrelated to corporation-management. Or, again, apply the test of popular deference, laudation, sycophancy and acclaim; are the British newspapers half as earnestly reverential towards the outpourings of any duke or earl as ours are to the casual chatter of one of this group when he can be induced to grant an interview? Apply the test of solidarity; their group-loyalties are stronger than most. Once in a while one hears of a titled Englishman breaking with his class for reasons of conscience or out of a sense of public duty; but who ever heard that any of Mr. Gerard's group had done so? The nearest approach to anything of the kind that I ever heard of was Mr. Ford's abrupt inauguration of the five-dollar minimum wage; and even this disloyalty turned out to be apparent only, not real. Apply analogous tests to our variant of an ecclesiastical hierarchy, and it will be found that except for the mere title and insignia of rank, we have a counterpart of the "lords spiritual" that is quite exact and of far greater political authority and power. Has the whole Bench of Bishops one-half the actual authority over the life of Great Britain's population that the Methodist-Baptist junto at Washington has over ours? Not one-half, not one-twentieth of one-half.

II

The fact of our having an upper class is natural and should not be surprising, for human society has regularly differentiated such a class, and usually by a regular formula. No nation ever purposefully started out to make itself a three-class affair, like steamships. The differentiation began when an alien group took possession of the soil and of other privileges, usually by conquest; then consolidating their position by outright assumption of the law-making power, and proceeding with the economic exploitation of the balance of the population lying outside their own group, through legislation forcibly imposed; such, for instance, as the Enclosures Acts of the British Parliament. The operations of the Japanese in Manchuria are a reversion to this primitive technique. Thus took place the stratification of society into two classes, an upper and lower, or, more strictly, an owning and exploiting class and a propertyless dependent class—Barbarians and Populace. After a long time an intercalary class began to coalesce and emerge, exerting a strong pressure both upward and downward; upward on the Barbarians and downward on the Populace. This was a class of merchants and industrial producers—capitalists in the true sense, not the Marxian sense—who made themselves felt through organizations like the Hansa and the City-State. Presently this class was reinforced and largely dominated—reinforced where there was an identity of interest and dominated where there was not—by a merger with it of monopolists, bankers, shavers, speculators, concessionaires, and latterly, stock-jobbers. This completed the division of society into three classes, upper, middle, and lower: Barbarian, Philistine, Populace.

Such, in general outline, is the historical formula by which societies have differentiated themselves into classes. In the United States, however, the case was somewhat different. Our society differentiated both its upper and lower classes out of fairly pure middle-class material, quite generally unaware that it was doing anything of the kind. It seems to have been thought—Mr. Jefferson notably thought so—that the resources of the country were sufficient permanently to preclude involuntary poverty and the rise of an exploitable proletariat. This was true enough, but the trouble was that these resources were so promptly preëmpted into legal ownership by a minority that a majority soon found itself practically dispossessed, exactly as whole populations of the English were dispossessed by the operation of the Enclosures Acts. Still, there is record that for some time there was no involuntary poverty in the country, even in its larger towns, and no labour-surplus sufficient to provoke a thoroughgoing economic exploitation. Many adventurous spirits pushed westward on the treks which our school-histories and early popular literature have so heavily romanticized, in search of unpreëmpted natural resources to bring them, first, independence, and second, the chance, for themselves or their descendants, of exercising economic exploitation in their turn; and this kept draining off the accumulation of exploitable labour-power from the industrial regions on the seaboard. But by the time the frontier was closed, about 1890,—that is to say, when practically all the natural resources of the country were preëmpted,—we had a considerable proletariat, not only industrial but in fair part also agricultural; and this has become progressively larger and more highly differentiated since that time. Our labour-surplus has been almost continuously sufficient to enable an economic exploitation that contemplates the subsistence-level; there have been some interruptions, but not serious or protracted. At the present moment this surplus is without precedent for size; I have seen its total estimated anywhere from five to seven millions, and the care of it has become one of our most costly public enterprises.

At the other end of the scale, our upper class has been differentiated by the one single qualification of success in accumulating wealth; that is to say, it has been differentiated according to a strictly middle-class canon. Our society imposes no other condition, absolutely none, for admission to its upper class. Nor does it put any definite expectation upon its upper class but to keep on accumulating and enjoying wealth, and to keep in motion the machinery by which the accumulation is got together. What expectation does it put, for example, on Mr. Gerard's fifty-nine corporation-heads, as class-representatives, but to keep their corporations running? I know of none. I am not taking account of such matters as distributing charity, endowing hospitals, founding colleges or serving on political commissions; for frankly, I see no sign that our society regards even these as an obligation specifically resting on its upper class. Its organs of opinion appear always to take them as an expression of pure generosity and to laud them accordingly. What I refer to is a set of distinctive class-ideals, class-excellences, class-responsibilities, such as an upper class has generally felt under a certain social pressure to accept; and as I said, I know of none in force but the one I mentioned. No society has ever asked less from its upper class than ours; none could very well ask less.

By way of example drawn from the present depression, we may remark that our upper class has largely extemporized itself into a last-minute organization for improving the condition of the poor—for giving back to the Populace by way of charity perhaps at most one-twentieth of what the Populace has lost in wages since the depression set in two years ago. It would seem fair for our society to say to this organization, Well, when poverty is all tided through, the depression over and prosperity restored—what then? Do you recognize any class-responsibility for an exercise of disinterested intelligence at all beyond what is required merely to keep your individual concerns going until another slump comes along? Do you admit that *noblesse oblige* comes in here and pointedly suggests a strong class-effort at self-transformation under the rule of intelligence? One hears nothing of any such demand.

In other societies, as a general thing, a member of the upper class is not supposed to make the accumulation of wealth his master-concern, or expected to be particularly good at it. His ancestors are supposed to have stolen enough in the first instance to enable him to rub along, merely taking care of what he has and devoting himself to other pursuits. The hoarding of wealth is not a serious infraction of the upper-class canon, though when it shows itself as a master-concern it is usually regarded with disfavour; but a master-concern with accumulation is not thought to comport with upper-class dignity. Recruitments of an upper class out of "trade," out of the instincts and abilities that built large fortunes on a foundation of penny-dreadfuls, beer or soap, are put down by general consent as a distinct adulteration. These instincts and abilities, focussed on the master-concern of accumulation, fall historically under the middle-class canon.

The United States, however, has differentiated its upper class by an application of the middle-class canon exclusively. The general membership of our upper class may be said, roughly, to be made up of those who have an income of two hundred thousand a year or more, and the regular trimmings, such as a yacht, a show-place here or there in America and another in Europe, and so on—who do, in short, the regular thing in the regular way. We have a petering-out remnant of human stock, "old families" as age goes in America, which still shows traces of class-qualities, ideals and standards that are not quite in the thoroughgoing middle-class tradition. It refuses to acknowledge the accumulation of wealth as the sole index of upper-class standing. It assents to the traditional obligation to maintain certain class-ideals of intelligence, breeding and culture as paramount. These distinctions, however, are so jealously disallowed by our society at large that this remnant has become encysted, and is as sterile and ineffectual in a social way as Robinson Crusoe. No longer is it of interest even to climbers, as it was up to, say, twenty years ago, before our upper class was full-formed and had organized itself into complete self-sufficiency.

We maintain, then, an upper class which is in all respects most substantially acknowledged in an informal way, but which we will not acknowledge formally, tending rather to get up a considerable patriotic warmth of dissent from the bare suspicion that we are maintaining an upper class. This might be taken as a culpable failure in intellectual integrity, as no doubt it is. Without laying any stress on that point, however, it may at least be taken as a failure in clarity about what we actually have; and what I wish to observe is that this lack of clarity is productive of extremely unfortunate social consequences. What we have actually done is to differentiate an upper class which we do not permit to act like an upper class; hence we lose the specific social benefits that are historically within the province of an upper class to disseminate.

III

Let us see how this is so. In other societies the upper class is supposed, in consideration of its privileges and immunities, to develop certain special class-ideals, class-standards, class-excellences; and there has always been a pressure of tradition upon its members to accept responsibility for them and keep to them with reasonable loyalty. *Noblesse oblige.* Default on these obligations, when it becomes flagrant, as in the France of 1789 or in present-day Russia, is the sole invariable antecedent to an upper class's overthrow. We, however, have made it impossible, through our lack of clarity, for our upper class to develop these characteristic ideals, standards and excellences. We insist that it must carry with it into its new status the ideals, standards and excellences of the middle class, and cleave only unto those. From its new vantage-point it must be always nervously looking back upon middle-class instabilities, uncertainties, trepidations, always faithfully reflecting the middle class's obscurantist prejudices, its narrow and ignoble prepossessions, its dogmatism, self-righteousness, self-sufficiency. The upper class's attainments, preoccupations, even its pleasures, must differ only in degree, not in quality, from those of the middle class; and in general, the strength of its influence and the weight of its authority are conditioned only by its power of agreement with the middle-class mind and spirit.

We have lately had before us a very striking illustration of the extreme stringency of this limitation. It is worth citing at length, even at the risk of throwing this essay somewhat out of balance. Mr. Hoover's relief-committee, a strictly upper-class organization headed by Mr. Gifford, published a series of advertisements last fall, addressed to the people at large, with a view to loosening up their purse-strings. We all remember those appeals; their tone was extremely interesting in the eloquence of its testimony on the point I am making. If the Duke of Devonshire should address the British people on a public matter of great urgency and importance, the people would expect him to address them in his class-character. If he adopted for the occasion a class-character not his own, they would be conscious of an anomaly more or less mortifying and painful. In addressing the American people, however, poor Mr. Gifford felt—or his advisers insisted—that he must get himself as far out of upper-class character and as far into middle-class character as he possibly could. He was not even permitted to talk like a gentleman. In one set of advertisements, for example, he must mimic the specious sales-talk of the Elk-Rotarian booster or the vulgar dog who used to whoop up patriotism amongst our theatre-audiences during the late war—this kind of thing:

Morale: it wins wars; it beats depressions; it lays the firm foundations for prosperity. America is engaged in a

mighty enterprise of morale-building. . . . Feel the thrill
that comes with victory. Go forward with America to the
better days ahead.

Again, as the price of a sympathetic response, the
middle-class canon required Mr. Gifford to impersonate a
plumber or bricklayer out of a job, and to talk the way
he thinks this unfortunate would talk—no, not exactly;
rather, the way he understands the middle-class canon
to prescribe as the right way for one of the unemployed
Populace to talk:

"I'll see it through if *you* will.
"They tell me there's five or six million of us out of
jobs.
"I know that's not your fault any more than it is
mine.
"But that doesn't change the fact that some of us now
are in a pretty tough spot, with families to worry about
and a workless winter ahead."

—and so forth; one simply can't go on with it, especially
since worse must follow. In the realm of intimate romance and sentiment the middle-class ideal is one of an
underbred self-abandonment, a complete enervation,
without restraint, without dignity; it is what one sees in
Mr. Will Hays's screen-drama and in the fiction written
for mass-production magazinedom. To meet this ideal,
therefore, the unfortunate spokesman for our upper class
must condescend to such neurasthenic drivel as this:

To-night say *this* to your wife; then look into her eyes.
"I gave a lot more than we planned. Are you angry?"
. . . It is true, the world *respects* the man who lives
within his income. But the world *adores* the man who
gives beyond his income.

No. When you tell her that you have given somewhat *more* than you had planned, you will see no censure in her eyes. But *love*.

Such a stringent limitation as this works badly. There has always been a social expectation, a sort of tacit understanding, that an upper class should do its best to become intelligent and that it should organize the progressive cultivation of intelligence within its own body, as the British upper class did in founding schools like Eton, Rugby and Harrow, and the universities of Oxford and Cambridge. I do not say that all the members of the British upper class have met the expectation put upon them, or that these institutions are beyond improvement. All I say is that the expectation existed, and that something, be it much or little, was done about it. Our society, on the contrary, discourages its upper class from cultivating intelligence. As the case of Mr. Gifford shows, it insists that the mind of the upper class shall run in middle-class sequences, and the middle class is not interested in intelligence; it is interested only in agreement.

An excellent demonstration of this is found in our upper class's utterances on the character, causes and probable duration of the depression signalized by the explosion of the stock-market in October, 1929. One can not bring oneself to speak of them at length. They should be enough, however, to convince any one that our society does not expect its upper class to become intelligent or has the faintest suspicion that it should do so. When a member of the British upper class, for example, talks wretched nonsense in public about some matter of national moment, he is at once reminded that there are certain class-criteria of intelligence by which what he says is to be judged. When Mr. Hoover, Mr. Ford, Mr. Rosenwald, Mr. Sloan, Mr. Gifford, Mr. Dawes, Mr. Schwab, Mr. Farrell, Mr. Strawn, talk nonsense, their words are not referable to any class-criteria, for none exists; their divagations are published widely, accepted complacently, lauded uncritically, and it goes for nothing that the mere passage of time proves them to be nonsense.

The complete bankruptcy of intelligence exhibited in these representative pronouncements from our upper class should make a clean sweep of the notion so often advanced to account for the low level of our general culture, that our best minds nowadays go into business. They do not. They do not go anywhere. There is nowhere for them to go. Our society has made no place for the individual who is able to think, who is, in the strict sense of the word, intelligent; it merely tosses him into the rubbish-heap, while picking out the stupidest millionaire in sight and placing him in the White House to the accompaniment of a deafening fanfare of adulation for his almost superhuman abilities. Intelligence is the power and willingness always disinterestedly to see things as they are, an easy accessibility to ideas, and a free play of consciousness upon them, quite regardless of the conclusions to which this play may lead. Intelligence, therefore, while not precisely incompatible with success in accumulating wealth, is unrelated to it; hence it is disallowed by our Philistines. It is ineffectual among our Populace, on account of that class's intense preoccupation with the hard problem of keeping body and soul together from day to day. The only class with which it might be effectual, our Barbarians, is virtually forbidden to transform itself by the cultivation of intelligence, because of society's strong insistence that it shall set up no class-ideals and class-criteria of its own, but shall keep steadfastly to those of the Philistines.

One may see evidence of this in the character of the great and rich educational institutions that our Barbarians have founded, as compared with those founded by the corresponding class in England. They are strictly middle-class institutions; that is to say, they are organized to do everything for the "average student," for the motor-minded, a great deal for the incompetent, the merely clever, the sagacious, but nothing whatever for the unconsidered minority which gives promise of some day becoming intelligent. If evidence of this be desired it may be had in any quantity from a perusal of Mr. Flexner's recent work on our universities and Mr. Learned's works on our colleges and our secondary schools. A significant book was published last winter under the title, *They Told Barron*. It is made up of notes taken down by the late Clarence W. Barron, publisher of the *Wall Street Journal*—notes of things told him by Mr. Gerard's "rulers of America" and others of high prominence in our upper class. Only the other day I came by accident on a review of it which contained this striking observation:

Of course it is well to remember that these are tales out of school, and such tales are never high lights of high-mindedness. . . . Yet the world which "told Barron" seems to me very different from any other society. . . . In all this talk of 361 pages by the "rulers" of our society, aged mostly between forty-five and seventy, there is hardly a line of good conversation, not a trace of real culture or plain good breeding, not the slightest evidence of even a fair formal education.

IV

Again, there has always been an understanding that in return for its immunities and privileges, an upper class should furnish an example of social life and manners. The value of this is imperfectly understood, as a rule; it lies in the inculcation of a really sound sentiment of patriotism. Burke said that "there ought to be a system of manners in every nation that a well-formed mind would be disposed to relish. *For us to love our country, our country ought to be lovely.*" This is just what our country is not; and our upper class is estopped from doing what it might to make it so because we jealously insist that its class-ideal of social life and manners shall be but a mere expansion or glorification of the middle-class ideal, limited, unintelligent, more than a little ignoble, and hence more than a little unlovely. The sentiment of patriotism pervading our society is, therefore, as everyone knows, correspondingly ignoble, brittle, meretricious. It is significant that our people are the only ones who expatriate themselves in large numbers because they do not wish to live at home. Others do it to better themselves in purse or in health; but thousands of Americans—often of a type, too, that no country alive to its best interests would willingly spare—do it because they find our civilization too unamiable to hold their sentimental allegiance. When Voltaire was asked what France ever really got out of the reign of Louis XIV, he replied acutely, *the social sense*. This sense has an immense power of attraction, its influence is edifying and binding; and where it has been diffused through a society its release has quite regularly been effected by the example and contagion of the manners of an upper class.

Again, there has always been a pretty general expectation put upon an upper class to develop a class-code whereby conduct is rated, not as legal or illegal, righteous or unrighteous, fashionable or unfashionable, but as becoming or unbecoming. These codes may be more or less unintelligently devised, more or less mechanically obeyed, but the essential thing about them is that they are bottomed on a strong sense of the place of dignity and self-respect in a sound social order. There is great social value in a class which sticks stoutly to its class-sense of conduct as becoming or unbecoming, and recognizes a fairly definite category of things that "aren't done." These things may be legal, fashionable, even by the going standards of morality they may be moral, but they are not felt to comport with dignity and self-respect and, therefore, one would just a little rather not do them.

Our upper class has no such code of conduct, nor can it develop one against the very strong social pressure upon it to retain the middle-class sanctions intact and unimproved. The middle-class ideal contemplates conduct primarily as legal or illegal; sometimes as moral or immoral according to a stark and mechanical notion of morality; sometimes also as fashionable or unfashionable. As far as other sanctions are concerned it tends towards letting every man do what is right in his own eyes. Specific illustrations of this tendency would probably be thought invidious, but one may supply them for oneself from almost any issue of any metropolitan newspaper. The journalistic history of the Harding and Coolidge administrations alone supplies plenty of them. It is no trouble to assure oneself that the middle-class ideal takes no great account of the claims of delicacy, dignity and self-respect in the realm of conduct; here again it is more than a little ignoble, and our society's devotion to this ideal has weakened the sense of these claims to the disappearing-point.

This is a disintegrating influence in our society, and one that has a free rein because the only class which is in a position to inaugurate any restraint upon it is estopped from doing so. Milton, himself a prophet of the middle class if ever it had one, has shown clearly the disintegrating effect of over-devotion to the middle-class ideal and its sanctions. His words are pretty closely descriptive of the courses that our society has taken, especially of late:

In every commonwealth, when it decays, corruption makes two main steps. First, when men cease to do according to the inward and uncompelled actions of virtue, caring only to live by the outward constraint of law, and turn this simplicity of real good into the craft of seeming so by law. . . . The next declining is when law becomes too strait for the secular manners, and those too look for the cincture of law. This brings in false and crooked interpretations to eke out law, and invents the subtle encroachments of obscure traditions, hard to be disproved.

Even with nothing else to its credit, an upper class that has maintained a sense of the "inward and uncompelled actions of virtue" and by force of example has recommended their "simplicity of real good" to the rest of the body politic, has pretty well paid its way.

Everybody is aware that we do not get much good out of our upper class, but perhaps is not so well aware that our lack of clarity about its status is a distinct interference with our getting any more. We have an upper class, we are bound to have one, for every society has always differentiated one, and ours is no exception. We may as well be clear about that; by any test of upper-class status that one may wish to apply, we have one. Well, then, since we have one, why not demand that it make itself useful, or at least allow it some reasonable chance and encouragement to make itself useful? There is a great deal to be got out of an upper class; but if we differentiate one on the sole condition of success in accumulating wealth, and put no further expectation on it, but insist that the differentiation shall stop with that, we are in no way to get much. If we differentiate it from the middle class, and then oblige it to go on with strictly middle-class ideals, standards, excellences, instead of developing distinctive class-ideals, standards and excellences of its own, how much better off are we for having it at all?

V

If no society ever got less from its upper class than ours—and this is true—it is fair to remember that no society ever asked less or made it so difficult to get more. The members of our upper class are, on the average, men of as good will as are to be found in a corresponding class elsewhere. They show an astonishing amount of really disinterested public spirit. The point is, however, first, that such spirit as they show is self-sprung; it is not elicited by a rational and definite expectation on the part of our society. Second, its expression follows implicitly the course set for it by middle-class custom and usage, never presuming to seek out and follow the courses of expression established by historical upper-class usage in other societies. Members of our upper class support museums, subsidize foundations, contribute to social-service enterprises, and attend Mr. Hoover's kaleidoscopic conferences; at present they are very busy taking care of the impoverished labour-surplus. They are generous, even lavish, in what they do, but nothing that they do suggests the slightest conscious effort at self-transformation, or any sense of responsibility for obligations that are historically distinctive of an upper class.

If it were suggested as a social obligation that they should turn away from incessantly looking backward at the middle class and create a set of distinctive and historical class-ideals, class-standards, class-excellences, such as an upper class has always felt under a certain social pressure to accept, it is quite possible that they would respond to this expectation also. Our society is unintelligent and without regard for intelligence; well, instead of accepting this state of things as natural and meritorious and falling in with it, an upper class can apply a considerable corrective, first by transforming itself to the best of its power, and then by giving an example of high respect for intelligence, and by taking measures for the discernment, appreciation and cultivation of intelligence at large. Our ideal of social life and manners is extremely imperfect; well, instead of acquiescing in its vulgarity as normal and proper, an upper class can do a great deal to refine and elevate it, and thus to liberate the only kind of patriotic sentiment that is worth anything. We have quite lost a sense of dignity and self-respect as sanctions of conduct or as elements making for stability in the social order; well, instead of condoning this defect or agreeing with middle-class tradition in erecting it into something like the status of a virtue, an upper class can exert a very powerful influence towards remedying it and forestalling its unfavourable consequences.

In these three directions an upper class has often made itself conspicuously useful and may do so again; and it is the only class that can. For one set of reasons a lower class can do very little for society in these directions; for another and wholly different set of reasons a middle class can do as little, perhaps less. Possibly our upper class would not accept obligations of this nature under any circumstances; it may be too firmly fixed in the middle-class tradition to see any reason why it should do so. But this is not the point; the point is that so long as strictly middle-class loyalties are so strenuously enforced upon it, it never can.

New York, October, 1931.

8

Thoughts on Utopia

THE first Utopian enterprise that I ever encountered was the one called the Kingdom of Heaven; such being, I suppose, the experience of many youngsters in my time, probably most of them. The project interested me mildly, although its specifications, as I remember, were rather vague. I never had them laid down to me in a dogmatic way, for the contemplation of heaven had no great part in the discipline of my bringing-up, and my information about it was got, for the most part, casually. My mother's family were chiefly responsible for this, as they had most to do with me in my early years. Originally they were French Protestants who had somehow managed to get out of Rochelle ahead of the sheriff in 1688, and crossed to America. Three generations of them were on earth in my childhood; I am now, I think, the last survivor, or almost the last. I was acquainted with some eighteen or twenty out of the lot, and I remember them now as being, without a single exception, the most clear-minded, free-thinking people I ever knew; and at the same time, with all their force of intellect and force of character, they were also the most gentle-spirited. More than anything, I believe, it was their immense humour that kept them free from any taint of hardness, pettiness, intolerance; they all had the saving grace of humour in the utmost abundance, and apparently it enabled them to look objectively, disinterestedly, at every concern of human life, no matter how intimate. I remember well my grandfather's quizzical gaze at two of the younger girls who were breathlessly bustling over some festivity in the local church. "I declare, children," he said, "you seem to be serving God to-day as if the devil were in you." Deeply religious as my mother's people were, they were staunch individualists in religion as in everything else; they were dead against authoritarianism, wherever found. They maintained the inalienable right of private judgment on all that goes on in the heavens above, the earth beneath, and the waters under the earth. They maintained it with the considerate tolerance becoming to a race of gentlefolk, but there was no doubt about their maintaining it. The old Creole gentleman in Cable's story brought their spirit before me very vividly when he said, "Remember, my boy, that none of your family line ever kept the laws of any government or creed."

Hence I can recall no pressure on me to take stock in the heavenly Utopia, or even any deliberate effort to make the prospect of going there especially attractive; so, naturally perhaps, I thought little about it. The essential feature of the heavenly society, as I understood it, was that everybody would be happy there; but as I thought myself quite happy where I was, this did not impress me particularly. As I remember, it was the geographical basis of heaven that most took my fancy. I had picked up the idea somewhere that this consisted mostly of gold and precious stones, which I thought would make a fine display, such as would be worth seeing. I also had a leaning towards the musical features of the celestial organization, for I had a great love of music and had been brought up amidst a most excellent practice of the art; with one exception, every member of my family on both sides was a good musician. I had no curiosity, however, concerning any other qualities or conditions of the heavenly life, and did not speculate about them.

Later, however, when I was sixteen or so, I began to be conscious of certain anomalies. I had always understood in a general way that to get into heaven one must be good. This seemed reasonable, and I was all for it; but now I began to see the need of a little more specific information about the nature of goodness. The entrance-requirements, as officially understood and accepted, seemed largely arbitrary, and for the most part incompetent; and hence they were bound to result in discriminations that appeared to me unfair. My personal associations at the time sharpened my sense of this. The people in our little community who most interested me were those whom the religious element put down unqualifiedly as men of sin. They drank, and I am afraid they swore, and dark hints passed among the elect that, like the hero of Bret Harte's little tale, they "useter go round with permiscous wimin"; and it was accepted *semper ubique et ab omnibus* that if they did not repent—which they seemed in no way whatever of doing—they would go to hell.

Circumstances put me close under the wing of these persons for some time; the point was that they saw in me a promising candidate for eminence in the realm of baseball, and were bent on developing my talents for the good of the local team, which, as bush-league teams went in those days, was a first-rate one. They were all much older than I; I suppose the difference averaged as much as ten years. They were bad men, so everybody said, yet the odd thing was that they were so unfailingly good to me; good, that is, even in the conventional sense. They watched over my manners, habits and morals with a much more lively and friendly concern than the elect displayed.

They cautioned me that liquor was a bad and dangerous thing, quite unnecessary; one got on much better without it; they themselves lifted in a little once in a while, but it was something I should leave strictly alone. Swearing was a low habit, nothing to be proud of, and while they themselves turned out some pretty artistic profanity on occasion, they did not want to hear any of it from me under any circumstances whatever. So it went, throughout all the categories of morals and manners; if I showed signs of going off the rails at any point of decent and gentlemanly behaviour, I heard about it on the spot. I will say for them that they were curiously careful, too, to give me as good an example as they could manage to improvise on short notice; when I was around they pretty well did their best to make a fair showing. I have always led a very temperate life, often bordering on the ascetic; and I mention this, not by way of putting on airs about it, for I have done it by pure choice and preference, but merely to show cause for my wondering, as I look back, how much of the credit for that preference—if there be any credit—is due to the strange admonitions of the strange beings with whom for two years I played ball, fished, swam and hobnobbed in Mr. Webster's "days of real sport," so long ago.

Among the elect, on the other hand, there were many who were thoroughly good, when measured by the criteria which my mother's family had set; these being the standards that I instinctively applied, and the only ones, really, that I knew and could use. The elect comprised others, however, for whose presence on the roster I could not account, except that they came up to a set of formal requirements which the scandalous and ungodly did not meet and seemed to make a point of not meeting.

There was, for example, Elder T., who earned his way by secular pursuits, some of which were said to be of a dubious nature, but carried on a collateral line of itinerant preaching in Baptist churches. He wore a gray goatee beard, shaped like a paintbrush; his eyes seemed faintly phosphorescent, like the eyes of a dead mackerel in the dark; and he had deep furrows down each side of his nose, which gave his face the fixed expression of one who smells a stench. Most people were against the Elder, freely saying that he was meaner than soapweed, and that they would not trust him alone in a room with a red-hot stove. Even apart from these little peculiarities, he was far from being what one would call a popular idol. I remember well the thick cloud of despondency that settled on the whole population when it was made known that what Mrs. Malaprop called "an unscrupulous Providence" had permitted the biggest maskalonge ever taken out of our favourite fishing-ground to be hooked by the Elder. Enraged eyewitnesses said that he was out only a few yards from shore in a very light canoe—

canvas, I think, though it may have been a light cedar clinker—fishing for panfish in three or four feet of water, with a borrowed tackle. When the maskalonge took his hook it frightened him so that he dropped his pole, but the reel caught under a thwart. The drag happened to be on, and by some miracle the line held; it ran out full, meanwhile communicating motion to the boat, and the maskalonge snaked the terrified Elder hither and yon until some of the boys put out from shore, and after a very pretty fight brought the fish in; it weighed forty-five pounds. This episode was regarded as a stain on the community. What most distressed our inveterate old professors of the sport, like Andy L. and Fred C., was that the wretched man had never dropped a hook in water before in all his life; this seemed the very last refinement of cosmic injustice. At first there was talk of taking some sort of reprisals on the Elder, but nothing was done.

A general view of the Elder, and of others whose case seemed as anomalous as his, made it clear to me that sheer goodness had less to do with getting one into the heavenly Utopia than one would think reasonable. It was not enough to be good; the main thing was to be good by prescription. The Elder, for instance, was sound in doctrine, he did not drink, swear or even smoke, never played cards, gambled, danced, never cast a desirous eye on any feminine charm. Hence he was certain of heaven; he could read his title clear. To me, however, the thought of prescription in any circumstances was utterly odious; and least of all could I reconcile it with the idea of any Utopia fit to live in. The men of sin did not employ prescription in their dealings with me, but always based their admonitions on grounds of reason; I could always see sense and wisdom in what they said. They did not tell me, for example, that swearing was by prescription sinful, and that it put one in jeopardy of hell; if they had, my instinct would have been to ask them how they knew that. On the contrary, they told me that it was a low, offensive sort of practice that one had best get on without; and my instinct was to agree at once.

Thus, as between the Elder and the men of sin, I perversely decided that if sense and reason played any part in the management of Utopia, I would cheerfully trade off his chances for theirs, at a ratio of sixteen to one. Stark prescription impressed me as likely to open the way for great numbers of people who were, in any other view, wholly ineligible. I did not wish to be like them, even for the sake of all the benefits that prescription could confer, and I plucked up courage finally to make up my mind that a society so heavily adulterated would be far from Utopian. Many years afterward I ran across something by the old Rhode Island Quaker, Thomas Robinson Hazard, in his delightful *Jonnycake Papers*, that reflected my youthful sentiments exactly. A robber named Mount had been hanged near Kingston, and as was more or less the fashion in those days when executions were public, the occasion gave rise to a sermon. Mr. Hazard says:

So far as I have learned, it may have been Elder Northup, or some other minister of one of the numerous out-branching sects of the Baptist persuasion, who performed the last sacred duties for Mount. The reverend gentleman's remarks on the occasion were generally held to be singularly appropriate and highly consolatory to the criminal, who, he declared, having repented and made a good confession before God's appointed minister, would doubtless be ushered into immediate glory as soon as the soul left the body; closing with a strong appeal to all present to go and do likewise with the sainted man about to suffer for Christ's sake and the good of his fellow-creatures, that they too might reap his reward, and like him, enter at once into the kingdom of heaven.

As the Elder closed his eloquent discourse, most, or all, present shed tears, excepting old Sim Hazard, who was heard to mutter to himself that if his "getting into heaven turned upon his becoming a damned thief, then they might set him down as one bound for hell."

II

The Utopian projects that came under my observation in later life were of a secular character; some of them had a religious flavouring or sugar-coating, but they were mostly mere naïve attempts at realizing an imaginary state of society on earth. About the time I have referred to, however, while I was still a lad, I ran across a curious group or sect of human-perfectibility people who, I suppose, might be said to have contemplated a sort of quietist Utopia. Their leader was an illiterate enthusiast, apparently quite innocent-minded and sincere. When in later life I read Turgeniev's little masterpiece called *A Strange Story*, it brought him back to mind. He did not exploit his followers or lay any kind of exactions on them, even though a few of them were pretty well-to-do. He pretended to be able to work miracles; people said, though I do not know how truly, that he had pretended to be able to walk on water, as Jesus did on the Sea of Galilee. Some of the boys heard of this and tossed him in the lake one day, which I remember thinking was rather a poor thing to do, since the man seemed never to have done anybody any actual harm. As I remember, he did not even proselytize; his disciples found their own way to him, and passed the word around among others.

His followers appeared to find their peculiar belief rather comforting. They were uneducated persons, weak-minded, and their simple creed suited them. They went a long step ahead of Rousseau, Condorcet, Price, Priestley—indeed, ahead of all who had ever dallied with the notion of human perfectibility. They were sure not only that perfection was attainable, but that they had attained it. I never heard of their having any preliminary discipline, or any more elaborate creed; they merely persuaded themselves that they were perfect and could do no wrong, and that was all there was "to it."

What chiefly struck me about these people was the sense of finality which their belief induced. They were perfect, so what more was there to do? Why read? Why think? Why do anything but the daily task whereby they lived? I never saw people more completely divested of any sense of responsibility to anybody, or for anything. This must have made more impression on me than I was aware of at the time, for always afterward my recollections of it came back promptly when I was considering the peculiarities of other persons engaged in the projection or promotion of Utopian ideas.

Presently I went to college, where I read Greek and Roman literature under the supervision of able and arbitrary persons who seemed to think that proficiency in this pursuit was the chief end of man. Here I encountered Plutarch's *Life of Lycurgus,* with its fine picture of the Utopia which that dignitary introduced into Sparta. This was no imaginary commonwealth like the one projected by Plato, which I had already put in good hard labour on examining, and which, if the truth must be told, I found a little dull, despite the fascinations of the pure Attic style. Plutarch's Utopia, on the contrary, purported to be historical; it was the real thing as it had actually existed, and I was prepared to respect it accordingly. I became convinced, however, that Plutarch was press-agenting Lycurgus a little too handsomely, and I presently discovered that authorities like Aristotle and Suidas bore out this notion. Nevertheless Plutarch's account was interesting, even if one took it subject to the regular discount, or a little better, and I therefore read it attentively.

Lycurgus established the New Deal in Sparta on the right idea; he believed in keeping his people poor, and his success seems to have been without precedent. He was the greatest leveler on record. Other rulers have managed to keep most of their people broke most of the time, but in Sparta everybody was broke all the time. Lycurgus did not need any Brain Trust to help him further this excellent enterprise; he was all the Brain Trust there was, and he was enough. He did not fiddle around at nicking partial values off the basic currency-unit; he devalued the whole currency right down to zero at one stroke, and substituted iron money so heavy that if by some miracle a Spartan accumulated a bank-roll of $165, he had to have a two-ox team to carry it around. Hence, obviously, Lycurgus had no trouble with predatory bankers; also he had no trouble about foreign exchange, for foreigners would not handle his money on any terms whatever, regarding it with what Homer finely calls "asbestos laughter," ἄσβεστος γέλως, which perhaps might be construed to mean the horse-laugh.

As an exponent of collectivism, Lycurgus must have made Marx, Engels, Lenin, *et al.*, look like bush-leaguers. With him the State was collectivist to a degree that made the individual's status determinable only by algebra. He had prescription down to what one might really call a fine point; and as for "social legislation," it seems to have been his specialty. Nobody could have any ornaments or even any clothes to speak of. Lycurgus believed in nudism on moral and social grounds as well as on hygienic grounds; Plutarch's observations on this point are worth the attention of those who are interested in such matters nowadays, as are also his observations on the arrangements instituted by Lycurgus for a sort of quasi-companionate or tandem marriage. Sumptuary laws extended even to haircutting; everyone had to have the same style of haircut. One could not wiggle out of compliance with Lycurgus's regulations by the aid of resourceful shysters; nor, on the other hand, did Lycurgus need a pliant contortionist judiciary to validate his incursions upon the liberties of the subject. The subject had no liberties, and there were neither lawyers nor lawsuits in Sparta—though prescription would seem to have been unnecessary on this latter point, for with everybody hopelessly busted, there was really nothing on which to found a lawsuit. Plutarch sums up the situation by saying that "no man was allowed to live as he pleased, the city being like one great camp, where all had their fixed allowance and knew their public duty."

So this was Utopia! This was the sort of collective existence that Spartans were supposed to like and be proud of! Perhaps they did like it; they may have done so, though Plutarch does not say specifically that they did. Knowing, however, that in such cases there is no great chance for dissenting opinion to find its way into history, I suspected that there might have been some few who in the long run became a trifle bored by the conditions of life in Lycurgus's Utopia. At any rate, I was sure that if I had been offered a chance at the smooth-running perfections of his Utopian régime, I should have civilly desired to be excused.

One thing remained with me permanently from my perusal of Plutarch. I observed with particular interest his saying that the Spartan system was philosophically perfect; that is, the way Lycurgus ran things was precisely the way that philosophers would say they should be run. He remarks that while the laws of Lycurgus remained in force, "Sparta was not so much under the political regulations of a commonwealth, as under the strict rules of a philosophic life." This observation could not be read without certain misgivings of a very serious nature; but Plutarch goes even further. He says that Lycurgus "produced a most inimitable form of government; and by showing a whole cityful of philosophers he confounded those who imagine that the much-vaunted strictness of a philosophic life is impracticable." I perceived then that if Plutarch was right about this, I had laid up another valuable criterion for future use, in addition to those I had garnered from previous observation. I had already made up my mind that my first test of any proposed Utopia would be a measure of its attitude towards prescription, and my second would be a very close measure of the sort of people whom it qualified for membership. Now that Plutarch had given me a line of direction on the kind of thing one might expect from philosophers if they were given a free hand, my third care would be to see how many of these gentry were on the board of managers.

III

For many years after my dealings with Plutarch I did nothing with Utopias except by desultory reading. At one time or another I dipped into More, Bacon, Cabet, Campanella, and so on down to Edward Bellamy and Mr. H. G. Wells, but I was not much interested in any of their proposals. The application of my three tests immediately raised a thick mist of fictitiousness and improbability about them which hid their merits. Even the demi-semi-Utopian projects of social reform and improvement that were rife among us in my earlier years went hard aground on one or another of my three criteria, or pretty regularly on all three at once. How many, many, of these enterprises there were in those days, and how fearfully in earnest they all were!—and, Lord, where be they now?

I saw the Uplift in all its protean forms, I think, from the endowed foundation down to the college settlement. I witnessed the impassioned advocacy of the Square Deal, the initiative, referendum and recall, the direct primary, the Wisconsin Idea, proportional representation, arbitration treaties, the World Court, the League of Nations and the devil and all of other devices directed towards some kind of millennial outcome. I saw the crusades of Bryan, Coin Harvey, Coxey, and I have a vague recollection of the searchings of heart caused by Senator Peffer and the Populists; I even remember a couple of stanzas of newspaper-verse that dates from this last period—how is it that such trash manages to fix itself so firmly in a boy's memory that one is like to remember it forever?

> I am Peffer, Peffer, Peffer,
>   From the wild and woolly West,
> And I have so many whiskers
>   That I never need a vest.

> I am Peffer, Peffer, Peffer,
>   And the breezes always sing
> When they meet me; to my sluggers
>   They don't do a blessed thing.

All these enterprises showed me plainly that the social and political reformer's main dependence is on prescription; it is the sinful Tammany ward-boss, whose knowledge of fundamental humanity is as "extensive and peculiar" as Sam Weller's knowledge of London, who does not employ it. Back in the days of Roosevelt the First and the Square Deal, I remember, when the forces of righteousness were on their way to Armageddon to fight the battle of the Lord in the hifalutinest, hymn-singingest political convention ever held in America, I worked out a bit of rough mathematics which showed that the ordinary citizen had something like seven times more margin of existence to dispose of as he pleased than he would have if the various proposals of the liberal and progressive reformers were carried into effect.

The only reformer abroad in the world in my time

who interested me in the least was Henry George, because his project did not contemplate prescription, but, on the contrary, would reduce it almost to zero. He was the only one of the lot who believed in freedom, or (as far as I could see) had any approximation to an intelligent idea of what freedom is, and of the economic prerequisites to attaining it. At the end of his book called *Progress and Poverty*, a work on fundamental economics, he sketches out a prospectus that I suppose is detailed enough to give him a place in the goodly fellowship of Utopia-builders, and I dare say that in the course of a few thousand years, say thirty or forty, it might be realizable. Although my lifetime overlapped the latter part of his career, I was too young to take much note of what went on in public affairs, so I really knew nothing of him at first hand, and never even saw him. It now seems clear, however, that he regarded himself as primarily an evangelist or crusader for a cause, and by taking his doctrine into politics, and making alignments with disaffected groups representing other causes which were really alien to his, he brought his own cause into a disrepute from which it has never recovered. One is immensely tickled to see how things are coming out nowadays with reference to his doctrine, for George was in fact the best friend the capitalist ever had. He built up the most complete and absolutely impregnable defense of the rights of capital that was ever constructed, and if the capitalists of his day had had sense enough to dig in behind it, their successors would not now be squirming under the merciless exactions which collectivism is laying on them, and which George would have no scruples whatever about describing as sheer highwaymanry.

Now, finally, when I had thought I was quite done with Utopias and Utopians, I find myself once more taking up my old post of observer, and surveying the impressive programme of the New Deal, which leads, so we are told, straight onward to the proletarian goal of the More Abundant Life. I had already looked over some specifications of the proletarian Utopia; Shakespeare puts them into the mouth of Jack Cade as a bid for the suffrage of the many-headed. They are so well worth a thoughtful perusal at the present time that I venture to cite them.

Cade. Be brave then, for your captain is brave, and vows reformation. There shall be in England seven halfpenny loaves sold for a penny; the three-hooped pot shall have ten hoops,[1] and I will make it felony to drink small beer; all the realm shall be in common; and in Cheapside shall my palfrey go to grass; and when I am king . . . there shall be no money; all shall eat and drink on my score; and I will apparel them all in one livery, that they may agree like brothers, and worship me their lord.
                    —*II King Henry VI*, Act iv, Scene ii

Applying my three tests to the New Deal's prospectus, one must see, I think, that it contemplates prescription carried to a degree that would win the admiring respect of Lycurgus himself. In the second place, if we are to be thus dragooned into the More Abundant Life, it strikes one as reasonable that one should ask for a much more prepossessing and much less disingenuous set of

---

[1] The ordinary drinking-mug or pot was of wood, with metal hoops which served as a sort of gauge of the contents. The reference to Cheapside seems to run parallel to the more modern notion of "making grass grow in Wall Street."

drill-sergeants, and also for a prospect of better company when we get there. When one thinks of even the most distant and formal association with Mr. Farley, Mr. Roosevelt, Mr. Tugwell, Mr. Ickes, Mr. Hopkins and their chief collaborators, the More Abundant Life seems hardly worth having at the price. In the third place, the scheme of the New Deal is said to have been worked out by philosophers; and after my vicarious experience with the architectonics of a philosopher's Utopia in Sparta and elsewhere, I for one would regard it *a priori* with the most profound distrust, and with no expectation whatever but that it would turn out much as it appears to be doing.

If, in fact, the More Abundant Life, or any other Utopian project, were realizable only under such guidance, by force of such associations, and on such philosophic principles, one is bound to question whether it would be worth the wholesale sacrifice of fundamental integrities that assent to these involves. One of the Church of England's really great prelates in the last century was Richard Whately, the redoubtable and uncompromising archbishop of Dublin. As things turned out, it seems strange that in his earlier days he collaborated with Newman on a textbook of logic; stranger still, perhaps, that he lent a hand with Heber at composing one of the very few English hymns that have any actual poetic quality. Whately had a Scots Calvinist servant-maid, with whom he used to amuse himself now and then by dragging her into argument about the probable number of the elect. He wound up one of these discussions, the last one they ever had, by telling her playfully that since she believed he was going to be damned anyway, the matter was hardly worth talking about. "Oh, no," she said, "indeed I believe nothing like that about your Grace. I firmly believe your Grace is going to be saved on account of your Grace's invincible ignorance." [2] It is said that the words were hardly out of her mouth before old Whately was jumping three feet high. He behaved in a most tremendous fashion for fully five minutes, staving around amidst the débris of his furniture, and declaring that he would rather his soul should be damned for ever and ever to thirty thousand wagonloads of black devils, than be saved on any such terms as those.

Even eternal salvation may conceivably come too high. It is conceivable also that national security and prosperity, even the continuance of a whole civilization, even a full realization of the More Abundant Life, might come too high. This thought occurred to me the other day when someone gave me to read a perfervid plea for the New Deal, by one of its principal fuglemen. A more disreputably disingenuous document I never saw; and I thought then that if the country had to be saved by such despicable misrepresentations of fact, it had far better be let go to the dogs in an honourable and self-respecting way. I handed the article back to my acquaintance, and said nothing; there was really nothing to say. The best I could do was to remind myself of the unhappy Frenchman who had to listen to some such outpouring of peculiarly odious nonsense. He must say something; he must also be polite; he was in an impasse. *"Monsieur,"* he said, austerely, *"je me permets d'invoquer l'auguste ombre du Général Cambronne."*

2 "A man is said to be in a state of invincible ignorance if . . . after reasonable effort he is unable to arrive at certain knowledge." *Encyclopædia of Religion and Ethics,* ed. Hastings, vol. VII, p. 403.

IV

When all comes to all, I am led to consider seriously, not whether this-or-that Utopia is practicable, but whether any Utopia is really desirable. Suppose a true Utopia could be worked out as a going concern, complete and perfect in every structural detail—well, how should we like it for warp and filling, and how long should we continue to like it? Would participation in it finally come to taking on the character of an endurance-test? Man's attitude towards perfection has always been strangely anomalous and inconsistent; he is feebly but persistently interested in perfection, tries feebly but persistently to realize it, and when he has succeeded in realizing what he thinks is some approximation to it, he is proud and contented for a while, then lapses into a vague dissatisfaction which he assuages by reverting to something distinctly imperfect, and glories in his shame. My enchanting friend Cassandre remarked the unfailing dominance of this instinct—for instinct it seems to be—when first she cast a clear Gallic eye upon our elaborate national apparatus of camps and dude ranches. "You do all you can with your infamous machinery," she said to me, "to destroy and defile your wilderness, for the sake of adding to what you call your comforts. Then you adore your comforts and conveniences, and hold them up for other nations to copy, meanwhile living such an intolerable life that you escape from it when you can, and pay great sums for the privilege of enjoying a poor imitation of what you have destroyed." Her reflections on our industrial and commercial Utopia (which was flourishing just then, and we were all delighting ourselves in its perfections) were undoubtedly severe; but there the facts were. Multitudes of people were going forth from comfortable homes at every opportunity, and sending their children forth, precisely as Cassandre said, *à grands frais,* to seek a palpably bogus counterfeit of the very discomforts that in my boyhood we used to enjoy free gratis for nothing, and in limitless abundance.

Canis reversus et sus lota, says the Apostle, citing a proverb that was old when Jesus walked the earth; so old is this tendency in the disposition of mankind. I myself have known the Perfect Husband (yea, even, tell it not in Gath, have I known the Perfect Wife to do likewise)—housebroken, loving, assiduous, devoted, dutiful, oh, everything—who every now and then left a beautiful and accomplished spouse to hoe her own row at home, while he spent the evening in an unimpeachably innocent and decorous flirtation with some female who would barely escape the Chamber of Horrors on her looks, and could not hold a job in a steam-laundry on her intelligence. There is no accounting for such divagations; they simply exist, as part and parcel of the creature of a "large discourse, looking before and after." In the Club Anonyme the other day, one of the members was lifting up his voice in bitter grievance against the management—nothing suited him—when Bill McN. plucked my sleeve, and whispered, "Harry won't be in heaven half an hour before you'll hear him say, 'Dammit, this gold hurts my feet.'" Truly it would appear that the complaint of Gilbert's captive king in *Princess Ida* was thrown up from the unplumbed depths of man's noblest endowment, his indefeasible cussedness:

Oh, don't the days seem lank and long
When all goes right and nothing goes wrong,
And is n't your life extremely flat
With nothing whatever to grumble at!

It is this noble endowment which makes things look
a little dark for the prospects of any Utopia that human
ingenuity can devise. One gets a pretty good idea of how
dark they do look by reading Mr. H. G. Wells's description of the Utopian hotel, where everything one may
wish for comes to pass at the mere touch of a button,
and where all is done by machinery. The reader may
be his own judge. Let him peruse that description slowly,
thoughtfully and with imagination—it amounts only to
a page or two—then let him stand forth, and with his
hand on his heart say truthfully how long he thinks he
could stand living in that hotel.

Climates of opinion, climates of thought, taste, even
of habit, seem to produce an effect of intolerable monot-
ony if one be exposed to them for any great length of
time, without the occasional relief of what someone, I
think it was William James, so well called a "moral holiday." Speaking of the weather in a certain region, Mark
Twain says that after two or three months of supreme
contentment with the unfailing brilliant sunshine and
exquisite mild air, one longs to watch dense black clouds
sweep overhead, to hear the rain and hail drive down,
with the thunder rattling and the wind roaring, and see
the lightning strike somebody. Perhaps the spirit of man
is a four-seasonal affair, sometimes even thriving on a
goodish stretch of "in-between"; and a four-seasonal
Utopia is something that no one has as yet been able
to contrive.

It may be thought—indeed, it is often said—that the complexities of modern life, brought about through the exercise of our boundless faith in machinery, act as an anodyne; that they have pretty well deadened this recalcitrant disposition out of the present race of men, and supplanted it with a porcine acquiescence which may be trusted to keep them permanently content with the conditions of a material and mechanical Utopia. The influences tending that way are undoubtedly very powerful, and one should not underestimate them. Still, one must remember that they have been at work but a relatively short time, that any essential change in this curiously tenacious nature of ours comes about far slower than one thinks, and also that each period—especially a period of great and rapid expansion—tends to regard itself as exceptional, whereas the unfolding of time usually exhibits it as quite otherwise. In spite of appearances, I suspect that the same inveterate dissatisfaction will arise against the new Utopias that one could predicate as so certain to arise against the old; and that it will still be strong enough to honeycomb them, and in the end will break them down.

Perhaps this disposition has come about by the purely accidental interplay of blind and purposeless "natural causes," whatever those are; perhaps it may be satisfactorily interpreted in terms of more or less plausibly sublimated *Kraft und Stoff,* whatever those are. Any other line of interpretation is so much out of fashion just now that going back to Paley and the argument from design seems almost an impertinence; or going back to Goethe, who put it simply that "if God had wished me otherwise, He would have made me otherwise." Still, under the license so happily accorded to literature nowadays, no tabu is sacred, and no sensibilities are shielded from shock. I therefore take advantage of this license to suggest boldly that the reason why no Utopia can be permanently satisfying is that our adorable Creator, in His wisdom, and in His loving-kindness, and for purposes of His own devising, does not wish it to be so.

What those purposes are I do not know, and do not care to know. All that interests me, inasmuch as the Divine veto seems to be clamped down tight on all attempts to organize human society around the Utopian principle, is to discern, if I can, some other principle around which it might be organized to better purpose than its present organization manifests; and here, since I have already made the plunge into the unpopular terms of a decayed superstition, I shall continue to use those terms in discussing the only principle I have been able to hit on as possibly workable.

Whenever I survey a crowd of people, I am overpowered by a sense of the most prodigious, the most stupendous miracle that can conceivably be performed, even by omnipotence. What miracle can one imagine, comparable with the annual and regular turning-out of millions of human beings, guaranteed positively no two alike? I can think of none. By comparison with this, raising the dead, cleansing lepers, multiplying loaves and fishes, seem most insignificant. Well, but, here that miracle is, here those beings are, and their infinite variety suggests to me that their Creator is not working this continuous miracle merely to show what He can do when He tries, but that He has some pretty distinct idea in mind when He does it. The thing is, therefore, to hit on some principle of social organization that comes nearest to corresponding with the conditions which this miracle appears to impose.

The only principle I can think of as coming anywhere near filling this bill is one that we have never tried— freedom. We have tried everything else with no great success, so even as a "flyer" or sporting venture, we might do worse than try freedom. It is fair to give warning, however, that a profitable application of this principle must go far beyond economic and political freedom, though these of course come first: economic freedom, meaning that each individual has free access to the primal source of his subsistence; and political freedom, meaning that government confines itself to exercising only the negative interventions of a *Polizeistaat*. But the principle must govern all the relations of life; and the essence of its successful application is that freedom should never be felt as permissive. As an illustration of what I mean, I may cite the amenities that we practice daily; they are actually exercises in true freedom. As things stand now, for example, the vegetarian devours his vapid fodder in pleasant converse with the husky beef-eater; the red-licker Democrat and the grape-juice Prohibitionist drink together on the best of terms. Neither party feels that he is acting on sufferance; the whole point is that neither party really notices what the other's choice is. This is the index of true freedom; well, why not extend indefinitely our application of the principle that so largely governs our existing amenities? In New York the other day, a magistrate refused to commit two girls for appearing naked on the stage, saying that mere nudity does not in itself connote a lewd performance. This is all very well, but one must see, I think, that the freedom which these girls now enjoy is purely permissive; it is freedom by prescription—that is to say, it is not freedom at all. True freedom in these premises would be found where, if the two walked naked on Fifth Avenue at noonday, no one would notice, unless quite casually or by afterthought, that they happened not to be wearing any clothes.

Whether in small matters or in great, the thorough-going application of this principle is, in short, an affair of the spirit; and while this principle is no foundation for a Utopia or anything remotely resembling one, it would seem to offer better terms for the organization of human society—terms corresponding much more closely with the nature of man—than those offered by any other principle of which we have knowledge.

New York, February, 1935.

9

American Education

COMPLAINT within the teaching profession about
the quality of education in America has lately
taken an interesting turn. For forty years, to my knowledge,—I do not know how much longer,—professional
criticism has confined itself pretty strictly to matters that
went on under the general system, and has not questioned the system itself. It has run to questions of pedagogic method and curricular content; to the *what* and
the *how*. One notices with satisfaction, however, that
within the past year some of our educators have gone
beyond these matters and touched the system's structural
principles. The presidents of Brown, Haverford and St.
Stephen's have spoken out plainly. Professor Giddings,
of Columbia, has been very explicit, and even the president of Columbia has made some observations that
might be construed as disparaging. These gentlemen
have spoken informally, mostly by implication, and not
pretending to present anything like a complete thesis on
the subject; nevertheless their implications are clear.

One wishes they had gone further; one hopes they may
yet do so. My own reason for writing is that perhaps a
layman's view of the situation may call out additional

professional comment on it. One need make no apology for the intervention, for the subject is quite within the layman's competence. Matters of content and method (the *what* and the *how*) are primarily a professional concern, and the layman speaks of them under correction. But the system itself is not a technical affair, and its points of strength and weakness lie as properly under lay review as under professional review. In any kind of fairness, indeed, if professional opinion takes responsibility for correctness in technical matters it has enough on its shoulders, and lay opinion may well take the lead on matters which are not technical.

I

On its moral and social side, our educational system is indeed a noble experiment—none more so. In all the history of noble experiments I know of none to match it. There is every evidence of its being purely an expression—no, one may put it even stronger than that, an organization—of a truly noble, selfless and affectionate desire. The representative American, whatever his faults, has been notably characterized by the wish that his children might do better by themselves than he could do by himself. He wished them to have all the advantages that he had been obliged to get on without, all the "opportunities," not only for material well-being but also for self-advancement in the realm of the spirit. I quite believe that in its essence and intention our system may be fairly called no less than an organization of this desire; and as such it can not be too much admired or too highly praised.

But unfortunately Nature recks little of the nobleness prompting any human enterprise. Perhaps it is rather a hard thing to say, but the truth is that Nature seems much more solicitous about her reputation for order than she is about keeping up her character for morals. Apparently no pressure of noble and unselfish moral earnestness will cozen the sharp old lady into countenancing a breach of order. Hence any enterprise, however nobly and disinterestedly conceived, will fail if it be not also organized intelligently. We are having a fine illustration of this great truth in the fate of the other noble experiment which Mr. Hoover commended on moral grounds in one of his campaign speeches; and an equally conspicuous illustration of it is furnished by the current output of our educational institutions.

Our educational pot has always been sufficiently astir; there can be no doubt of that. It would seem that there is no possible permutation or combination in pedagogic theory and practice that we have not tried. The roster of our undergraduate and secondary courses reads like the advertisement of a bargain-counter. One of our pioneer women's colleges offers, among other curious odds-and-ends, some sort of "course" in baby-tending! Our floundering ventures in university-training have long been fair game for our cartoonists. Only this morning I saw a capital cartoon in a New York paper, prompted by a news-item on some new variant of a cafeteria or serve-self educational scheme vamped up in one of our top-heavy state universities. But now, after all this feverish and hopeful fiddling with the mechanics of education, the current product seems to be, if anything, a little poorer than any that has gone before it.

This statement may rest as it lies. I see no point in a digression to define education or to describe the marks that set off an educated person. If I were writing on oyster-culture, I should consider it a waste of space to define an oyster, because everyone likely to read my paper would know well enough what an oyster is; at least, he would know very well what it is not. Similarly, everyone likely to read this essay may be presumed to know an educated person from an uneducated person. But if this seems a cavalier way of dealing with one's readers, one may establish a perfect understanding by a reference to Mr. James Truslow Adams's paper in the November 1929 issue of the *Atlantic Monthly*. It is enough to say that one who, by whatever means, has compassed just the discipline intimated by Mr. Adams,— a discipline directed as steadily towards *being* and *becoming* as towards *doing* and *getting*,—and who in all his works and ways reflects that discipline, is an educated person. One who has not compassed it, and whose works and ways do not reflect it, may not properly be called an educated person, no matter what his training, learning, aptitudes and accomplishments may be.

Mr. Adams's paper makes it clear that the educated American is not often to be met with; and there is a pretty complete consensus that he is at present much scarcer than he was, say, twenty-five years ago. An Italian nobleman of high culture, who has seen a great deal of our college and university life, lately told me that he had made a curious observation while here, and asked me whether I thought it was a fair one, and if so, how I should account for it. He said he had now and then met Americans who were extremely well educated, but they were all in the neighbourhood of sixty years old; he had not seen a single person below that age who impressed him as having been even respectably educated, although interest in the matter had led him to look everywhere. It is unsafe to generalize from a single opinion, but it may be worth remembering that this reference is the judgment of one foreign observer of experience and distinction.

This state of things is obviously not due to any deficiency in our mechanical equipment. What impresses one most, I think, at sight of the Continental school, is the very moderate character of its plant and general apparatus of learning, as compared with ours. I have elsewhere remarked that no live-wire, up-to-date, go-getting American college president would look twice at the University of Poitiers or the old university at Brussels. Even Bonn, the aristocrat of German universities, is a very modest and plain affair in its physical aspects. The secondary schools of France and Belgium have in our eyes an appearance of simplicity almost primitive. Yet see what comes out of them. Compare the order of disciplined intelligence that somehow manages to squeeze itself out of Poitiers and Brussels with that which floats through one of our universities. With every imaginable accessory and externality in his favour, the American simply makes no comparison. Put a cost-accounting system on education in France and America, with reference to the quality of the product,—if such a thing were possible,—and the result would be, I think, a most disquieting surprise.

Nor have the French and Belgians any natural advantage over us in respect of raw material. I firmly believe

that the run-of-mine American is just as intelligent as
the run-of-mine Frenchman, and the picked American
as the picked Frenchman. The trouble is not there, nor
can I see that it lies anywhere in the technique of pedagogy; I must needs be shown wherein our pedagogy is
not entitled to a clean bill. Yet the fact is that with relatively poor equipment, with no better raw material and
no better pedagogy than ours, French institutions turn
out extremely well-educated men, and ours do not.

The whole trouble is that the American system from
beginning to end is gauged to the run-of-mine American
rather than to the picked American. The run-of-mine
Frenchman does not get any nearer the university than
the adjacent woodpile. He does not get into the French
equivalent of our undergraduate college. If he gets
through the French equivalent of our secondary school,
he does so by what our ancestors called the uncove-
nanted mercies of Providence, and every step of his progress is larded with bitter sweat. The chief reason why
my Italian friend found no educated Americans under
sixty years of age is that forty years ago the run-of-mine
American did not, as a rule, get much nearer the founts
of the higher learning than the run-of-mine Frenchman
does to-day, and for the same reason—he could not,
speaking strictly, "make the grade." The newspapers
some time ago quoted the president of Columbia as saying that during the past half-century the changes in
school and college instruction, as to both form and content, have been so complete that it is probably safe to
say that to-day no student in Columbia College, and perhaps no professor on its faculty, could pass satisfactorily

the examination-tests that were set for admission to Columbia College fifty years ago.

The root-idea, or ideal, of our system is the very fine one that educational opportunity should be open to all. The practical approach to this ideal, however, was not planned intelligently, but, on the contrary, very stupidly; it was planned on the official assumption that everybody is educable, and this assumption still remains official. Instead of firmly establishing the natural limit to opportunity—the ability to make any kind of use of it—and then making opportunity as free as possible within that limit, our system says, Let them all come, and we will scratch up some sort of brummagem opportunity for each of them. What they do not learn at school, the college will teach them; the university will go through some motions for them on what the college failed to get into their heads. This is no jaunty exaggeration. I have a friend who has spent years in a mid-Western state university, trying to teach elementary English composition to adult illiterates. I have visited his classes, seen what they were about, seen his pupils, examined their work, and speak whereof I know. A short time ago, in another enormous university,—a university, mind; not a grade school, but a university dealing with adult persons,—two instructors published samples of the kind of thing produced for them by their students. Here are a few:

Being a tough hunk of meat, I passed up the steak.
Lincoln's mind grew as his country kneaded it.
The camel carries a water tank with him; he is also a rough rider and has four gates.
As soon as music starts, silence rains, but as soon as it stops it gets worse than ever.

College students as a general rule like such readings that will take the least mental inertia.

Modern dress is extreme and ought to be checked.

Although the Irish are usually content with small jobs, they have won a niche in the backbone of the country.

At the hands of some upper-classmen and second-year men, Shakespeare fared as follows:

Edmund, in *King Lear,* "committed a base act and allowed his illegitimate father to see a forged letter." Cordelia's death "was the straw that broke the camel's back and killed the king." Lear's fool "was prostrated on the neck of the king." "Hotspur," averred a sophomore, "was a wild, irresolute man. He loved honor above all. He would go out and kill twenty Scotchmen before breakfast." Kate was "a woman who had something to do with hot spurs."

Also Milton:

"Diabetes was Milton's Italian friend," one student explained. Another said, "Satan had all the emotions of a' woman, and was a sort of trustee in heaven, so to speak." The theme of *Comus* was given as "purity protestriate." Mammon, in *Paradise Lost,* suggests that the best way "to endure hell is to raise hell and build a pavilion."

Would it be unfair to ask the reader how long he thinks that order of intelligence would be permitted to display itself at the University of Brussels or the University of Poitiers?

II

The history of our system shows a significant interplay between the sentiment for an indiscriminate and prodigal distribution of "opportunity" and certain popular ideas or pseudo-ideas that flourished beside it. One of these was the popular conception of democracy. It is an interesting fact that this originally got its currency through the use of the word by politicians as a talking-point. Practically all publicists now quite arbitrarily use the word "democratic" as a synonym for "republican"—as when, for instance, they speak of the United States and France as "great democracies." The proper antithesis of democracy is not autocracy, monarchy, or oligarchy, but absolutism; and, as we all know, absolutism is much deeper entrenched in these republican countries than in monarchical Denmark, say. The term, too, became debased in its more special uses. In the America which Dickens visited, a democratic society meant one in which "one man was just as good as another, or a little better"; this phrase itself is of sound American coinage current with the merchant. Democratic manners to-day, as a rule, mean merely coarse manners; for instance, the ostentatiously "democratic" luncheon-etiquette of our booster clubs means that all hands shall, under some sort of penalty, call each fellow member by his given name, regardless of previous acquaintance or the lack of it.

Thus the educational free-for-all sentiment got a very powerful endorsement. It was democratic. Poverty-stricken Tom, from the slashes, should go through school, college and university hand in hand with Dick the scion of Wall Street, and toplofty Harry of the Back Bay. Democracy so willed it, in spite of Nature's insuperable differentiations whereby Tom had first-rate school-ability, Harry had excellent ability in other directions but no school-ability, and Dick was a *Dummkopf* with no ability of any kind. Privately these differ-

entiations might be recognized, indeed must be, but it
was of the essence of democracy that there should be
no official or institutional recognition of them. The un-
speakable silliness of our truant laws, which make com-
pulsory attendance a matter purely of school-age instead
of school-ability, appropriately expresses this limitation.

The very human but rather ignoble tendency to self-
assertion which led us to put the label of democracy
on what was merely indiscriminate or vulgar led us also
to put the label of greatness on what was merely big.
With a whole civilization groveling in the unintelligent
worship of bigness, a great school must be a big school.
The thing to notice is how admirably this fell in with
pseudo-democratic doctrine and also with the noble but
ill-starred sentiment pervading our system. To make a
big school, students must be got; to get them, standards
of eligibility must be brought down to a common denominator of intelligence, aptitude and interest. Then,
when they are got, something has to be found for them
to do that they can do, or at least upon which they are
able to mark time,—such as "courses in English," the
number of which exhibited annually by our institutions
will amaze the reader, if he has curiosity enough about
it to look it up,—and this means a profound sophistication of requirements. It can be seen at once how solidly
sentiment and pseudo-democratic doctrine stood behind
these developments and encouraged them.

By another interesting coincidence—these coincidences
in the history of our system are really remarkable—
these developments also met, as if made to order, the
great and sudden expansion of the nation's industrial
life, the glorification of profit-making, and the implied

disparagement of all intellectual, æsthetic, and even
moral processes which did not tend directly or indirectly
to profit-making. It was promptly perceived that the
ineducable person might become a successful banker,
industrialist, broker, bond-salesman or what not; plenty
such there were who could manage no more than to read
the stock-quotations and write their own signatures—
Daniel Drew, for instance, and Cornelius Vanderbilt.
Thus vocationalism came at once to the burdened system's aid. Circumstances were created whereby the ineducable person might bear directly on the business of
banking, brokerage, industry, and so on, with the prestige of a college or university career thrown in. The
elective bargain-counter was extended all over the academic floor-space; its limit was only at the line where
imaginative ingenuity broke down and ceased to work;
and certain fragile windflowers, such as "courses in
English," were distributed over it here and there, partly
by way of garnishment, partly as camouflage. Thus
everything was made satisfactory all round. The ineducable person was taken care of with an academic career
to all appearances as respectable as anybody's; sentiment
was assuaged; democratic doctrine was satisfied; the
general regard for size was satisfied, and so was the general preoccupation with profit.

III

In discussing the effect of all this, I wish to make it
as clear as possible that I am not laying the slightest
blame upon our educators. They had to take the system
as they found it; its faults were none of their making.

They had to meet measurably the egregious demands of a noble but undiscriminating sentiment, a preposterous misconception of the democratic principle, a childish reverence for bigness, and an exclusive preoccupation with profit-making. It is a large order; if in practice they were able to meet these demands by ever so little obliquely, one might reasonably ask no more. With this clearly understood, we may observe that one immediate effect is a calamitous overlapping of effort, whereby the lines marking off the school from the college and the college from the university have been obliterated. As in the case I cited, the university is doing work that by the handsomest possible concession one would say should be done in the eighth grade. The secondary school and the undergraduate college, again, are overlapping on the university in their furtherance of vocationalism. Hence, whatever may be done for sentiment or democracy or the promotion of profit-making, none of them are doing anything for education. An institution, like an individual, has only twenty-four hours a day, and only a limited amount of attention at its disposal; and so much of time and attention as it devotes to one pursuit must be taken from another.

This overlapping, indeed, gives rise to a great deal of justifiable avoidance on the part of educators, or what I understand is better known as "passing the buck." In looking over an undergraduate college last year, I remarked to the president that, on the one hand, he seemed to be doing a good deal of rather elementary school-work, and at the same time trespassing pretty heavily on the university, especially in his science courses; so that on the whole his college made me think of the small boy's objection to some asparagus that his mother offered him—it tasted raw at one end and rotten at the other. He said this was so; he had to give way to vocationalism somewhat—much more than he wished; he was doing his best against it. As for the other matter, it was the fault of the schools; they left ragged holes in the boys' preparation. "Don't you think we should do something for the poor fellows who come to us with these deficiencies?"

"Certainly," I replied. "Fire them."

"Ah, but then we should have no students, and should be obliged to shut up shop."

"Well, but at that," I suggested, "would it really be such a killing misfortune?"

"Possibly so, I think," he answered, after a moment's reflection. "My ideas are the same as yours precisely, but needs must when the devil drives. We are doing only half a job, I know,—perhaps not that,—but we are doing it better than any other college, and perhaps that justifies us in keeping on."

There may be something in this,—I personally doubt it,—but that is another matter. The point is that we can see clearly just what it is to which this lamentable situation runs back. The secondary school must take in all the shaky material sent up from the grade-school, for of such is the kingdom of democracy. In its turn the grade-school must take in all the enormous masses of human ineptitude that are dumped on it by the truant laws; and thus from one end of our system to the other do we see the ramification of the four social principles that our civilization has foisted on it as fundamental.

A second immediate effect is the loss, in practice, of

any functional distinction between formative knowledge and instrumental knowledge. Formerly a student gave up, in round numbers, the first twenty years of his life to formative knowledge; his pursuits during this time were directed exclusively toward the *being* and *becoming*. That was the stated business of the school and college, and they kept him so busy with it that he hardly knew there was such a thing as instrumental knowledge in the world. He got his introduction to that later, at the university or technical school, where first he began to concern himself with the *doing* and *getting*. I have not space to discuss this aspect of our system at length,—done properly, it would take many pages,—but I think the reader will have no trouble about perceiving it in all its relations with what has been said already.

A third effect is the grotesque and monstrous shift of responsibility from the student to the teacher. Formerly the teacher had none of it; now he has practically all of it. The student who formerly presented himself was capable of learning; that was what he was there for; it was "up to" him to do it, and he did it. The teacher directed him, perhaps helped him a little,—precious little, in my experience,—but took no responsibility whatever for the student's progress. The run-of-mine student now arrives, incapable of anything, usually indifferent and incurious toward everything. Well, what is to be done? He may be relied on to do nothing particularly striking for himself,—Nature has attended to that,—therefore what is done must be done either for him or with him; and thus the burden of responsibility immediately passes to the teacher, and there it remains.

IV

For some reason that I have never been able to discover, Mr. Jefferson seems to be regarded as a great democrat; on public occasions he is regularly invoked as such by gentlemen who have some sort of political axe to grind, so possibly that view of him arose in this way. The fact is that he was not even a doctrinaire republican, as his relation to the French Revolution clearly shows. When Mr. Jefferson was revising the Virginia Statutes in 1797, he drew up a comprehensive plan for public education. Each ward should have a primary school for the three R's, open to all. Each year the best pupil in each school should be sent to the grade-school, of which there were to be twenty, conveniently situated in various parts of the state. They should be kept there one year or two years, according to results shown, and then all dismissed but one, who should be continued six years. "By this means," said the good old man, "twenty of the best geniuses will be raked from the rubbish annually"—a most unfortunate expression for a democrat to use! At the end of six years, the best ten out of the twenty were to be sent to college, and the rest turned adrift.

As an expression of sound public policy, this plan has never been improved upon. Professor Chinard, who has lately put us all under great obligations by his superb study—by far the best ever made—of Mr. Jefferson's public life, thinks it quite possible that those who formed the French system had this plan before them. Whether so or not, the French system is wholly in accord with

Mr. Jefferson's hard good sense in accepting the fact that the vast majority of his countrymen were ineducable, and with his equally hard realism in permitting this fact to determine the fundamentals of his plan. The Faculty of Literature at the University of Poitiers is domiciled in the Hôtel Fumée, an exquisitely beautiful family mansion, built about 1510 by a rich lawyer. From an outside view, which is all I ever had of either property, I should say the Hôtel Fumée carries about as much floor-space as Mr. James Speyer's residence on Fifth Avenue. I venture to say that if Columbia University cleared out all its ineducable students, root and branch, its Faculty of Literature could do a land-office business in a house the size of Mr. James Speyer's, with maybe a room or two to rent.

From what Professor Giddings and the presidents of Brown, Haverford and St. Stephen's have said, I infer that this is the season of repentance. Whether or not it will lead to a season of good works is another matter; I think it highly improbable. Nevertheless it seems useful at the present time that the situation should be diagnosed, and its "indications," as the doctors say, taken into account. Artemus Ward once said the trouble with Napoleon was that he tried to do too much and did it. Just this is the trouble with American education. In my judgment, the indications are simply that the whole school-population of the country, above the primary grade, should be cut down by ninety per cent. If anyone thinks that this proportion is too high, let him take it out on Mr. Jefferson, who is much bigger than I am; my figures are fairly liberal as compared with his. With him on my side I make bold to believe that nine-tenths of our student population, in university, college, grade schools and secondary schools, have no more justification for being where they are than they would have for an intrusion upon the French Academy or the Royal Society; and that unless and until this mass is cut adrift, the prospects for American education will show no improvement worth considering.

Professional criticism has already suggested that the college and university—and I believe there has been some similar hint about the secondary school—should slough off the otiose bulk of those brought to them by the mere *vis inertiæ,* and those who present themselves because it is the thing to do, or as a liberation from home or a furlough for parents; likewise those who are going in for contacts, athletics, husbands, the atmosphere and flavour of college life, or for what I understand the authorities now delicately call "extra-curricular activities," whereof the coonskin coat and pocket-flask are said to be the symbols. At present this would no doubt account for sixty per cent of Mr. Jefferson's "rubbish," probably seventy, but that is not enough. The intention of Mr. Jefferson's plan was to off-load all ineducable persons, no matter what their disposition, and to have this relief applied continuously at every point in the system above the primary school.

This reform seems unlikely to be carried out, and I do not urge it or even recommend it. Conversance with human history begets a deal of respect for Nature's well-established policy of progress by trial and error, and a profound circumspection about trying to anticipate it. The experienced person regards root-and-branch reforms, even good ones, with justifiable doubt. One may be by no means sure—far from it—that it would be a good thing "by and large" and in the long run for the United States to produce any educated people, or that in its present summary sacrifice of its educable individuals it is not taking precisely the right way with them. I am not disposed to dogmatize either way, and hence I do not recommend this reform, or, indeed, any reform. I am merely recording observations of certain social phenomena, placing them in their right relations and drawing the conclusions that seem warranted in the premises. As to the final desirability of the state of things contemplated by these conclusions, I have nothing to say.

V

Still, education seems as yet to be a subject of experiment with us, and I observe with interest that, according to some educators, the next experiment will be with the revival of the small college. There is obviously no more saving grace in smallness than in bigness; everything depends upon what the small college is like. The forecast, however, sets one's fancy going. Perhaps—one must have one's doubts about it, but perhaps—without too much infringement on Nature's policy, or deflection of our great moral and social mission to the world at large, one small laboratory experiment might be tried, such as has never yet been tried by us. I mean an experiment in educating educable persons only. It would be interesting and possibly useful to set up two small institutions, a school and an undergraduate college, both so well endowed as not to care a straw whether a student came near them or not, and both committed wholly to the pursuit of formative knowledge; the school's attendance limited, say, to sixty, and the college's to two hundred. The school should take pupils at the age of eight, and carry them on until they could meet the college's requirements. Neither institution should take any account whatever of bogus democratic doctrine, the idolatry of mass, vocationalism or the pretended rights of ineducable persons. If such persons presented themselves they should be turned away, and if anyone got in and afterward was found for any reason or to any degree ineducable, he should be forthwith bounced out.

These institutions should be largely a reversion to type, their distinction being that of representing the pure type, without a trace of hybridization. Requirements for entrance to the college should be the ability to read and write Latin and Greek prose with such ease and correctness as to show that language-difficulties were forever left behind; knowledge of arithmetic and of algebra up to quadratics; nothing more. The four years' course in college should cover the whole range of Greek and Latin literature from Homer's time to that of Erasmus, mathematics as far as the differential calculus, a compendium of formal logic, and one of the history of the English language (not literature), and nothing more; and this should lead to the degree of Bachelor of Arts, the only degree that the college should confer.

My notion is that the instructors in these institutions could pretty well follow their own devices for five years, having no students to teach, but that in ten years things would look up a little, and that in fifty years a review of the experiment would be interesting. One could then make the observations and comparisons necessary to determine what it was worth. I can not say flatly that I recommend this experiment; I merely say that it would be interesting, might be useful enough to be worth its cost, and incidentally some poor few, at least, of our educable fry would lay up out of it a treasure more to be desired than gold—yea, than much fine gold. Yet it is nothing that I would urge, for quite possibly the Larger Good requires that things should go on as they are now going.

Probably, however, I should give (though in all diffidence) some decorous hint about the sort of thing I should look for from it, if it were carried out under strictly aseptic experimental conditions. The literature of Greece and Rome represents the longest continuous record available to us,—a matter of some twenty-five hundred years or more, if mediæval and Renaissance literature were included, as it should be,—as well as the fullest and most diversified record, of what the human mind has ever been busy about. Therefore the one great benefit of the "grand old fortifying classical curriculum," as far as it went, was that on one's way through it one saw by centuries instead of weeks, by whole periods instead of years, the operation of the human mind upon every aspect of collective human life, every department of spiritual, industrial, commercial and social activity; one touched the theory and practice of every science and every art. Hence a person came out from this discipline with not only a trained mind but an experienced mind. He was like one who had had a profound and weighty experience. He was habituated to the long-time point of view, and instinctively brought it to bear on current affairs and happenings. In short, he was mature.

"Sobald er reflektirt," said Goethe of Lord Byron, *"ist er ein Kind."* Byron was one of the great natural forces in literature,—all praise to him for that,—but of maturity, the best assurance of a right interpretation and right use of personal experience of the world and its affairs, he had none. So, too, the composite American is one of the greatest natural forces that have ever appeared in human society. Perhaps it is as such, and such only, that Nature proposes to use him, and she may intend to fade him out and supersede him when this function in her inscrutable economy is fulfilled,—she has never been any too scrupulous about turning such tricks,—and, if so, it would be hazardous to tamper with the fundamentals of a training that fits him for her purpose. Our system seems to have been constructed in anticipation of just this purpose on the part of Nature; it confirms him in a perpetual adolescence, permits his inner adjustment to the world and its affairs to proceed by a series of juvenile, casual and disorderly improvisations—*sobald er reflektirt ist er ein Kind.*

New York, December, 1930

10

The Value of Useless Knowledge

IN CONVERSATION with a learned friend lately, our talk ran on various definitions of culture, and on the fact that for one reason or another we found them all unsatisfactory. This led us to ponder the notion that culture is one of those things that are perhaps better understood by not being too closely defined, like certain stars that become visible only when one looks a little away from them. We recalled the profound observation of Joubert, that "it is not hard to know God, provided one does not trouble oneself to define Him." There are many such matters, an astonishing number when one comes to count them up; astonishing, too, when one remarks how competent our working knowledge of them may be, notwithstanding our best definitions of them are so incompetent.

In regard to these matters, Truth shows herself the unscrupulous flirt that her devoted lover Ernest Renan finally declared her to be. A direct approach to her, a direct drive upon her coquettish reserve, is fatal to one's chances. A teasing wench, she lures one on by every imaginable charm, but at the moment one thinks to take her by force she slips out of one's grasp and is gone.

Indeed, one never succeeds with her completely by any art of seduction; she is of the Rommany breed, and is bound to break one's heart at last, like Tchertapkhanov's gypsy Masha. One must make up one's mind to that. But, again like Masha, each time one approaches her indirectly, tentatively, now by this side and now by that, never overpressing her coyness, she will make some little concession; and at the end of a lifetime of devotion one finds that the sum of her concessions is really considerable—not what one hoped for, certainly, but a fair reward, though platonic. One thankfully sorts them over and assembles them in terms of definition, though well aware that one's formulas are partial and provisional, and that one can never make them more than that.

II

It is perhaps only in this humble fashion that one may attempt a definition of culture; first of culture as a process, and then of culture as a possession. Concerning culture as a process, one would say that it means learning a great many things and then forgetting them; and the forgetting is as necessary as the learning. Diligent as one must be in learning, one must be as diligent in forgetting; otherwise the process is one of pedantry, not culture. The trouble with the pedant is not that he has learned too much, for one can never do that, but that he has not forgotten enough. In the view of culture, the human spirit is somewhat like the old-fashioned hectograph, which had to be laid aside for a day or so after each use, to let the surface-impression sink down into the gelatine pad. The pedant's learning remains too long

on the surface of his mind; it confuses and distorts suc-
ceeding impressions, thus aiding him only to give himself
a conventional account of things, rather than leaving his
consciousness free to penetrate as close as possible to
their reality, and to see them as they actually are.

It would appear, though, that half the process of culture has been neglected in practice; or, worse than that,
it has been disallowed and reprehended. Learning has
always been made much of, but forgetting has always
been deprecated; therefore pedantry has pretty well
established itself throughout the modern world at the
expense of culture. To cite perhaps the most conspicuous instances, it is no trouble to see how thoroughly
pedantry has pervaded the world's practice of politics
and economics. Nietzsche made the interesting observation that in the drama of politics the comic rôle has always been played by professors. This is very true, but
when one considers the way in which the public affairs
of most countries have been managed for the past two
decades, one perceives that professors have no monopoly
of pedantry. It is hard to believe that the drama of politics could have degenerated more swiftly and hopelessly
into a roaring farce if the curtain had been rung up
twenty years ago with nothing but professors in the cast.
Pedantry pervades economics, dealing with them as it
does with politics, by policies of sheer prestidigitation.
The upshot of pedantry in politics is government by
sleight-of-hand; its upshot in economics is a régime of
extemporization. It can not be otherwise, because the
essence of pedantry is to satisfy oneself wholly with a
limited, partial and conventional account of things, then

to assume that other people should and will satisfy themselves wholly with the same account, and then to become puzzled and indignant when it turns out that they do not.

The essence of culture is the exact opposite of all this; and here one may see where the importance of the second step in the process comes in. When the smart boy from the East Side or the farm-girl from the Mississippi Valley knocks at the gate of the college and declares for culture, one should say, "Youngster, this is a hard business that you are proposing, and a very long business. Are you sure it is what you want to undertake? Culture may not be quite what you think it is. The essence of culture is never to be satisfied with a conventional account of anything, no matter what, but always instinctively to cut through it and get as close as you can to the reality of the thing, and see it as it actually is. Culture's methods are those of exercising the consciousness in a free and disinterested play over any object presented to it, unchecked by prepossession and uncontrolled by formula. This exercise will keep you very busy for many years. In preparation for it, you must spend a great deal of time in learning a great many things, and then you must spend more or less time in forgetting them. Are you up to it? If you think you can manage the learning (for it must be actual learning—we shall see to that if you come here), what sort of fist do you think you can make at the forgetting? In any case, now that you have some idea of what it really is that you say you are after, does the thing strike you as worth trying? Do you believe you are equal to it?"

III

Our definition, however, is not quite explicit enough, because it does not specify the kind of knowledge that the process of culture contemplates. We all know that useful knowledge gains value by being remembered, and loses value by being forgotten; and it has most value when best remembered. Useless knowledge, on the contrary, gains value only as it is forgotten; and the point to be brought out is that useless knowledge alone is the concern of culture. Our definition, then, may be made more precise—perhaps as precise as any that can be made —if we put it that culture, considered as a process, means acquiring a vast deal of useless knowledge, and then forgetting it.

Perhaps the prevalence of pedantry may be largely accounted for by the common error of thinking that, because useful knowledge should be remembered, any kind of knowledge that is at all worth having should be remembered too. By overlooking the fact that useless knowledge, if properly forgotten, has value, the common assumption is that the only kind of knowledge one should try to get is the kind that must be remembered. Here one has a crow to pick with the universities for promoting this error, for this is the ground of resentment against their wholesale adoption of ideals and methods that belong naturally and properly to the scientific school; and this too is the ground of particular resentment against their taking the scientific school into full partnership as a member of the academic organization. The university's undiscriminating attitude toward learn-

ing, its failure to establish a clear line between useful
and useless knowledge, its misapprehension of values and
its consequent misdirection of responsibility—all this the
believer in culture is bound to regard as most unfortunate.

For *quid Athenis et Hierosolyma?* The business of a
scientific school is the dissemination of useful knowledge,
and this is a noble enterprise and indispensable withal;
society can not exist unless it goes on. The university's
business is the conservation of useless knowledge; and
what the university itself apparently fails to see is that
this enterprise is not only noble but indispensable as
well, that society can not exist unless it goes on. The attitude of the university being what it is, one scarcely sees
how the exceeding great value of useless knowledge is
ever going to be properly appraised; and this is a hard
prospect for the student of civilization to contemplate.

We all remember Mr. Stephen Leacock's account of
his visit to Oxford, and his delightful portrayal of Oxford as the complete and perfect conservator of useless
knowledge; a place where professors never lecture but
by request, and then wretchedly,—Mr. Leacock was told
that some had not lectured for thirty years,—where tutors
seem to do nothing much but smoke, and students seem
to do little but live in mouldy mediæval quarters, eat
food cooked in Henry VIII's kitchen, and sleep in an
unwholesome mess of age-old ivy. We recall his sly pretense of puzzlement when he compared the ways of Oxford with those of the universities that he was acquainted
with on this side of the Atlantic, and finally his reluctant
admission that somehow, dead against every conceivable
possibility, Oxford "gets there," and his dark suspicion

that it will continue to get there for many generations to come. No one in America knows the value of useless knowledge better than Mr. Leacock, and his fascinating sketch of Oxford makes it clear that the business of a university is to do what for centuries Oxford has been doing, and to turn out the kind of human produce that for centuries Oxford has been turning out.

But the traditional faculties of a university are those of Literature, Law, Theology, and Medicine; and by their professional side, the side first presented to the intending practitioner, the mastery of these subjects is a matter of science, a matter of absorbing much useful knowledge. True; but "the four learned professions" are very old, they have a long and heavily documented tradition, and in the course of their history they have laid all sorts and kinds of useless knowledge under continuous contribution, thus building up a thick accretion which, for the purposes of culture, is most valuable. It seems a fair question, then, whether the university should not occupy itself with this, and leave the professional side of the subjects to be dealt with by the scientific schools.

It seems fair to suggest, for example, that a true Faculty of Law at Harvard ought not to be equipping aspirants with useful knowledge in the way of getting up briefs, badgering witnesses, and steering flagitious enterprises with skill enough to keep their promoters out of jail. Let a good law-school do all that; the Faculty of Law should be taking on eligible products of the law-school, and filling them up bung-full of useless knowledge. In a word, the law-school should be producing sheer practitioners, giving them every chance at all the science, all the useful knowledge, that there is; the Faculty of Law should be producing practitioners like Sir Henry Maine, Maitland, Lord Penzance, or the Lord Chief Justice Coleridge. Let some medical school teach intending practitioners how to track down sinus-trouble and operate for appendicitis; the Faculty of Medicine at Johns Hopkins should be producing practitioners like William Osler, Mitchell, Draper, Pancoast, shoveling into them all the prodigious mass of useless knowledge that these men acquired, and then bidding them go forth and forget it as handily as these men did. There are enough divinity-schools in operation here and there to give students for the ministry all the useful knowledge necessary to a successful exercise of their profession. Let them attend to this, and meanwhile let the Faculty of Theology at Yale attend to its own business. If it did so, who knows but it might produce some theologians like the Cambridge Platonists, religious philosophers like Bishop Butler, moralists like the doctors of Salamanca? Things being as they are, we could do with a good many such just now, if we had them, and if we may not look to the university for them, where are we to look?

IV

So much, then, for culture when considered as a process. Considered now as a possession, one may define culture as the residuum of a large body of useless knowledge that has been well and truly forgotten. In order to see how this is so, let us take the simplest possible illustration. Let us suppose that I say to you, "Plato says so-and-so." You reply, "I think not. I can not speak positively, for I have long forgotten every word of Plato that I ever read. But all of Plato that I have read and forgotten, taken together with all I have read of a great many other authors and likewise forgotten, has left me with a clear residual impression that Plato never said anything like that." Then you look it up and find that you are right.

Being right about a saying of Plato is perhaps not important in itself, and this illustration must not be taken to imply that it is important. All this depends on what the saying is, and the connexion in which it is brought forward. Plato said a great many fine things that are no doubt worth recalling on occasion, but the illustration is meant only to give a clearer notion of the kind of thing that a residuum of useless knowledge is, and how it works on the mind of the person who has it. The value of useless knowledge is another matter. I have already suggested that it has great value, and another type of illustration may serve to show in part what that value is. The field of useless knowledge is so vast that one might multiply illustrations almost indefinitely, and establish a tolerably complete set of values by their aid; but here, where there is no room for a treatise, we will keep to a single line of illustration, and a single line of values.

The prime example of useless knowledge that occurs to me for this purpose is a knowledge of history. Alchemy, astrology, sociology, horoscopy—it is wildly conceivable that if one went in for any of these he might somewhere by some chance strike a trifling streak of "pay dirt"; whereas in the case of history such a thing is inconceivable, at least by me. Whether or not the best example, however, history seems to offer a very good example, as good as any I can bring to mind, of knowledge which is utterly useless except as it be forgotten; but which, when forgotten, becomes of great value. "The only thing that history teaches us," said the German philosopher, "is that history teaches us nothing"; and we may put the point of his epigram in still fewer words by saying merely that remembered history is valueless.

Let us suppose the case of one who, back in the bad old times when the university made a point of doing such jobs pretty thoroughly, had been loaded to the guards with history, perhaps by some Mommsen, Niebuhr or Guizot, and then turned loose to take the world as he found it. When he is well past middle age a war breaks out, and publicists, propagandists, pedants and professors lift up their voices with one accord to tell him that the cause of the war is absolutely this-or-that, the object of the war is absolutely thus-and-so, and that the character of one and another of the belligerents is absolutely such-and-such. If he has not forgotten his useless learning, if any of it remains on the surface of his mind, these affirmations encounter it and blend with it in a blur; and it is ten to one—nay, a hundred to one —that the account he gives himself of these matters, the account with which he finally satisfies himself, will be as purely conventional as any of those that the pedants and propagandists offer.

But suppose his useless learning is gone. Life has obliged him to remember so much useful knowledge that he has lost not only his history, but his whole original cargo of useless knowledge; history, languages, literatures, the higher mathematics, or what you will—all are gone. The Carthaginian wars and the battle of Pavia are but names to him, or not even names. When they were fought, and where, and "how come," and who won, and why, and what the consequences were—of all this, or any of it, he knows nothing. All that aniline has sunk down into the hectograph pad, leaving no trace of a definite pattern; but it has diffused itself throughout the texture of the pad and imparted its colour to the gelatine. Therefore the affirmations of the pedants encounter no confusing surface-impressions, but encounter only a general cast of thought that has been coloured by purely residual learning. Hence he replies, "I think not. I think this war came about in quite another way, and that it has quite another set of objects"; and the mere passage of time brings proof that he is right.

Again, let us say that in the same circumstances an association of governments is proposed, to bring about permanent peace, to promote disarmament, to ensure the rights of racial minorities, to safeguard democracy, to protect small nations from molestation, and to further various other laudable purposes. The proposal is taken up and vigorously pushed by energumens who declare that this association is meant to do all these things and will unfailingly do them. The man who has forgotten all his useless learning was once aware that this proposal would be nothing new, that similar associations similarly advertised have already appeared in history under similar circumstances; but now he remembers nothing about any of them, not even its name. He says, however, "No, I believe this association is proposed for quite different purposes, and that it will never accomplish any of the things you say it will"; and, again, the mere passage of time proves that he is right. It may appear, indeed he himself may think, that his reaction is instinctive, but it is not; it is due to the residuum of useless and forgotten learning.

Thus it may be seen how useless knowledge can be made directly contributory to a force of sound and disinterested public opinion. We are told nowadays that such opinion will never prevail in a republic, and indeed, as things stand, it seems unlikely to do so; if for no other reason, because it is inimical to well-established political interests, and to the general auspices under which public affairs are managed. The business of a practical politician, as Edmund Burke said, is "still further to contract the narrowness of men's ideas, to confirm inveterate prejudices, to inflame vulgar passions, and to abet all sorts of popular absurdities." He is all for the theory that moral questions are determinable by a plebiscite; that right and wrong, truth and falsehood, come down in the last instance to a matter of counting noses, and therefore their practical test is always, as we say, "what one can get away with." This being so obviously the case, there is small chance that a force of sound and disinterested public opinion can prevail. Nevertheless it is generally thought desirable that such a force should exist in society, and, if that be so, any discipline likely to generate it must be regarded as valuable.

The discipline of useless knowledge, moreover, moves a person always to "run to the short way" in his estimate of public enterprises, to strike through to their first principles and "the reason of the thing," instead of being caught and held by their more manifest aspects. When someone tells him, for example, what a good thing for Rome it was to win the Carthaginian wars, cabbage all the trade of Carthage, and set up a great Mediterranean empire, he replies that it was certainly impressive, but, as to its being a good thing for Rome, he would first have to know what the Romans were like when they got through doing it. Thus he cuts straight through to the first principle so often cited by Mr. Jefferson, that a public enterprise is to be judged, not by its direct effect on commerce, finance, industry, employment and the like, but by its effect on collective human character; and a discipline which moves him invariably to judge it in this way has value.

V

We hear on all sides that the world is in a bad way, so bad as to give but slim assurance that anything worth doing can be done about it. Some think we are plunging into the chaos of the Dark Ages; others think we are at the end of an era, and entering into a new mediæval-ism. One suspects that these views of our situation may be a little excessive, or at least that while waiting for the crash we have time to be cheerful. If it be true, however, that the world is actually perishing before our eyes, there is perhaps some sort of melancholy interest in the thought that it may be perishing largely of inat-tention to the value of useless knowledge.

Nothing shows more clearly how profound this inatten-tion is than the nature of current comment on the New Deal. This comment runs to millions of words, and covers every conceivable question suggested by our public enterprises except the one that the man of forgotten learning most wants to hear discussed. He is naturally interested in the outcome of these enterprises, interested to see how the American variant of Statism and corporalism is going to work, and therefore he is glad to read all the intelligent comment on it, pro and con, that comes his way; but the previous question always rises in his mind. Suppose our adventure in Statism works perfectly, suppose the New Deal scores a clean success at every practical point, what kind of people are we going to be when it has done so?

This, in his view, is the really important question raised by the recrudescence of Statism in Europe. He is aware that Bolshevism, Fascism, Hitlerism, are all essentially identical, all branches off the same tree planted by the German idealist philosophers in the early years of the last century. They all mean, in essence, that the State is everything, the individual nothing. Fichte put it that "the State is the superior power, ultimate and beyond appeal, absolutely independent," and Hegel said that "the State is the general substance, whereof individuals are but accidents." There is the general formula for all variants of the common doctrine of Statism.[1] Well, then, what one really wants to know is the effect that this doctrine is likely to produce in the long run upon the character of those who swallow it. In the long

[1] This seems to be officially acknowledged. Compare this formula with Mussolini's declaration that "the State embraces everything, and nothing outside the State has value. The State creates right"; with Hitler's assertion that "the State dominates the nation because it alone represents it"; and with Lenin's frank admission that "it is nonsense to make any pretense of reconciling the State and liberty."

run, what will Mussolini's Italians be like, or Hitler's Germans, or Stalin's Russians?

Certain features of the American variant of Statism raise the same question about ourselves, but they are never discussed; one never hears anything about them. They are four in number: first, according to Mr. Hopkins's report published on the day I write this, thirty million persons, nearly one-fourth of our population, are being subsidized by the Federal Government; second, a vote-controlling bureaucracy has been prodigiously expanded; third, executive control over legislation has been made almost absolute through the distribution of money in the Congressional districts; fourth, centralization has been made almost absolute by federal grants to the states, or, as one writer puts it very well, these subsidies have set up a carpetbag government in every state.

These features of the New Deal impress the man of forgotten learning so unfavourably that he gets out his dusty books and looks up his history to see if perchance he may be wrong; and he finds that he is not wrong. His impression is abundantly made good. Curiously, too, the instance that most conspicuously corroborates it is one where no blame, no disparagement, no breath of suspicion, could rightfully be directed against the executive authority, but quite the opposite; and this pleases him, because he likes to consider all such matters, or indeed all matters, as impersonally as possible.

At the end of the first century, Rome had already seen how easily a republic slides off into a despotism, and despotism into ruinous tyranny. Things had been at low tide in the empire for some time; the Flavian dynasty had petered out to the tune of something that one could really call a depression. Meanwhile mendicancy and subvention had been erected into a permanent political asset, not at first embracing one fourth of Rome's population, probably, but well on its way to do so. Bureaucracy, which in earlier times hardly counted, began to spread wide and grow rapidly. Centralization busily undermined the large measure of self-rule that had prevailed in the provinces and even more largely in the cities. Quite in the tone of Mr. Jefferson, Plutarch speaks bitterly of this decay of local public spirit, saying that those who refer every twopenny detail of public life to Rome must share the spiritual fate of the hypochondriac who will neither bathe nor eat but as the doctor tells him.

Then a remarkable thing happened. For the next eighty years the empire was governed by an unbroken succession of extraordinarily able and good rulers, each one better than his predecessor. The short and good reign of Nerva bridged the turn of the century. Then came Trajan, the most just, frugal and energetic of all Rome's emperors, so far. Then Hadrian, who added to Trajan's virtues great wisdom and foresight, breadth of view, and range of sympathy. Then Antoninus Pius, whom to name is enough, and then one who need not even be named; the world has not once looked upon his like, and his praise is for ever and ever. Yet hardly was the breath out of his body before the rotten social fabric of Rome disintegrated, and the empire crumbled to pieces.

If ever rulers were disinterested, these were. None of

them wished to set up a carpetbag government in the provinces and cities. They clearly foresaw the upshot of organized mendicancy and subvention, of the growing power of bureaucracy, of the growing tendency to centralization. They did the best they could to check these malignant growths, but could do nothing. The combination of job-holders, prætorian guards, frontier soldiers and subsidized Roman rabble could turn out any disobliging government on short notice by the simple expedient of cutting a disobliging emperor's throat. The mere suspicion that Nerva was for a general policy of retrenchment brought sudden fate on him, and even Trajan, the most heavy-handed of the lot, could do little worth doing in the way of reform. The emperors of the second century remind one of nothing so much as an array of the world's best physicians striving to reclaim a hopeless cancer-patient.

The thing could not be done; there is the whole story. The cancer of organized mendicancy, subvention, bureaucracy and centralization had so far weakened its host that at the death of Marcus Aurelius there was simply not enough producing-power left to pay the bills. Under the exactions of the job-holders, nobody could do any business, fields went untilled, and even the army had to be recruited among foreigners. But to the man of useless learning these matters are only relatively important. In his view the significant thing is that, under the conditions existing, eighty years of continuous effort by five of the world's best and ablest rulers could not prevent the Roman populace from degenerating into the very scum of the earth, worthless, vicious, contemptible, sheer human sculch.

A rather long-winded illustration, possibly, in support of my thesis that useless knowledge has value, but the fact that no one else is saying anything on the subject may perhaps serve as its excuse.

Brussels, December, 1933.

11

The Disadvantages of Being Educated

MY INTEREST in education had been comfortably asleep since my late youth, when circumstances waked it up again about six years ago. I then discovered that in the meantime our educational system had changed its aim. It was no longer driving at the same thing as formerly, and no longer contemplated the same kind of product. When I examined it I was as far "out" on what I expected to find as if I had gone back to one of the sawmills familiar to my boyhood in Michigan, and found it turning out boots and shoes.

The difference seemed to be that while education was still spoken of as a "preparation for life," the preparation was of a kind which bore less directly on intellect and character than in former times, and more directly on proficiency. It aimed at what we used to call training rather than education; and it not only did very little with education, but seemed to assume that training *was* education, thus overriding a distinction that formerly was quite clear. Forty years ago a man trained to proficiency in anything was respected accordingly, but was not regarded as an educated man, or "just as good," on the strength of it. A trained mechanic, banker, dentist or man of business got all due credit for his proficiency, but his education, if he had any, lay behind that and was not confused with it. His training, in a word, bore directly upon what he could do or get, while his education bore directly on neither; it bore upon what he could become and be.

Curiosity led me to look into the matter a little more closely, and my observations confirmed the impression that the distinction between training and education was practically wiped out. I noticed, too, that there was a good deal of complaint about this: even professional educators, many of them, were dissatisfied with it. Their complaints, when boiled down, seemed to be that education is too little regarded as an end in itself, and that most of the country's student-population take a too strictly vocational view of what they are doing, while the remainder look at it as a social experience, encouraged largely in order to keep the cubs from being underfoot at home, and reciprocally appreciated mostly because it puts off the evil day when they must go to work; and that our institutions show too much complacency in accommodating themselves to these views.

These complaints, I observed, were not confined to educators; one heard them from laymen as well, and the laymen seemed to be as clear in their minds about the difference between education and training as the professional educators were. For example, one of America's most distinguished artists (whom I am not authorized to quote, and I, therefore, call him Richard Roe) told a friend of mine that when his ship came in he proposed to give magnificent endowments to Columbia, Harvard, Princeton and Yale on the sole condition that they should shut up shop and go out of business forever. Then he proposed to put up a bronze plate over the main entrance to each of these institutions, bearing this legend:

CLOSED

THROUGH THE BENEFACTION

OF

RICHARD ROE

AN HUMBLE PAINTER

IN BEHALF OF EDUCATION

As I saw the situation at the moment, these complaints seemed reasonable. Training is excellent, it can not be too well done, and opportunity for it can not be too cheap and abundant. Probably a glorified crèche for delayed adolescents here and there is a good thing, too; no great harm in it anyway. Yet it struck me as apparently it struck others, that there should also be a little education going on. Something should be done to mature the national resources of intellect and character as well as the resources of proficiency; and, moreover, something should be done to rehabilitate a respect for these resources as a social asset. Full of this idea, I rushed into print with the suggestion that in addition to our present system of schools, colleges and universities which are doing first-class work as training-schools, we ought to have a few educational institutions. My notion was that the educable person ought to have something like an even chance with the ineducable, because he is socially useful. I thought that even a society composed of well-trained ineducables might be improved by having a handful of educated persons sifted around in it every now and then. I, therefore, offered the suggestion, which did not seem exorbitant, that in a population of a hundred and twenty-odd million there should be at least one set of institutions, consisting of a grade-school, a secondary school and an undergraduate college, which should be strictly and rigorously educational, kept in perpetual quarantine against the contagion of training.

II

This was five years ago, and about eighteen months ago I repeated the suggestion. My modest proposal was hardly in print before I received a letter from a friend in the University of Oxford, propounding a point which —believe it or not—had never occurred to me.

But think of the poor devils who shall have gone through your mill! It seems a cold-blooded thing . . . to turn out a lot of people who simply can't live at home. Vivisection is nothing to it. As I understand your scheme, you are planning to breed a batch of cultivated, sensitive beings who would all die six months after they were exposed to your actual civilization. This is not Oxford's superciliousness, I assure you, for things nowadays are precious little better with us. I agree that such people are the salt of the earth, and England used to make some kind of place for them. . . . But now—well, I hardly know. It seems as though some parts of the earth were jolly well salt-proof. The salt melts and disappears, and nothing comes of it.

As I say, I had never thought of that. It had never occurred to me that there might be disadvantages in being educated. I saw at once where my mistake lay. I had been looking at the matter from the point of view of an elderly person to whom such education as he had was just so much clear gain, not from the point of view of a youth who is about to make his start in the world. I saw at once that circumstances, which had been more or less in favour of my educated contemporaries, were all dead against the educated youngster of to-day. Therefore, last year, when I was appointed to deal again with the subject in a public way, I went back on all I had said, and ate my ration of humble-pie with the best grace I could muster.

Every shift in the social order, however slight, puts certain classes irrevocably out of luck, as our vulgarism goes. At the beginning of the sixteenth century the French feudal nobility were out of luck. They could do nothing about it, nobody could do anything about it, they were simply out of luck. Since the middle of the last century, monarchs and a hereditary aristocracy are out of luck. The *Zeitgeist* seems always arbitrarily to be picking out one or another social institution, breathing on it with the devouring breath of a dragon; it decays and dissolves, and those who represent it are out of luck. Up to a few years ago an educated person, even in the United States, was not wholly out of luck; since then, however, an educated young man's chance, or an educated young woman's, is slim. I do not here refer exclusively to the mere matter of picking up a living, although, as I shall show, education is a good bit of hindrance even to that; but also to conditions which make any sort of living enjoyable and worth while.

So in regard to my championship of education it turned out again that everybody is wiser than anybody, at least from the short-time point of view, which is the one that human society invariably takes. Some philos-

ophers think that society is an organism, moving instinctively always towards the immediate good thing, as certain blind worms of a very low order of sensibility move
towards food. From the long-time point of view, this may
often be a bad thing for the worm; it may get itself
stepped on or run over or picked up by a boy looking
for fish-bait. Nothing can be done about it, however, for
the worm's instinct works that way and, according to
these philosophers, so does society's, and the individual
member of society has little practical choice but to go
along.

Hence our institutions which profess and call themselves educational, have probably done the right thing—
the immediate right thing, at any rate—in converting
themselves, as our drugstores have done, into something
that corresponds only very loosely to their profession.
No doubt the lay and professional complaint against this
tendency is wrong; no doubt the artist Richard Roe's
proposal to close up our four great training-schools is
wrong. No doubt, too, our young people are right in
instinctively going at education, in the traditional sense
of the term, with very long teeth. If I were in their
place, I now think I should do as they do; and since I
am in the way of recantation, as an old offender who
has at last seen the light of grace, I may be allowed to
say why I should do so—to show what I now plainly see
to be the disadvantages of being educated.

III

Education deprives a young person of one of his most
precious possessions, the sense of co-operation with his

fellows. He is like a pacifist in 1917, alone in spirit—a depressing situation, and especially, almost unbearably, depressing to youth. "After all," says Dumas's hero, "man is man's brother," and youth especially needs a free play of the fraternal sense; it needs the stimulus and support of association in common endeavour. The survivor of an older generation in America has had these benefits in some degree; he is more or less established and matured and can rub along fairly comfortably on his spiritual accumulations; and besides, as age comes on, emotions weaken and sensitiveness is dulled. In his day, from the spiritual and social point of view, one could afford to be educated—barely and with difficulty afford it perhaps, but education was not a flat liability. It netted enough to be worth its price. At present one can afford only to be trained. The young person's fellows are turning all their energy into a single narrow channel of interest; they have set the whole current of their being in one direction. Education is all against his doing that, while training is all for it; hence training puts him in step with his fellows, while education tends to leave him a solitary figure, spiritually disqualified.

For these reasons: education, in the first place, discloses other channels of interest and makes them look inviting. In the second place, it gives rise to the view that the interest which absorbs his fellows is not worth mortgaging one's whole self, body, mind and spirit, to carry on. In the third place, it shows what sort of people one's fellows inevitably become, through their exclusive absorption in this one interest, and makes it hard to reconcile oneself to the thought of becoming like them. Training, on the other hand, raises no such disturbances;

it lets one go on one's chosen way, with no uncertainty, no loss of confidence, as a man of the crowd. Education is divisive, separatist; training induces the exhilarating sense that one is doing with others what others do and thinking the thoughts that others think.

Education, in a word, leads a person on to ask a great deal more from life than life, as at present organized, is willing to give him; and it begets dissatisfaction with the rewards that life holds out. Training tends to satisfy him with very moderate and simple returns. A good income, a home and family, the usual run of comforts and conveniences, diversions addressed only to the competitive or sporting spirit or else to raw sensation—training not only makes directly for getting these, but also for an inert and comfortable contentment with them. Well, these are all that our present society has to offer, so it is undeniably the best thing all round to keep people satisfied with them, which training does, and not to inject a subversive influence, like education, into this easy complacency. Politicians understand this—it is their business to understand it—and hence they hold up "a chicken in every pot and two cars in every garage" as a satisfying social ideal. But the mischief of education is its exorbitance. The educated lad may like stewed chicken and motor-cars as well as anybody, but his education has bred a liking for other things too, things that the society around him does not care for and will not countenance. It has bred tastes which society resents as culpably luxurious, and will not connive at gratifying. Paraphrasing the old saying, education sends him out to shift for himself with a champagne appetite amidst a gin-guzzling society.

Training, on the other hand, breeds no such tastes; it keeps him so well content with synthetic gin that a mention of champagne merely causes him to make a wry face. Not long ago I met a young acquaintance from the Middle West who has done well by himself in a business way and is fairly rich. He looked jaded and seedy, evidently from overwork, and as I was headed for Munich at the moment, I suggested he should take a holiday and go along. He replied, "Why, I couldn't sell anything in Munich—I'm a business man." For a moment or two I was rather taken aback by his attitude, but I presently recognized it as the characteristic attitude of trained proficiency, and I saw that as things are it was right. Training had kept his demands on life down to a strictly rudimentary order and never tended to muddle up their clear simplicity or shift their direction. Education would have done both; he was lucky to have had none.

It may be plainly seen, I think, that in speaking as he did, my friend enjoyed the sustaining sense of co-operation with his fellows. In his intense concentration, his singleness of purpose, and in the extremely primitive simplicity of his desires and satisfactions, he was completely in the essential movement of the society surrounding him; indeed, if his health and strength hold out, he may yet become one of those representative men like Mr. Ford, the late Mr. Eastman or Mr. Hoover, who take their tone from society in the first instance and in turn give back that tone with interest. Ever since the first westward emigration from the Atlantic seaboard, American civilization may be summed up as a free-for-all scuffle to get rich quickly and by any means. In so far as a person was prepared to accept the terms of this free-for-all and engage in it, so far he was sustained by the exhilaration of what Mr. Dooley called "th' common impulse f'r th' same money." In so far as he was not so prepared, he was deprived of this encouragement.

To mark the tendency of education in these circumstances, we need consider but one piece of testimony. The late Charles Francis Adams was an educated man who overlived the very fag-end of the period when an American youth could afford, more or less hardly, to be educated. He was a man of large affairs, in close relations with those whom the clear consenting voice of American society acclaimed as its representative men, and whose ideals of life were acclaimed as adequate and satisfying; they were the Fords, Eastmans, Owen Youngs, Hoovers, of the period. At the close of his career he wrote this:

As I approach the end, I am more than a little puzzled to account for the instances I have seen of business success—money-getting. It comes from rather a low instinct. Certainly, as far as my observation goes, it is rarely met in combination with the finer or more interesting traits of character. I have known, and known tolerably well, a good many "successful" men—"big" financially—men famous during the last half-century; and a less interesting crowd I do not care to encounter. Not one that I have ever known would I care to meet again, either in this world or in the next; nor is one of them associated in my mind with the idea of humour, thought or refinement. A set of mere money-getters and traders, they were essentially unattractive and uninteresting. The fact is that money-getting, like everything else, calls for a special aptitude and great concentration; and for it I did not have the first to any marked degree, and to it I never gave the last. So, in now summing up, I may account myself fortunate in having got out of my ventures as well as I did.

This is by no means the language of a man who, like my acquaintance from the Middle West, is sustained and emboldened by the consciousness of being in co-operation with his fellows—far from it. It will be enough, I think, to intimate pretty clearly the divisive and separatist tendency of education, and to show the serious risk that a young person of the present day incurs in acquiring an education. As matters now stand, I believe that he should not take that risk, and that any one advising or tempting him to take it is doing him a great disservice.

IV

An educated young man likes to think; he likes ideas for their own sake and likes to deal with them disinterestedly and objectively. He will find this taste an expensive one, much beyond his means, because the society around him is thoroughly indisposed towards anything of the kind. It is preëminently a society, as John Stuart Mill said, in which the test of a great mind is agreeing in the opinions of small minds. In any department of American life this is indeed the only final test; and this fact is in turn a fair measure of the extent to which our society is inimical to thought. The president of Columbia University is reported in the press as having said the other day that "thinking is one of the most unpopular amusements of the human race. Men hate it largely because they can not do it. They hate it because if they enter upon it as a vocation or avocation it is likely to interfere with what they are doing." This is an interesting admission for the president of Columbia to make—interesting and striking. Circumstances have enabled our society to get along rather prosperously, though by no means creditably, without thought and without regard for thought, proceeding merely by a series of improvisations; hence it has always instinctively resented thought, as likely to interfere with what it was doing. Therefore, the young person who has cultivated the ability to think and the taste for thinking is at a decided disadvantage, for this resentment is now stronger and more heavily concentrated than it ever was. Any doubt on this point may be easily resolved by an examination of our current literature, especially our journalistic and periodical literature.

The educated lad also likes to cultivate a sense of history. He likes to know how the human mind has worked in the past, and upon this knowledge he instinctively bases his expectations of its present and future workings. This tends automatically to withdraw him from many popular movements and associations because he knows their like of old, and knows to a certainty how they will turn out. In the realm of public affairs, for instance, it shapes his judgment of this-or-that humbugging political nostrum that the crowd is running eagerly to swallow; he can match it all the way back to the politics of Rome and Athens, and knows it for precisely what it is. He can not get into a ferment over this-or-that exposure of the almost incredible degradation of our political, social and cultural character; over an investigation of Tammany's misdoings; over the Federal Government's flagitious employment of the income-tax law to establish a sleeping-partnership in the enterprises of gamblers, gangsters, assassins and racketeers; over the wholesale looting of public property through official connivance; over the crushing burden which an ever-increasing bureaucratic rapacity puts upon production. He knows too much about the origin and nature of government not to know that all these matters are representative, and that nothing significant can be done about them except by a self-sprung change of character in the people represented. He is aware, with Edmund Burke, that "there never was for any long time a corrupt representation of a virtuous people, or a mean, sluggish, careless people that ever had a good government of any form." He perceives, with Ibsen, that "men still call for special revolutions, for revolutions in politics, in externals. But all that sort of thing is trumpery. It is the soul of man that must revolt."

Thus in these important directions, and in others more or less like them, the educated youth starts under disadvantages from which the trained youth is free. The trained youth has no incentive to regard these matters except as one or another of them may bear upon his immediate personal interest. Again, while education does not make a gentleman, it tends to inculcate certain partialities and repugnances which training does not tend to inculcate, and which are often embarrassing and retarding. They set up a sense of self-respect and dignity as an arbiter of conduct, with a jurisdiction far outreaching that of law and morals; and this is most disadvantageous. Formerly this disadvantage was not so pressing, but now it is of grave weight. At the close of Mr. Jefferson's first term, some of his political advisers thought it would be a good move for him to make a little tour in the North and let the people see him. He replied, with what now seems an incomprehensible austerity, that he was "not reconciled to the idea of a chief magistrate parading himself through the several States as an object of public gaze, and in quest of an applause which, to be valuable, should be purely voluntary." In his day a chief magistrate could say that and not lose by it; Mr. Jefferson carried every northern State except Connecticut and every southern State except Maryland. At the present time, as we have lately been reminded, the exigencies of politics have converted candidacy for public office into an exact synonym for an obscene and repulsive exhibitionism.

Again, education tends towards a certain reluctance about pushing oneself forward; and in a society so notoriously based on the principle of each man for himself, this is a disadvantage. Charles Francis Adams's younger brother Henry, in his remarkable book called *The Education of Henry Adams,* makes some striking observations on this point. Henry Adams was no doubt the most accomplished man in America, probably the ablest member of the family which as a whole has been the most notable in American public service since 1776. His youth was spent in acquiring an uncommonly large experience of men and affairs. Yet he says that his native land never offered him but one opportunity in the whole course of his life, and that was an assistant-professorship of history at Harvard, at four dollars a day; and he says further that he "could have wept on President Eliot's shoulder in hysterics, so grateful was he for the rare good-will that inspired the compliment." He recalls that at the age of thirty:

No young man had a larger acquaintance and relationship than Henry Adams, yet he knew no one who could help him. He was for sale, in the open market. So were many of his friends. All the world knew it, and knew too that they were cheap; to be bought at the price of a mechanic. There was no concealment, no delicacy and no illusion about it. Neither he nor his friends complained; but he felt sometimes a little surprised that, as far as he knew, no one seeking in the labour-market even so much as inquired about their fitness. . . . The young man was required to impose himself, by the usual business methods, as a necessity on his elders, in order to compel them to buy him as an investment. As Adams felt it, he was in a manner expected to blackmail.

Such were the disabilities imposed upon the educated person fifty years ago, when as Adams says, "the American character showed singular limitations which sometimes drove the student of civilized man to despair." Owing to increased tension of the economic system, they are now much heavier. Even more than then, the educated youth emerges, as Adams and his friends did, to find himself "jostled of a sudden by a crowd of men who seem to him ignorant that there is a thing called ignorance; who have forgotten how to amuse themselves; who can not even understand that they are bored."

One might add a few more items to the foregoing, chiefly in the way of spiritual wear and tear—specific discouragements, irritations, disappointments—which in these days fall to the lot of the educated youth, and which the trained youth escapes; but I have mentioned enough for the purpose. Now, it is quite proper to say that the joys and satisfactions of being educated should be brought out as an offset. One can not get something for nothing, nor can one "have it going and coming." If an education is in itself as rewarding a thing as it is supposed to be, it is worth some sacrifice. It is unreasonable to court the joy of making oneself at home in the world's culture, and at the same time expect to get

Standard Oil dividends out of it. Granted that your educated lad is out of step, lonesome, short on business acumen and concentration, and all the rest of it—well, he has his education; nobody can get it away from him; his treasure is of the sort that moth and rust do not corrupt, and stock-market operators can not break through and mark down quotations on it. Agreed that if Charles Francis Adams had not been an educated gentleman he might have become another Gould, Fisk, Harriman, Rockefeller, Huntington, Morgan; but given his choice, would he have swapped off his education and its satisfactions for the chance to change places with any of them? Certainly not.

Certainly not; but times have changed. If economic opportunity were now what it was even in Henry Adams's day, a young person just starting out might think twice about balancing the advantages of an education against its disadvantages. In that day, by a little stretching and with a little luck, a young person might come to some sort of compromise with society, but the chance of this is now so remote that no one should take it. Since the closing of the frontier, in or about 1890, economic exploitation has tightened up at such a rate that compromise is hardly possible. It takes every jot of a young person's attention and energy merely to catch on and hang on; and as we have been noticing these last two years, he does not keep going any too well, even at that. The question is not one of being willing to make reasonable sacrifices; it is one of accepting every reasonable prospect of utter destitution. The joys and satisfactions of an education are all that Commencement orators say they are, and more; yet there is force in the Irishman's question, "What's the world to a man when his wife's a widdy?"

V

Things may change for the better, in time; no doubt they will. Economic opportunity may, by some means unforeseen at present, be released from the hold of its present close monopoly. The social value of intellect and character may some day be rediscovered, and the means of their development may be rehabilitated. Were I to be alive when all this happens, I should take up my parable of five years ago, and speak as strongly for education as I did then. But I shall not be alive, and I suspect also that none of the young persons now going out into the world from our training-schools will be alive; so there is no practical point to considering this prospect at present. Hence I can only raise my voice in recantation from the mourner's bench, a convert by force of expediency if not precisely in principle—rice-Christian style, perhaps, and yet, what is one to say? I belong to an earlier time, and for one reason or another the matter of rice does not present itself as an over-importunate problem, but nevertheless I see that the Christians have now "cornered" all the rice, so I can not advise young persons to do as I and my contemporaries did. No, they are right, their training-schools are right; Richard Roe and I are wrong. Let them be honest Christians if they can possibly manage the will-to-believe—one can make astonishing successes with that sometimes by hard trying—but if not, let them be rice-Christians, they can do no better.

Gastein, June, 1932.

12

The Quest of the Missing Link

A FRIEND remarked to me with great disfavour the other day that, what with the magazines bringing their aims and methods ever consciously closer to those of stark journalism, if one picks up a magazine three months old it is like picking up a week-old newspaper; one finds nothing worth reading, still less worth keeping. Reading it is like reading so much "dead copy." This is no doubt true; and perhaps the worst of it is that it induces a corresponding attitude on the part of readers. They tend to assume that all they find in a magazine was written for the moment, and if by any chance something turns up there that was not written for the moment, they tend to regard it as a mere *jeu d'esprit,* or as a piece of journalism that has somehow missed its mark and may therefore be passed by.

A little over two years ago there appeared in a popular magazine an article that was not written for the moment.[1] Its title was "Why We Do Not Behave Like Human Beings"; its author was the distinguished architect, Mr. Ralph Adams Cram. It ably and plausibly presented what

[1] It appeared in the *American Mercury* of September, 1932.

226

is virtually a brand-new idea about the nature of man and his relation to other forms of life; and the implications of this idea are so great, so far-reaching and so revolutionary, that if the article had been published thirty-five or forty years ago, when magazines had neither lot nor part with journalism,—when they addressed themselves more to reflective thought and less to mere sensation,—it would have raised a fine breeze from one end of the country to the other.

Things being as they are, however, this article raised no breeze. I observed with considerable astonishment that nobody took it up for rebuttal or even for discussion. In particular, our anthropologists had nothing to say about it, whereas I expected that they would have quite a little to say. My own interest in the subject was presently sharpened by a very remarkable book called *Immortability*, by Dr. S. D. McConnell, whose incidental findings gave solid support to Mr. Cram's thesis. Then when the Spanish philosopher, Ortega y Gasset, came along with his *Revolt of the Masses*, I saw that this also squinted steadily in Mr. Cram's direction. Finally, after waiting some time to hear from my betters, I published a brief paper, suggesting that Mr. Cram's brilliant speculation seemed to be of great practical consequence, and asking the anthropologists to take it up and let us hear about it. This was all that a poor disparaged man of letters could properly do in the premises. Not being one of this present world's elect, he could not presume to discuss the matter himself; it was not down his street. All he could do was to exercise the right of petition, and that was all I ventured to do.

The anthropologists, however, paid no attention to

my humble overture. Perhaps I should have addressed the psychologists instead, but if so, my mistake was so clearly one of ignorance that a kindly word would have set it right. Perhaps they held it *infra dig.* to encourage secular curiosity; yet it is hard to associate this cavalier attitude with those of them I know—with my old friends Mr. Lowie and Mr. Sapir, for example. What actually happened, I think, was that since my paper, like Mr. Cram's, was published in a popular magazine, they regarded it as a bit of more or less playfully sensational journalism rather than as an honest inquiry; or, even more probably, that they never saw it.

II

Mr. Cram's thesis, stated simply, is that most of us do not behave like human beings because most of us are not human beings; not only are not, but never were, and—which is most important—never shall be. The great, the overwhelming majority of us are merely the raw material out of which the occasional human being has been, and still is, produced by an evolutionary process, the exact nature of which is undetermined, but is probably catastrophic. What Dr. McConnell calls "the presumption that all those living creatures classed as Man on physical grounds are also Man on psychical grounds" is simply contrary to fact. The zoölogical classification *Homo sapiens* is competent for physical structure and function, but no further. Not everyone who answers to *Homo sapiens* is a human being; in fact, the immense majority are not. Psychically, the human being is a distinct species; and Mr. Cram acutely points out that in our graduated, popular scale of speech our instinct has always led us to classify him as such.

Moreover, Mr. Cram synopsizes ten thousand years of history to the effect that the whole prodigious residue of *Homo sapiens,* the mass-man,[2] has never shown, and does not now show, any development worth speaking of in the direction set by the occasional evolutionary product; it has never brought itself a jot nearer the psychical character that differentiates the "human" species, properly so called. Hence the search for what used to be known as the "missing link" (the intercalary form between *Homo sapiens* and the anthropoids) is not properly in the province of zoölogy, as has hitherto been supposed. In Dr. McConnell's words, its concern begins not at the point "which separates man from brute, but at that which separates one kind of man from the rest." Or, as Mr. Cram puts it, "the just line of demarcation should be drawn, not between Neolithic Man and the anthropoid ape, but between the . . . human being and the Neolithic mass which was, is now, and ever shall be."

What moves me to bring this matter up again is the receipt of a letter a few days ago, enclosing a précis of some findings made by a man of science concerning the

[2] One wishes idly that there were some way once and for all to dispose of the imbecile notion that when one speaks of the mass-man one means the poor man, the labouring man or the proletarian. I suppose the best one can do is to remember the blessed Apostle's exhortation to suffer fools gladly, say what one means, and let be made of it what will. If I were picking a half-dozen standard specimens of the mass-man now among us, four would be inordinately rich, one most eminent in the federal judiciary, another equally eminent in elective office.

"missing link." It would be improper for me to describe them in advance of their publication, if they are to be published, which I presume is the case. There is no impropriety, however, I trust, in my remarking their complete consistency with Mr. Cram's belief that the missing link is not actually missing at all, nor has ever been, but that it exists in vast numbers everywhere around us, and has always done so. It occurs to me now that if at last a man of science is examining the status of *Homo sapiens* from this point of view, a layman's observations on the importance of his quest might be interesting, perhaps even helpful. In my former paper I said as little as possible about this, because my object was only to ask the men of science for a discussion by which I and the rest of the unlearned might profit; and I thought it was becoming to avoid any appearance of suggesting terms for such a discussion. It now seems that this consideration no longer holds, and I may therefore remark some of the changes, not only in our thought but in our feeling, that are likely to ensue upon the verification of this doctrine of the missing link.

III

In New York last November I left my lodgïngs uncommonly early one morning, and saw a man salvaging odds-and-ends out of a garbage-barrel. It made a most painful impression on me; the memory of it still persists. Half a block away I saw a dog engaged in the same occupation; it did not impress me painfully. As it happened, neither object was, in the ordinary sense, especially pitiable. The man's clothes were as warm as mine and not much shabbier, and he did not seem weak or broken or dejected.

He was not old, fairly healthy, fairly strong, fairly cheerful-looking, and I thought his general condition was pretty good; and I could say the same of the dog.

What differentiated my view of these two objects was a sense that the dog was living up to the measure of his own capacities, while the man was not. In the one case I had no sense of a come-down from a higher spiritual estate, while in the other I had. I also felt that the man had been somehow estopped from regaining this estate, and I had no such feeling towards the dog. Hence I could sentimentalize the one case, and not the other. I was governed, in short, by the presumption that the man was a human being, and the certainty that the dog was not. Such indeed, I hasten to add, may the man have been. As Mr. Cram is careful to show, the occasional human being often, in fact pretty regularly, lives and dies in poverty and neglect. It is most important to remember that no test of this kind is applicable, nor are the tests set by the conventional criteria of intelligence; the only competent test is psychical. Still, while the man I saw may have been a human being by Mr. Cram's classification, the probabilities are so strongly the other way that this proviso may be dismissed. Well, then, if Mr. Cram is right, one's feeling for the man would obviously change, not in strength or quality, but in kind. Abstract the sense of a human estate from which one may fall, and to which one may revert, and I would regard the man quite as I would the dog; that is, with every wish for his well-being and happiness, and every repugnance to his mistreatment or abuse, but nothing more.

Most forms of humanitarian enterprise seem to me to hang upon the belief that the evolution of humanity is progressive rather than catastrophic, that zoölogical man is also psychical man, and that he is psychically capable of indefinite improvement, provided conditions are right; and with this goes, as a kind of corollary, the belief that "society" is responsible for the wrongness of conditions, and therefore responsible for the arrest of his spiritual development. Given favourable conditions,—economic security, proper food and housing, more leisure, better education, better cultural opportunities, and so on,—the "Neolithic mass" which Mr. Cram says has lain spiritually inert for ten thousand years to our knowledge, and no one may say how much longer, will show itself capable of spiritual mass-development to an indefinite degree; logically, perhaps (granted the further postulate of indefinite time), to a degree as high as the highest now known.

This perfectionist doctrine is highly respectable; one might almost call it official. Many of us would say, at least officially, that they believe in it, and no doubt some of us actually do. The modern institutional church is based on it, and our leading social reformers have accepted it, apparently without question. With Henry George, for example, this belief served as his only spring of action. His crusade for economic freedom was for nothing but what he regarded as the first and indispensable condition of spiritual mass-progress. It may be observed that, although we have done more with this doctrine in a practical way than has been done in any other country, the results, so far, are not convincing; but, on the other hand, it is perhaps a little early yet to measure results, and one must also allow for the effect of many and powerful countervailing influences. If it could be shown beyond doubt, however, that this belief is without foundation, that the Neolithic mass is incapable of humanizing itself under whatever conditions, I think our whole code of humanitarian practice would be revised. It would still be important that the Neolithic mass should have every chance and encouragement towards such development as its subhuman capacities indicate as possible, because, while not itself human, it is the raw material out of which the human being is occasionally produced; but any effort to encourage an impossible spiritual development would appear at once as useless.

One may observe in passing that there is perhaps some significance in the fact that just this revision appears to be taking place. I have no notion of carrying ammunition to feed Mr. Cram's artillery, but I fancy he has already found some evidential value in the estimate that the Neolithic mass puts upon its own spiritual capacities, as shown in the rationale of the institutions it creates. There can be no doubt, I think, that Western society at large is now purely an organization of the Neolithic mass, that all its institutions reflect the ideals and aspirations of the mass, and that therefore these may be taken as showing pretty clearly what the mass thinks of itself. I can discern in them no intimation that it thinks of itself as more than zoölogically human; no intimation of man as "a creature of a large discourse, looking before and after," but rather as concerned first and last with what Saint Paul calls the ἐπίγεια—his god is his belly. The mass-organization here, as in Italy, Russia, Germany, appears to contemplate no attribute that might not be taken on mimetically from the mass-organization of ants, bees, beavers, wolves, and extended in a purely quantitative fashion. The qualitative difference, or psychical "spread," between the highest and lowest forms of *Homo sapiens*—between Confucius, Socrates, Marcus Aurelius, and the Akka, the bushman, the tropical pygmy—is far greater than between these latter and the anthropoid; and there is nothing to show that the mass-organization consciously contemplates a reduction of that spread. The estimate of *Homo sapiens* that appears, for instance, in official Hitlerism, Bolshevism, Fascism and, the New Deal, is set forth in terms that are strictly non-psychical; one might say, in sheer terms of food, shelter, training and amusement. In just such terms, it seems to me, might the dog I saw the other day give an account of his species, if one could but somehow dig the information out of him.

On the score of a deep sensibility, therefore, the issue raised by Mr. Cram appears to be important. As I said, there are some of us who still hold to the early-Victorian universalist doctrine that all men, even the bushman, even the Akka, are psychically differentiated as a distinct species, capable of an improved and strengthened psychical life; and this belief is the basis of our humanitarian disposition. If it be shown that this belief is illusory, the ground will be cleared between us and the accepted interpreters of the Neolithic mass, and we may give ourselves and them the benefit, whatever it amounts to, of a definite common understanding.

IV

From the point of view of politics it seems equally important that Mr. Cram's thesis should be either verified or exploded. The doctrine of popular sovereignty, as set forth by Mr. Jefferson in the Declaration, has now pretty well covered the Western world. Mostly in form, largely in fact, the State has almost everywhere become republican. It stands, as always, an all-powerful engine for the distribution of economic advantage, and republicanism has made it the pliant organ of such segments of the Neolithic mass as can get at it, one after another, and work it for their own behoof, and for the disservice of extruded segments. The whole history of republicanism in America might be summed up as a record of violent collisions among segments of the mass, incurred in the headlong effort to get at this machine and pull its levers. During the earlier post-war period, for example, Mr. Bottles, Mr. Plugson of Undershot, Mr. Murdstone, Mr. Ralph Nickleby and Mr. Arthur Gride managed the machine, and were, as we say, "getting theirs"; and now another segment has shouldered them aside, and Mr. Micawber, Mr. Quinion, Jacques Bonhomme, Couche-tout-nu and Gouge-le-Bruant are by way of getting theirs.[3]

Surveying the upshot of all this as it appears at the moment, I think one must admit that republicanism has made rather a mess of things. Mr. Cram puts it mournfully that "we confront a situation so irrational and apparently hopeless of solution that there is not a scientist, a politician, an industrialist, a financier, a philosopher or a parson, who has the faintest idea how we got that way, or how we are to get out of it." This is as it may be. We content ourselves with observing that the record of re-

[3] On the day I write this, the Associated Press reports that more than 25,500,000 persons, one fifth of our population, are now being subsidized by the State!

publicanism bears witness to very little that is human in the character of the Neolithic mass. It is, in fact, a record of continuous, reciprocal and progressive corruption between *Homo sapiens* and the State. The Neolithic mass corrupts the State, and in turn the State still further corrupts the Neolithic mass; and this brings about a general condition which appears to be increasingly difficult and unsatisfactory, as well as increasingly repulsive and degrading.

There are two ways of regarding this state of things, and which of the two we take depends entirely upon the answer we give to this very question whether the Neolithic mass is psychically improvable, or whether in literal truth, as Alexander Hamilton said, "the people is a great beast." For my own part, I think it is improvable, and therefore I am a republican. I admit that Mr. Cram has shaken me up frightfully, and also that all the evidence available, every scrap of it, positive and negative, looks straight his way. Yet, perhaps because I am too old a dog to learn any new tricks, I must still put myself down, at least provisionally, as a Jeffersonian and Georgite of sorts. Unless the anthropologists come out with something pretty substantial, I may in time, probably shall, go over to the opposition; but as yet I have not done so. My expectations, doubtless, run to a much more distant future than Mr. Jefferson's or Mr. George's, but I am still, perhaps quite irrationally, on their side.

This is in itself of no consequence; I mention it only to account for my conviction that all of us who think— or think we think—as I do, should be staunch republicans. If the mass be improvable, it may be expected ultimately to work out for itself a satisfactory mode of political self-expression, and obviously the only way to that lies through a free and unlimited succession of trial and error; and when all comes to all, this is precisely what republicanism means. Therefore those who think that the mass is psychically capable of sometime getting itself somewhere are all for giving the mass its head, and taking the untoward incidental consequences as best one can. Such messes as we are now in are quite as difficult and deplorable as Mr. Cram depicts them, but they are part of the process, and we accept them philosophically as a test of faith, quite aware that in the nature of things there will be many more and far worse messes to be put up with before the millennial end is reached.

Therefore, with the great example of Socrates always before our eyes, we are strongly against any attempt to interfere with the political self-direction of the Neolithic mass, and especially chary about offering any advice to clear and aid it when it has got itself in circumstances of unusual difficulty. When Socrates was charged with being a bad citizen because he took no part in Athenian public affairs—which were in an extremely poor way just then—he replied good-humouredly that this only proved that he and his followers were the very best politicians in Athens. We do not even discountenance the peculiarly despicable type of political leadership that the mass accepts by an inveterate choice as old as the days of Moses and Aristides; for how is the mass to make progress in spiritual discernment save through a long course of intensive bilking and dragooning? In short, we are against any attempt at interference with orderly causation. Emerson calls cause and effect "the chancellors of God," and we have too wary a respect for them ever to hoodwink ourselves with the notion that an officious tampering with their sequences can possibly turn out well in the long run. Bishop Butler gave our disingenuous race a great lesson in the fundamental integrities when he said that "things and actions are what they are, and the consequences of them will be what they will be; why, then, should we desire to be deceived?"

Hence, when Professor Ortega y Gasset declares that mass-control and mass-operation of the State are at present ruinous, we quite agree with him. When we are told that a general domination by the mass is bringing Western civilization to an appalling end, we quite agree. When we are told that a recurrence of the Dark Ages is at hand, we reply that it is highly probable. When, however, in the face of these prospects, we are invited to abjure republicanism and take up with this or that anti-republican nostrum in order to avert them, we say that we can not possibly contemplate doing anything of the kind. Joubert's dictum of "force till right is ready" is attractive, but specious. If applied ably and disinterestedly as a political emergency-doctrine, it is with a view so much beyond the mass's power of perception that the sense of tutelage resents it and in the end nullifies it; and if applied otherwise, it merely anæsthetizes the mass's sense of responsibility, with the result that right either is never ready or, if perchance ready, is repressed and overborne. Republicanism holds it as axiomatic that the only permanent good that can be worked out for the mass—the only good which does not indirectly cost more than it comes to—is what it works out on its own.

Sub specie æternitatis, the recurrent wreck of civilizations is an incident in the progress of the Neolithic mass towards collective self-improvement. Recurrent dark ages are the interval in which the mass's self-preserving instinct scrabbles around, and cobbles up the beginnings of a new civilization. As Mr. Cram observes, these recurrences have taken place repeatedly; no doubt they will take place again and again until the Neolithic mass has learned how to manage something like a satisfactory collective life for itself. The mass, if human, learns in the only way human beings can learn, by experience; and these recurrences represent experience, and are to be regarded and respected accordingly.

But if the mass be not human, and therefore not psychically improvable, the case is very different. Republicanism is then preposterous in theory, and monstrously vicious in practice. A political system based on the principles of the Declaration is by hypothesis doomed to rapid degeneration and quick dissolution. The mass-man then is to be regarded, as Mr. Cram says he should be, as only the raw material out of which the occasional human being is produced, and, aside from this, as having no political value or respectability whatever. An ideal political system would take no account of him in any other capacity. He would be the political ward of a human oligarchy; not exploited, not discouraged from any enterprise lying within the purview of his faculties, but in all respects treated with exclusive reference to the occasional human product that in some uncomprehended fashion he brings forth.

Any such system as this is so obviously impracticable that the mere mention of it seems absurd. The political ascendency of the Neolithic mass is now everywhere overwhelming, it can not be checked, nor can the preponderance of the mass be broken up. Hence, while by our first hypothesis republicanism's distressing mess is bad enough, it is not hopeless; whereas, by our second, it is. Neither on this mess nor on those worse messes which naturally must ensue can one predicate anything but a progressive degeneration from which there is neither escape nor recovery. Republicanism is a doctrine of mass-preponderance, pure and simple; and by our second hypothesis, mass-preponderance means the political extinction of the human being, and the calculated subversion of any but a purely animal instinct or intention in the conduct of public affairs.

> *Prosilit ad prædam rapidus Leo; Cæsar ad orbis*
> *Imperium; finis, fateor, diversus utrique,*
> *At non dissimilis pugna, labor unus et idem,*
> *Quo cænam Fera, quo regnum sibi comparat Heros.*

At Athens, in Plato's time, the Neolithic mass was in the saddle with a vengeance, as it was at Rome in the time of Marcus Aurelius; and both these worthies surveyed the scene with a sense of great despondency and helplessness. Half-lettered persons nowadays say they find an unpleasant affectation and priggishness in Marcus Aurelius's view of his fellow-Romans, but such persons either simply do not know what sort of folk those Romans were, or else are incapable of understanding how the quality of their collective life would impress a human being. Historians tell us that their views of life and their demands on life were exactly what one sees reflected in the professedly "smart" publications of the present day. With all that might be said for it,—and as much might be said for it as Juvenal says for the collective life of certain animals,—their collective life showed no trace whatever of a specifically human quality.

Plato, in his middle years, raised the question of what the human being can do with himself under such circumstances. He anticipated Alexander Hamilton in likening the Neolithic mass to a pack of wild beasts. The human being, he says, can not make himself one of them; and if he expose himself to them, they will smell him out and destroy him; and there are not enough of him to resist them effectively. All he can do, "like a man sheltering himself behind a wall against a hurricane," is to keep out of their way, cultivate his own virtues as best he can, and wait quietly for the inevitable end.

This end came so quickly to Athens that Plato lived to see it. The story is worth a digression. Plato lived into the administration of Eubulus; he was an old man then. Now, this Eubulus stands perhaps unmatched in history as a type and pattern of the best there is in Neolithic political mass-leadership. He was one of the ablest politicians that ever lived. A most attractive public figure, his manners were charming, his temper unvarying, his smile indelible, and his bearing always showed the most pleasing admixture of informality and easy dignity. His ambitions wore the guise of public spirit, he was a first-class executive, a good financier, and a tireless worker. He was immensely popular, and his administration, which lasted something over fifteen years, was to all appearances quite successful. If the human being, or the "lover of virtue," as Plato calls him, could find no good word to say for such political leadership as this, the Athenians might have thought he was hard to suit. But for all that, the end of Eubulus's administration was also the end of Athens.

"Live as on a mountain," Marcus Aurelius admonished himself sadly. Well, if the Neolithic mass be really what it appears to be when seen in the twilight of Athens and of Rome, that is about the best a human being can do.

V

If Mr. Cram's thesis could be made to hold water, it would enforce a radical change upon one's whole social outlook. Philosophical anarchism, with its profound belief in the essential goodness of *Homo sapiens,* becomes less than tenable; it becomes grotesque. The inflated ideas of *Homo sapiens* "in a state of nature," as put forth by Rousseau and Chateaubriand, are mere wind and confusion. Any moral quality that has been associated with the various forms of collectivism vanishes at once; and the doctrine of natural rights, proclaimed by Mr. Jefferson, is attenuated well-nigh to the disappearing-point. Human beings may conceivably be endowed by their Creator with certain unalienable rights as against one another; and by some slight stretching of terms the Neolithic mass may be said to have certain natural rights as against the human being; but terms will hardly stretch far enough to let us make out, on Mr. Cram's thesis, that members and segments of the mass have any natural rights as against one another. It is interesting to observe that the mass-instinct seems to attest this difficulty, for it has become a cardinal point of doctrine with the mass-interpreters that *Homo sapiens* has no natural rights whatever, but that all his rights are of social origin, and therefore purely provisional.

All this means that the human being may be easily reconciled to many of his present circumstances that in his former view seemed intolerably depressing. For example, when judged by the Jeffersonian estimate of man's nature and capacities, the course of mass-education under a republican régime is about as bad as it can be, but no question it matches the mass's estimate of its own capacities extremely well. Quite inappropriate to human attributes, it answers admirably to the mass's attributes, as Mr. Cram describes them. Hence the human being may excuse himself from expostulating with the mass, or from trying to foist an alien ideal and alien methods upon it, since he sees that in an educational way the mass is doing very well as it is, and since he is aware also that the mass is incapable of understanding his admonitions or carrying out his suggestions, and is therefore instinctively indisposed to entertain either. Instead, he recalls the example of Socrates, and the austere words of the *Santissimo Salvatore*,[4] and devotes all his energies to the humbler task of continually clearing and educating himself.

Thus, too, in a great many other directions the human being's sense of social responsibility is similarly simplified. If he be proved a psychical alien in a Neolithic civilization, he will survey most of the aspects and social phenomena of that civilization from an alien point of view, and reconcile himself to them as lying wholly within the order of nature, and hence beyond not only

[4] Matthew vii. 6.

his power of interference, but his right and duty of interference as well. In this frame of mind he may edify himself by sometimes observing how sound the Neolithic mass-instinct almost always is, from its characteristic short-time point of view on its own designs, and how much more competent in the premises its suggestions are than a good Jeffersonian would like to think them. For example, the mass-interpreters say that war is an indispensable regulatory provision of what they call "human nature"; and those of us who have lived through a war have remarked the bedlamite enthusiasm with which the mass-instinct bears this view out. The Jeffersonian and Georgite regard this demonstration as sheer insanity, and if it reflected a human instinct, they would be right. But clearly, if the Neolithic mass be not human, its instinct is as sound as that of any group of anthropoids in the jungle. The onslaught of war is inexorable, it is as strictly within the order of nature as the precession of the equinoxes, and the human being regards it as the hero of Bret Harte's story regarded the onslaught of the bulls of the Blessed Trinity.

VI

Discussing Mr. Cram's thesis the other day, a clerical friend who knows Mr. Cram very well, and whose sense of humour is hung on a hair-trigger, said to me, "What a thundering joke it would be if Ralph Cram and the anthropologists should bring old John Calvin back!" In view of Mr. Cram's vast distaste for Calvin, in which I fully concur, it would be rather amusing if his own thesis should clear the ground for a neo-Calvinist doctrine of predestination and election. Something of the sort seems possible. It is in the realm of religion, perhaps, that the Neolithic mass gives the most downright account of itself. By all his works and ways, the mass-man gives himself out as a non-religious being; well, possibly again his instinct is sound. In the nature of things, according to Mr. Cram, that is quite what he would be. The general temper of his civilization, as Dr. McConnell observes, is especially strong, for example, against the idea of a persistence of psychical life after physical death, an idea with which religion concerns itself considerably; well, again that is quite what one would expect.

Dr. McConnell most logically suggests that the consideration of persistence should not begin where traditional theology begins it,—that is, at the point of differentiation between *Homo sapiens* and the anthropoids,—but at the point of differentiation between psychical Man and zoölogical Man; or, as Mr. Cram might put it, between the human being and the Neolithic raw material out of which the human being is now and then brought forth. This seems reasonable, for it is fair to presume that, if psychical man were a distinct species, this species would be the only one to have any experience of a kind of life with which the idea of persistence could at all plausibly be associated. Therefore, since no one knows, or apparently can know, what the process is by which the occasional human being is produced, it seems to me that a pretty fair case for some neo-Calvinistic theory of predestination and election might be made out.

I know nothing whatever about theology, and therefore I approach these matters of doctrine with great caution; but on looking over the Thirty-nine Articles, the only doctrinal manual I have handy at the moment, I think I see how some of the other old formulas constructed back in Cranmer's time—nearly all of them, in fact—might have something to say for themselves. Leaving theological theory aside, however, it seems certain that the verification of Mr. Cram's thesis would powerfully affect the current practices and applications of organized Christianity. In that case, for instance, would not the Church cease from presenting to the Neolithic mass an ideal of life that the mass must of necessity find unintelligible and directly opposed to all the testimony of its own experience? Would it not turn to the exclusive business of nourishing and improving the psychical life of the human being?—which seems, by the way, as well as I can make it out, to have been the only business it originally had. My clerical friend, of whom I spoke just now, was about starting off on a missionary enterprise at the time of our conversation, so I playfully suggested that he let the heathen rage, and devote himself instead to an extension of the monastic principle into secular life. Something like this, it seems to me, would be the sole interest of organized Christianity in the circumstances contemplated.

But I may no longer "occupy myself in great matters which are too high for me." The only points in Mr. Cram's dissertation on which I am entitled to an opinion are his history, his logic, and his personal observations of the mass's bearing and behaviour. His history is sound, his logic is airtight, and I have made observations precisely like his. Concerning his main conclusion I can of course say nothing, except provisionally. In this way, however, I may have said enough to show how important the issue that Mr. Cram raises is to the human being, to the Neolithic mass itself, and in particular to the anthropologist, the psychologist, the political theorist, the social philosopher and the theologian. One might pursue the hypothesis much further and in many more directions, but I have not space for that, nor probably is it necessary; imagination will carry the argument on to any desired length. Perhaps the matter will be settled by the test of experience, *solvitur ambulando;* I incline to the belief that it can be finally settled only in that way. Yet, as Bishop Butler said, probability is the guide of life; and the men of science, to whom the question is of considerable consequence, can, if they will, go a long way towards determining the probabilities at issue.

New York, December, 1934.

13

Isaiah's Job

ONE evening last autumn I sat long hours with a European acquaintance while he expounded a politico-economic doctrine which seemed sound as a nut, and in which I could find no defect. At the end he said with great earnestness, "I have a mission to the masses. I feel that I am called to get the ear of the people. I shall devote the rest of my life to spreading my doctrine far and wide among the populace. What do you think?"

An embarrassing question in any case, and doubly so under the circumstances, because my acquaintance is a very learned man, one of the three or four really first-class minds that Europe produced in his generation, and naturally I, as one of the unlearned, was inclined to regard his lightest word with reverence amounting to awe. Still, I reflected, even the greatest mind can not possibly know everything, and I was pretty sure he had not had my opportunities for observing the masses of mankind, and that therefore I probably knew them better than he did. So I mustered courage to say that he had no such mission and would do well to get the idea out of his head at once; he would find that the masses would not care two pins for his doctrine, and

still less for himself, since in such circumstances the popular favourite is generally some Barabbas. I even went
so far as to say (he is a Jew) that his idea seemed to show
that he was not very well up on his own native literature. He smiled at my jest, and asked what I meant by
it; and I referred him to the story of the prophet Isaiah.

It occurred to me then that this story is much worth
recalling just now when so many wise men and sooth-
sayers appear to be burdened with a message to the
masses. Dr. Townsend has a message, Father Coughlin
has one, Mr. Upton Sinclair, Mr. Lippmann, Mr. Chase
and the planned-economy brethren, Mr. Tugwell and
the New Dealers, Mr. Smith and the Liberty Leaguers—
the list is endless. I can not remember a time when so
many energumens were so variously proclaiming the
Word to the multitude and telling them what they must
do to be saved. This being so, it occurred to me, as I say,
that the story of Isaiah might have something in it to
steady and compose the human spirit until this tyranny
of windiness be overpast. I shall paraphrase the story in
our common speech, since it has to be pieced out from
various sources; and inasmuch as respectable scholars
have thought fit to put out a whole new version of the
Bible in the American vernacular, I shall take shelter
behind them, if need be, against the charge of dealing
irreverently with the Sacred Scriptures.

The prophet's career began at the end of King Uzziah's
reign, say about 740 B.C. This reign was uncommonly
long, almost half a century, and apparently prosperous.
It was one of those prosperous reigns, however, like the
reign of Marcus Aurelius at Rome, or the administration
of Eubulus at Athens, or of Mr. Coolidge at Washing-

ton, where at the end the prosperity suddenly peters out, and things go by the board with a resounding crash.

In the year of Uzziah's death, the Lord commissioned the prophet to go out and warn the people of the wrath to come. "Tell them what a worthless lot they are," He said. "Tell them what is wrong, and why, and what is going to happen unless they have a change of heart and straighten up. Don't mince matters. Make it clear that they are positively down to their last chance. Give it to them good and strong, and keep on giving it to them. I suppose perhaps I ought to tell you," He added, "that it won't do any good. The official class and their intelligentsia will turn up their noses at you, and the masses will not even listen. They will all keep on in their own ways until they carry everything down to destruction, and you will probably be lucky if you get out with your life."

Isaiah had been very willing to take on the job; in fact, he had asked for it; but this prospect put a new face on the situation. It raised the obvious question why, if all that were so, if the enterprise were to be a failure from the start, was there any sense in starting it? "Ah," the Lord said, "you do not get the point. There is a Remnant there that you know nothing about. They are obscure, unorganized, inarticulate, each one rubbing along as best he can. They need to be encouraged and braced up, because when everything has gone completely to the dogs, they are the ones who will come back and build up a new society, and meanwhile your preaching will reassure them and keep them hanging on. Your job is to take care of the Remnant, so be off now and set about it."

II

Apparently, then, if the Lord's word is good for anything,—I do not offer any opinion about that,—the only
element in Judæan society that was particularly worth
bothering about was the Remnant. Isaiah seems finally
to have got it through his head that this was the case;
that nothing was to be expected from the masses, but
that if anything substantial were ever to be done in
Judæa, the Remnant would have to do it. This is a very
striking and suggestive idea; but before going on to
explore it, we need to be quite clear about our terms.
What do we mean by the masses, and what by the Remnant?

As the word *masses* is commonly used, it suggests agglomerations of poor and unprivileged people, labouring people, proletarians, and it means nothing like that;
it means simply the majority. The mass-man is one who
has neither the force of intellect to apprehend the principles issuing in what we know as the humane life, nor
the force of character to adhere to those principles steadily and strictly as laws of conduct; and because such
people make up the great, the overwhelming majority
of mankind, they are called collectively *the masses*. The
line of differentiation between the masses and the Remnant is set invariably by quality, not by circumstance.
The Remnant are those who by force of intellect are
able to apprehend these principles, and by force of character are able, at least measurably, to cleave to them;
the masses are those who are unable to do either.

The picture which Isaiah presents of the Judæan

masses is most unfavourable. In his view the mass-man, be he high or be he lowly, rich or poor, prince or pauper, gets off very badly. He appears as not only weak-minded and weak-willed, but as by consequence knavish, arrogant, grasping, dissipated, unprincipled, unscrupulous. The mass-woman also gets off badly, as sharing all the mass-man's untoward qualities, and contributing a few of her own in the way of vanity and laziness, extravagance and foible. The list of luxury-products [1] that she patronized is interesting; it calls to mind the women's page of a Sunday newspaper in 1928, or the display set forth in one of our professedly "smart" periodicals. In another place [2] Isaiah even recalls the affectations that we used to know by the name of the "flapper gait" and the "debutante slouch." It may be fair to discount Isaiah's vivacity a little for prophetic fervour; after all, since his real job was not to convert the masses but to brace and reassure the Remnant, he probably felt that he might lay it on indiscriminately and as thick as he liked—in fact, that he was expected to do so. But even so, the Judæan mass-man must have been a most objectionable individual, and the mass-woman utterly odious.

If the modern spirit, whatever that may be, is disinclined towards taking the Lord's word at its face value (as I hear is the case), we may observe that Isaiah's testimony to the character of the masses has strong collateral support from respectable Gentile authority. Plato lived into the administration of Eubulus, when Athens was at the peak of its great jazz-and-paper era, and he speaks

[1] Isaiah iii. 18-23.
[2] Chap. iii. 16.

of the Athenian masses with all Isaiah's fervency, even comparing them to a herd of ravenous wild beasts. Curiously, too, he applies Isaiah's own word *remnant* to the worthier portion of Athenian society; "there is but a very small *remnant,*" he says, of those who possess a saving force of intellect and force of character—too small, precisely as in Judæa, to be of any avail against the ignorant and vicious preponderance of the masses.

But Isaiah was a preacher and Plato a philosopher; and we tend to regard preachers and philosophers rather as passive observers of the drama of life than as active participants. Hence in a matter of this kind their judgment might be suspected of being a little uncompromising, a little acrid, or as the French say, *saugrenu.* We may therefore bring forward another witness who was preëminently a man of affairs, and whose judgment can not lie under this suspicion. Marcus Aurelius was ruler of the greatest of empires, and in that capacity he not only had the Roman mass-man under observation, but he had him on his hands twenty-four hours a day for eighteen years. What he did not know about him was not worth knowing, and what he thought of him is abundantly attested on almost every page of the little book of jottings which he scribbled offhand from day to day, and which he meant for no eye but his own ever to see.

This view of the masses is the one that we find prevailing at large among the ancient authorities whose writings have come down to us. In the eighteenth century, however, certain European philosophers spread the notion that the mass-man, in his natural state, is not at all the kind of person that earlier authorities made him out to be, but on the contrary, that he is a worthy object of interest. His untowardness is the effect of environment, an effect for which "society" is somehow responsible. If only his environment permitted him to live according to his best lights, he would undoubtedly show himself to be quite a fellow; and the best way to secure a more favourable environment for him would be to let him arrange it for himself. The French Revolution acted powerfully as a springboard for this idea, projecting its influence in all directions throughout Europe.

On this side of the ocean a whole new continent stood ready for a large-scale experiment with this theory. It afforded every conceivable resource whereby the masses might develop a civilization made in their own likeness and after their own image. There was no force of tradition to disturb them in their preponderance, or to check them in a thoroughgoing disparagement of the Remnant. Immense natural wealth, unquestioned predominance, virtual isolation, freedom from external interference and the fear of it, and, finally, a century and a half of time—such are the advantages which the mass-man has had in bringing forth a civilization which should set the earlier preachers and philosophers at naught in their belief that nothing substantial can be expected from the masses, but only from the Remnant.

His success is unimpressive. On the evidence so far presented one must say, I think, that the mass-man's conception of what life has to offer, and his choice of what to ask from life, seem now to be pretty well what they were in the times of Isaiah and Plato; and so too seem the catastrophic social conflicts and convulsions in which his views of life and his demands on life involve him.

I do not wish to dwell on this, however, but merely to observe that the monstrously inflated importance of the masses has apparently put all thought of a possible mission to the Remnant out of the modern prophet's head. This is obviously quite as it should be, provided that the earlier preachers and philosophers were actually wrong, and that all final hope of the human race is actually centred in the masses. If, on the other hand, it should turn out that the Lord and Isaiah and Plato and Marcus Aurelius were right in their estimate of the relative social value of the masses and the Remnant, the case is somewhat different. Moreover, since with everything in their favour the masses have so far given such an extremely discouraging account of themselves, it would seem that the question at issue between these two bodies of opinion might most profitably be reopened.

III

But without following up this suggestion, I wish only, as I said, to remark the fact that as things now stand Isaiah's job seems rather to go begging. Everyone with a message nowadays is like my venerable European friend, eager to take it to the masses. His first, last and only thought is of mass-acceptance and mass-approval. His great care is to put his doctrine in such shape as will capture the masses' attention and interest. This attitude towards the masses is so exclusive, so devout, that one is reminded of the troglodytic monster described by Plato, and the assiduous crowd at the entrance to its cave, trying obsequiously to placate it and win its favour, trying to interpret its inarticulate noises, trying to find out what it wants, and eagerly offering it all sorts of things that they think might strike its fancy.

The main trouble with all this is its reaction upon the mission itself. It necessitates an opportunist sophistication of one's doctrine which profoundly alters its character and reduces it to a mere placebo. If, say, you are a preacher, you wish to attract as large a congregation as you can, which means an appeal to the masses, and this in turn means adapting the terms of your message to the order of intellect and character that the masses exhibit. If you are an educator, say with a college on your hands, you wish to get as many students as possible, and you whittle down your requirements accordingly. If a writer, you aim at getting many readers; if a publisher, many purchasers; if a philosopher, many disciples; if a reformer, many converts; if a musician, many auditors; and so on. But as we see on all sides, in the realization of these several desires the prophetic message is so heavily adulterated with trivialities in every instance that its effect on the masses is merely to harden them in their sins; and meanwhile the Remnant, aware of this adulteration and of the desires that prompt it, turn their backs on the prophet and will have nothing to do with him or his message.

Isaiah, on the other hand, worked under no such disabilities. He preached to the masses only in the sense that he preached publicly. Anyone who liked might listen; anyone who liked might pass by. He knew that the Remnant would listen; and knowing also that nothing was to be expected of the masses under any circumstances, he made no specific appeal to them, did not accommodate his message to their measure in any way, and did not care two straws whether they heeded it or not. As a modern publisher might put it, he was not worrying about circulation or about advertising. Hence, with all such obsessions quite out of the way, he was in a position to do his level best, without fear or favour, and answerable only to his august Boss.

If a prophet were not too particular about making money out of his mission or getting a dubious sort of notoriety out of it, the foregoing considerations would lead one to say that serving the Remnant looks like a good job. An assignment that you can really put your back into, and do your best without thinking about results, is a real job; whereas serving the masses is at best only half a job, considering the inexorable conditions that the masses impose upon their servants. They ask you to give them what they want, they insist upon it, and will take nothing else; and following their whims, their irrational changes of fancy, their hot and cold fits, is a tedious business, to say nothing of the fact that what they want at any time makes very little call on one's resources of prophecy. The Remnant, on the other hand, want only the best you have, whatever that may be. Give them that, and they are satisfied and you have nothing more to worry about. The prophet of the American masses must aim consciously at the lowest common denominator of intellect, taste and character among 120,000,000 people; and this is a distressing task. The prophet of the Remnant, on the contrary, is in the enviable position of Papa Haydn in the household of Prince Esterhazy. All Haydn had to do was to keep forking out the very best music he knew how to produce, knowing it would be understood and appreciated by those for whom he produced it, and caring not a button what anyone else thought of it; and that makes a good job.

In a sense, nevertheless, as I have said, it is not a rewarding job. If you can touch the fancy of the masses, and have the sagacity to keep always one jump ahead of their vagaries and vacillations, you can get good returns in money from serving the masses, and good returns also in a mouth-to-ear type of notoriety:

Digito monstrari et dicier, Hic est!

We all know innumerable politicians, journalists, dramatists, novelists and the like, who have done extremely well by themselves in these ways. Taking care of the Remnant, on the contrary, holds little promise of any such rewards. A prophet of the Remnant will not grow purse-proud on the financial returns from his work, nor is it likely that he will get any great renown out of it. Isaiah's case was exceptional to this second rule, and there are others, but not many.

It may be thought, then, that while taking care of the Remnant is no doubt a good job, it is not an especially interesting job, because it is as a rule so poorly paid. I have my doubts about this. There are other compensations to be got out of a job besides money and notoriety, and some of them seem substantial enough to be attractive. Many jobs which do not pay well are yet profoundly interesting, as, for instance, the job of the research-student in the sciences is said to be; and the job of looking after the Remnant seems to me, as I have surveyed it for many years from my seat in the grandstand, to be as interesting as any that can be found in the world.

IV

What chiefly makes it so, I think, is that in any given society the Remnant are always so largely an unknown quantity. You do not know, and will never know, more than two things about them. You can be sure of those—dead sure, as our phrase is—but you will never be able to make even a respectable guess at anything else. You do not know and will never know who the Remnant are, or where they are, or how many of them there are, or what they are doing or will do. Two things you know, and no more: first, that they exist; second, that they will find you. Except for these two certainties, working for the Remnant means working in impenetrable darkness; and this, I should say, is just the condition calculated most effectively to pique the interest of any prophet who is properly gifted with the imagination, insight and intellectual curiosity necessary to a successful pursuit of his trade.

The fascination and the despair of the historian, as he looks back upon Isaiah's Jewry, upon Plato's Athens, or upon Rome of the Antonines, is the hope of discovering and laying bare the "substratum of right thinking and well-doing" which he knows must have existed somewhere in those societies because no kind of collective life can possibly go on without it. He finds tantalizing intimations of it here and there in many places, as in the Greek Anthology, in the scrapbook of Aulus Gellius, in the poems of Ausonius, and in the brief and touching tribute *Bene merenti* bestowed upon the unknown occupants of Roman tombs. But these are vague and fragmentary; they lead him nowhere in his search for some kind of measure of this substratūm, but merely testify to what he already knew *a priori,* that the substratum did somewhere exist. Where it was, how substantial it was, what its power of self-assertion and resistance was—of all this they tell him nothing.

Similarly, when the historian of two thousand years hence, or two hundred years, looks over the available testimony to the quality of our civilization and tries to get any kind of clear, competent evidence concerning the substratum of right thinking and well-doing which he knows must have been here, he will have a devil of a time finding it. When he has assembled all he can get and has made even a minimum allowance for speciousness, vagueness, and confusion of motive, he will sadly acknowledge that his net result is simply nothing. A Remnant were here, building a substratum, like coral insects,—so much he knows,—but he will find nothing to put him on the track of who and where and how many they were, and what their work was like.

Concerning all this, too, the prophet of the present knows precisely as much and as little as the historian of the future; and that, I repeat, is what makes his job seem to me so profoundly interesting. One of the most suggestive episodes recounted in the Bible is that of a prophet's attempt—the only attempt of the kind on record, I believe—to count up the Remnant. Elijah had fled from persecution into the desert, where the Lord presently overhauled him and asked what he was doing so far away from his job. He said that he was running away, not because he was a coward, but because all the

Remnant had been killed off except himself. He had got away only by the skin of his teeth, and, he being now all the Remnant there was, if he were killed the True Faith would go flat. The Lord replied that he need not worry about that, for even without him the True Faith could probably manage to squeeze along somehow, if it had to; "and as for your figures on the Remnant," He said, "I don't mind telling you that there are seven thousand of them back there in Israel whom it seems you have not heard of, but you may take My word for it that there they are."

At that time probably the population of Israel could not have run to much more than a million or so; and a Remnant of seven thousand out of a million is a highly encouraging percentage for any prophet. With seven thousand of the boys on his side, there was no great reason for Elijah to feel lonesome; and incidentally that would be something for the modern prophet of the Remnant to think of when he has a touch of the blues. But the main point is that if Elijah the Prophet could not make a closer guess on the number of the Remnant than he made when he missed it by seven thousand, anyone else who tackled the problem would only waste his time.

The other certainty which the prophet of the Remnant may always have is that the Remnant will find him. He may rely on that with absolute assurance. They will find him without his doing anything about it; in fact, if he tries to do anything about it, he is pretty sure to put them off. He does not need to advertise for them, or resort to any schemes of publicity to get their attention. If he is a preacher or a public speaker, for example, he may be quite indifferent to going on show at receptions, getting his picture printed in the newspapers, or furnishing autobiographical material for publication on the side of "human interest." If a writer, he need not make a point of attending any pink teas, autographing books at wholesale, or entering into any specious free-masonry with reviewers. All this and much more of the same order lies in the regular and necessary routine laid down for the prophet of the masses; it is, and must be, part of the great general technique of getting the mass-man's ear—or as our vigorous and excellent publicist, Mr. H. L. Mencken, puts it, the technique of boob-bumping. The prophet of the Remnant is not bound to this technique. He may be quite sure that the Remnant will make their own way to him without any adventitious aids; and not only so, but if they find him employing such aids, as I said, it is ten to one that they will smell a rat in them and will sheer off.

The certainty that the Remnant will find him, however, leaves the prophet as much in the dark as ever, as helpless as ever in the matter of putting any estimate of any kind upon the Remnant, for, as appears in the case of Elijah, he remains ignorant of who they are that have found him, or where they are, or how many. They do not write in and tell him about it, after the manner of those who admire the vedettes of Hollywood nor yet do they seek him out and attach themselves to his person. They are not that kind. They take his message much as drivers take the directions on a roadside signboard; that is, with very little thought about the signboard, beyond being gratefully glad that it happened to be there, but with very serious thought about the directions.

This impersonal attitude of the Remnant wonderfully

enhances the interest of the imaginative prophet's job. Once in a while, just about often enough to keep his intellectual curiosity in good working order, he will quite accidentally come upon some distinct reflection of his own message in an unsuspected quarter; and this enables him to entertain himself in his leisure moments with agreeable speculations about the course his message may have taken in reaching that particular quarter, and about what came of it after it got there. Most interesting of all are those instances, if one could only run them down (but one may always speculate about them), where the recipient himself no longer knows where or when or from whom he got the message; or even where, as sometimes happens, he has forgotten that he got it anywhere, and imagines that it is all a self-sprung idea of his own.

Such instances as these are probably not infrequent, for, without presuming to enroll ourselves among the Remnant, we can all no doubt remember having found ourselves suddenly under the influence of an idea, the source of which we can not possibly identify. "It came to us afterward," as we say; that is, we are aware of it only after it has shot up full-grown in our minds, leaving us quite ignorant of how and when and by what agency it was planted there and left to germinate. It seems highly probable that the prophet's message often takes some such course with the Remnant.

If, for example, you are a writer or a speaker or a preacher, you put forth an idea which lodges in the *Unbewusstsein* of a casual member of the Remnant, and sticks fast there. For some time it is inert; then it begins to fret and fester until presently it invades the man's conscious mind and, as one might say, corrupts it. Meanwhile he has quite forgotten how he came by the idea in the first instance, and even perhaps thinks he has invented it; and in those circumstances the most interesting thing of all is that you never know what the pressure of that idea will make him do.

V

For these reasons it appears to me that Isaiah's job is not only good but also extremely interesting; and especially so at the present time when nobody is doing it. If I were young and had the notion of embarking in the prophetical line, I would certainly take up this branch of the business; and therefore I have no hesitation about recommending it as a career for anyone in that position. It offers an open field, with no competition; our civilization so completely neglects and disallows the Remnant that anyone going in with an eye single to their service might pretty well count on getting all the trade there is.

Even assuming that there is some social salvage to be screened out of the masses, even assuming that the testimony of history to their social value is a little too sweeping, that it depresses hopelessness a little too far, one must yet perceive, I think, that the masses have prophets enough and to spare. Even admitting in the teeth of history that hope of the human race may not be quite exclusively centred in the Remnant, one must perceive that they have social value enough to entitle them to some measure of prophetic encouragement and consolation, and that our civilization allows them none whatever. Every prophetic voice is addressed to the masses, and to them alone; the voice of the pulpit, the voice of education, the voice of politics, of literature, drama, journalism—all these are directed towards the masses exclusively, and they marshal the masses in the way that they are going.

One might suggest, therefore, that aspiring prophetical talent may well turn to another field. *Sat patriæ Priamoque datum*—whatever obligation of the kind may be due the masses is already monstrously overpaid. So long as the masses are taking up the tabernacle of Moloch and Chiun, their images, and following the star of their god Buncombe, they will have no lack of prophets to point the way that leadeth to the More Abundant Life; and hence a few of those who feel the prophetic afflatus might do better to apply themselves to serving the Remnant. It is a good job, an interesting job, much more interesting than serving the masses; and moreover it is the only job in our whole civilization, as far as I know, that offers a virgin field.

New York, March, 1936.

14

Free Speech and Plain Language

RECENTLY, under the title, "So Conceived and So Dedicated," Mr. William F. Russell published an excellent paper,[1] which starts an interesting train of thought. It shows that the author is a true believer in free speech. It ends with an appeal for freedom, which I found most exhilarating; so exhilarating that I at once determined to take it as a text, as I now do. Speaking of the American people's progress in safety and happiness, and of the means to be employed in promoting that progress, Mr. Russell says, "Our only hope is full, free, frank, open discussion from all sides, open propaganda, open influence upon the press, upon public opinion, upon our Congress and legislators, and upon our governors and President. Whoever thinks, let him speak. Whoever would muzzle another, let him stay his hand. Bring on the opposition. Let it be heard. Then shall we have all the forces in full play."

These are noble and inspiring words; well, just what do they mean? I am not asking what they mean to Mr. Russell. I take it that he is a literal-minded person, like

[1] The *Atlantic Monthly*, May, 1935.

the statesman of the last century who said that the way
to resume specie payment is to resume. If I might do
so without impropriety, I would ask Mr. Russell's permission to place myself beside him in that category. To
such as Mr. Russell and myself, then, free speech means
simply free speech, whether the words be conveyed by
sound or by writing or by printing. That is that, and
that is all there is, and there isn't any more—use no
hooks. Moreover, it would appear to us that the plain
provisions of the Bill of Rights mean nothing else, nor
can be made to mean anything else, save through one
of those processes of interpretation whereby, as a contemporary of Bishop Butler said, anything can be made
to mean anything—processes, in other words, of sheer
and patent shysterism. But I may remind Mr. Russell
that the world seems to be rapidly going away from old-
fashioned people of our kind, and it is therefore necessary to consider what free speech means to others who
are not like us, and especially to those who are in a position more or less to prescribe the courses in which public sentiment concerning such matters shall run.

A little story occurs to me in this connexion, which I
shall tell, partly because it is amusing, but also because
it tends somewhat to show what I am driving at.

In the interregnum following the fall of the Tsarist
régime, Petersburg was full of spellbinders haranguing
the crowds in the public squares, and telling them what
they must do to be saved. Some were emissaries of foreign governments. One of my friends was there; he entertained himself all day and every day by wandering
around among the crowds with an interpreter, to find
out what was going on. In one group that was being

addressed in very thick Russian, he found a knot of five or six proletarians, took them aside and questioned them about their odd attitude of docility towards the speaker. "Don't you know that this man is an agent of the German Government?"

"Yes."

"Well, then, he is a dangerous fellow. Why do you listen to him? Why don't you throw him out?"

"Anything the German Government has to say to us, we ought to hear."

This was a stupefying surprise. My friend, being a man of great humour, saw his chance, and went on:

"Is that the way you people generally feel about it?"

"Yes."

"That is your notion of free speech, is it?"

"Yes."

"But you don't seem to know the difference between liberty and license."

"No; what is it?"

"Well, when some perfectly respectable person gets up and says something that everybody agrees to, that is liberty."

They ruminated on this awhile, finally got it down, and then asked, "What is license?"

"Why, license is when some infernal scoundrel, who ought to be hanged anyway, gets up and says something that is true."

The men drew apart and had a long powwow with the interpreter, who finally came forward and said, "These men say there must be some misunderstanding on your part, probably owing to differences in language. They say we are not for liberty at all; we are for license."

I take it that, in the circumstances set forth in Mr. Russell's article, he and I are for license; but the fact remains, I fear, that most of our fellow-citizens are very strong for liberty; very strong indeed.

II

This addiction seems to be the natural fruitage of another addiction which is more or less common to all men, but with us is so inveterate and so ingrained that we might almost take out a process-patent on it; and that is, the addiction to expediency as the supreme law of conduct. Among the many observers who came over from Europe to study us in the early days of our republic, the ablest and most profound was one who for some reason is also most neglected. This was the eminent economist and Saint-Simonian, Michel Chevalier. One never hears of him; yet he is probably worth more to us, especially at the moment, than all the Tocquevilles, Bryces, Chateaubriands and Halls put together. I wish I might prevail on some enterprising editor to arrange with Professor Chinard, who not only knows our history so well but understands it so thoroughly, to write an essay on Chevalier which should bring him out of a most unmerited obscurity and introduce him to us.

Chevalier, who spent four years among us exactly a century ago, traveling everywhere, has a great deal to say about the blind devotion to expediency which he found prevailing throughout our society. He found, in short, that in any circumstances, in any matter small or great, whenever considerations of expediency collided with principle, law, precept or custom, it was invariably the latter that must give way.

Witnessing these collisions, he would ask such questions as, "Where are your principles of action? What about the doctrine set forth in the Declaration of Independence? What about your belief in the natural rights of man?"—and he would get but the one answer, that the action taken in the premises must be regulated by expediency.

Truly, it would seem that Americans of Chevalier's day were temperamentally more ill-fitted for the undertaking of self-government by written statutes, and under a written constitution, than any people who had passed beyond the patriarchal stage of political development. In this very matter of free speech which we are discussing, it is worth remembering that the ink was barely dry on the Bill of Rights when the Sedition Act was passed; and since then the history of free speech in America has pretty well been a history of efforts to show, as Mr. Dooley said, "that th' Constitution iv th' United States is applicable on'y in such cases as it is applied to on account iv its applicability."

So I believe it is unquestionably the inveterate devotion to expediency that has left Mr. Russell and myself standing together in this rather forlorn hope for the future of free speech. It is coercion based on expediency that suppresses what we loosely call "Communist propaganda." It is coercion based on expediency that enforces silence about this or that flagitious transaction in public affairs; and so on. As an abstract issue, free speech comes in for a good deal of discussion now and then, for instance during the late war, when coercion based on expediency was widely applied; and the general run of argument pro and con is probably well enough known. There is one line of argument, however, that is not often brought out. It proceeds from the fact that while, as a rule, action based on pure expediency gets the immediate results it aims at, those results always cost a great deal more in the long run than they are worth; and moreover, the most expensive items in the bill are those that were not foreseen and never thought of.

For example, expediency suggested that the evils of the liquor-traffic be suppressed by coercion. It got results, after a fashion, but it got them for us at the price of making corruption and hypocrisy respectable. A heavy price—were they worth it? Again, expediency suggested that the care of our poor be made a government job. It gets results, but at what price? First, the organization of mendicancy and subvention into a permanent political asset. Second, the indoctrination of our whole citizenry with a false and dangerous idea of the State and its functions—that the State is something to be run to in any emergency, trivial or serious, to settle matters out of hand.

This idea encourages, invites, nay, insists upon what Professor Ortega y Gasset rightly calls the gravest danger that to-day threatens civilization: the absorption of all spontaneous social effort by the State. "When the mass suffers any ill-fortune, or simply feels some strong appetite, its great temptation is that permanent, sure possibility of obtaining everything—without effort, struggle, doubt or risk—merely by touching a button and setting the mighty machine in motion."

There is no trouble about seeing how deeply our people are penetrated with this idea; even the cartoons in our newspapers show it. I saw one not so long ago, a caricature of the Revolutionary reveille, the fine old picture that everybody knows, of the old man, his son and grandson, marching three-abreast, with banner, drum, and fife. The cartoon showed three ill-looking adventurers marching on Washington and their banner bore the word, "Gimme."

This degrading enervation of a whole people is rather a heavy offset to the benefits gained through a policy of expediency. The devotees of expediency, however, never consider the final cost of their policies; they are after the immediate thing, and that only. Their case was never better put than by Mr. George Horace Lorimer, in his observations on the young man who pawned a razor for fifteen cents to get a shave.

I had a desultory talk with one devotee of expediency not long ago, a good friend and a thoroughly excellent man. He was all worked up over the activities of Communists and what he called pink Socialists, especially in the colleges and churches. He said they were corrupting the youth, and he was strong for having them coerced into silence. I could not see it that way. I told him it seemed pretty clear that Mr. Jefferson was right when he said that the effect of coercion was "to make one half the people fools and the other half hypocrites, and to support roguery and error all over the earth"; look at Germany and Italy! I thought our youth could manage to bear up under a little corrupting—they always have— and if they were corrupted by Communism, they stood a first-rate chance to get over it, whereas if they grew up fools or hypocrites, they would never get over it.

I added that Mr. Jefferson was right when he said that "it is error alone which needs the support of government; truth can stand by itself." One glance at governments anywhere in the world proves that. Well, then, the surest way to make our youth suspect that there may be something in Communism would be for the government to outlaw it.

"That is all very well for Mr. Jefferson," my friend said, "but think of this: Some years ago an anarchist agitator went up and down the land, preaching the doctrine of terrorism. A weak-minded young man heard it, was unbalanced by it,[2] went forth and shot President McKinley. The State executed him and buried his body in quicklime to show its abhorrence of the deed, but nothing was done about the agitator who provoked it. Is this logical? Lincoln did not think so. When a delegation of liberals complained to him about the Sedition Act, he said, 'Must I shoot a simple-minded soldier-boy who deserts, while I must not touch a hair of the wily agitator who induces him to desert?' "

This is, of course, a sound argument, provided one accept the premise implied. On the other hand, one might suggest that in shooting simple-minded boys and burying lunatics in quicklime, the State is not taking precisely the right way with them under any circumstances. We avoided this digression, however, and returned to the subject in hand.

"McKinley's death was a shocking thing, truly," I said, "but let us try to strike a balance. Don't you think, when

[2] My friend may have been misinformed. This story was current at the time, but no evidence of it was ever brought forward, and it was probably an invention.

all comes to all, that the life of a President, now and then, maybe,—such things seldom happen,—is a moderate price for keeping you free of a civilization made up half of fools and half of hypocrites? Men have thought so before now, and pretty good men too. On the occasion of Shays's Rebellion, Mr. Jefferson said, 'If the happiness of the mass of the people can be secured at the expense of a little tempest now and then, or even of a little blood, it will be a precious purchase. *Malo libertatem periculosam quam quietam servitutem.*' Again," I added, "you remember that when Sir Robert Peel proposed to organize a police-force for London, Englishmen said openly that half a dozen throats cut annually in the Whitechapel district was a cheap price to pay for keeping such an instrument of potential tyranny out of the hands of the government.

"That sounds rather cold-blooded, but the immense augmentation and strengthening of the police-forces in all countries in the past fifty years go far to show that they were right. Get up in one of our industrial centres to-day and say that two and two make four, and if there is any financial interest concerned in maintaining that two and two make five, the police will bash your head in. Then what choice have you, save to degenerate either into a fool or into a hypocrite? And who wants to live in a land of fools and hypocrites?

"Mr. Jefferson was right," I continued. (I could not resist winding up with a little flourish.) "Error is the only thing that needs the backing of government, and when you find the government backing anything you are pretty safe in betting that it is an error. Truth is a very proud old girl, and if you or any crew of ignorant blackguards in public office think she cares two pins for your patronage, or that you can put her in debt to you, you have another guess coming. She will look at your little efforts with an amused eye, perhaps give you one or two mild Bronx cheers, and then when she gets around to it—in her own good time, no hurry, she is never in a hurry—she will stand you on your head. Rome, Moscow and Berlin papers, please copy."

To be on the popular side at the moment is not especially interesting; the thing is to be on the right side in the long run. As I see it, the best argument for free speech is what the suppression of it does to the character of a people. This is the only thing in the whole contention that interests me, though I have every respect for the Bill of Rights. Mr. Jefferson said that "it is the manners and spirit of a people which preserve a republic in vigour. A degeneracy in these is a canker which soon eats to the heart of its laws and constitution." Nothing promotes this degeneracy more effectively than a check on free speech. We all remember, for example, what the "spirit of a people" was like in 1917, when free speech was suppressed, and when any low-minded scoundrel might make character for himself by spying and eaves-dropping. The Bill of Rights is all very well, so long as it has the manners and spirit of a people behind it; but when these are hopelessly impaired, it is not worth the paper it was written on.

But, as Mr. Jefferson saw clearly, we can not hope to get something for nothing; and here, I think, is probably the real issue between old-fashioned persons like Mr. Russell and myself, and the believer in expediency like my good and honoured friend whom I have just now cited. My friend unquestionably wants the manners and spirit of our people kept up to par,—it would be a base slander to suggest the contrary,—but when it comes to digging up for it, he boggles at the price; in short, he wants to get something for nothing, and this simply can not be done. The whole order of nature is against it.

I believe I may count on Mr. Russell being with me when I say that, if the spirit of a people is worth maintaining, we must be prepared to accept the offenses, inconveniences and injuries incidental to its maintenance. We must take a chance on terrorists, pink Socialists, Communists and what not; a chance on a fracas or two, on a few youths being corrupted, maybe on losing a President once in a long while, and all the rest of it. Possibly those chances are not quite so desperate as the believer in expediency imagines; I think it very likely. I have a letter just now from a French friend, who says that *quand les Américains se mettent à être nerveux, ils dépassent tout commentaire;* and I too have often thought I noticed something of the kind. However, desperate or not, those chances must be taken.

Julius Cæsar went unattended; he said that life was not worth having at the expense of an ignoble solicitude about it. Considering the outcome, the believer in expediency might say this was quixotic. Yet, on the other hand, it is conceivable that this example was better for the spirit of the Roman people than the spectacle of a *Führer* guarded by squads of secret-service men and plug-uglies. One of the greatest men that England ever produced was Lucius Cary, Viscount Falkland; he was killed in the battle of Newbury, at the age of thirty-three. He held the job of Secretary of State for a year, just when things were warming up nicely for the Civil War. He refused to employ spies or to censor correspondence; he would not open a single private letter. Horace Walpole sneers at this, saying that it "evinced debility of mind." Well, no doubt it incurred the chance of considerable inconvenience, even of some injury; but Falkland seemed to think it better to run that chance, rather than turn loose a swarm of sneaking vermin to deprave the spirit of the people.

So the issue is that "you pays your money and you takes your choice." The believer in expediency appreciates the benefits of freedom, but thinks they are likely to come too high. The old-style doctrinaire, like Mr. Russell and myself, is doubtful that they will come so high as all that, but never mind. Let them cost what they may, he is for them. He is for them unreservedly and unconditionally and world without end.

III

Thought on this subject opens the way for a few words about plain language; and here I must party company with Mr. Russell, for nothing in his article warrants the assumption that he would go with me, though he might —his article intimates nothing either way.

I am thinking particularly about the current treatment of public affairs, though in general I wish we were in the habit of conveying our meanings in plain explicit terms rather than by indirection and by euphemism, as we so regularly do. My point is that habitual indirection in speech supports and stimulates a habit of indirection in thought; and this habit, if not pretty closely watched, runs off into intellectual dishonesty.

The English language is of course against us. Its vocabulary is so large, it is so rich in synonyms, it lends itself so easily and naturally to paraphrase, that one gets up a great facility with indirection almost without knowing it. Our common speech bristles with mere indirect intimations of what we are driving at; and as for euphemisms, they have so far corrupted our vernacular as to afflict us with a chronic, mawkish and self-conscious sentimentalism which violently resents the plain English name of the realities that these euphemisms intimate. This is bad; the upshot of our willingness to accept a reality, provided we do not hear it named, or provided we ourselves are not obliged to name it, leads us to accept many realities that we ought not to accept. It leads to many and serious moral misjudgments of both facts and persons; in other words, it leads straight into a profound intellectual dishonesty.

The glossary of business has many such euphemisms; for example, when you hear that a concern is being "reorganized," it means that the concern is bankrupt, unable or unwilling to meet its bills; it is busted. "Bankruptcy" has, however, become an unfashionable word; we are squeamish and queasy and nasty-nice about using it or hearing it used. We prefer to fall back on the euphemism of "reorganization."

The glossary of politics is so full of euphemistic words and phrases—as in the nature of things it must be—that one would suppose politicians must sometimes strain their wits to coin them. For example, when Secretary A. tells Congressman B. that unless he votes right on a certain measure there will be no more pork-barrel funds distributed in his district, that is blackmail,—there is no other name for it,—but we prefer to lump off transactions of this sort under the general and euphemistic term "patronage." Sometimes we find a euphemism on a euphemism; for example, what we used to call an indemnity is what our ruder ancestors called booty, plunder, which is precisely what it is. But the word "indemnity" became in turn unfashionable, for some reason,—overwork, perhaps,—and for the last few years we have been saying "reparations." Some literary artist spread himself to give us "unemployment relief," when it became evident that the good and sound word "dole" was a little heavy for our pampered stomachs; and while we all know well enough what "mandated" territory is, and what "mandates" are, we are quite indisposed to saying what they are, or to hearing anyone say what they are.

A person never sees so clearly how absurd these euphemisms are until he translates a few of them from another language into his own. The French language has a small vocabulary, and its genius is rather against euphemism,—as much against it as English is for it,—but it can turn out a few very handsome ones. Embezzlement, for instance, is known as an "indelicacy"; you will read in French newspapers that yesterday's cashier who made off with the contents of the safe "committed an indelicacy." Italian newspapers, reporting a bad accident on the railway, will begin by telling you that the Sunrise Express "disgraced itself" yesterday morning, at such-and-such time and place; casualties, so-and-so many. These sound as ridiculous to us as our pet euphemisms must sound to a Frenchman or an Italian; the reason being that all such sophistications of speech are intrinsically ridiculous. They sound silly because they are silly; and, being silly, they are debilitating.

Bad as euphemism is, however, indirection is worse. I notice that a writer in a recent magazine gives this advice to budding newspaper men:

Even where opinion is admitted, as on the editorial page, fact is often more desirable than opinion. Thus it is better to scrap an editorial calling the mayor a liar and a crook, and to write another which, by reciting facts without using adjectives and without calling names, makes it obvious that the mayor is a liar and a crook.

In the view of journalism, that is first-class good advice, because we are all so accustomed to indirection that a lapse from it affects us unpleasantly and sets us against the person or organ that indulges in any such lapse; and that will not do for journalism, because it makes people stop their subscriptions.

In the view of intellectual integrity, on the other hand, this advice seems to me about the worst imaginable. In the first place, if the mayor is a liar and a crook, saying so is certainly "reciting facts." It is not "calling names," it is not uttering abuse or vituperation; it is a simple and objective recital of fact, and only a weak and sticky supersensitiveness prevents our seeing it as such. In the second place, indirection is so regularly the vehicle of propaganda that the use of it marks the man with an axe to grind. The advice which I have just cited contemplates a person who is more concerned with producing an effect on people's minds than he is with the simple expression of truth and fact. This may be good journalism,—I am not entitled to an opinion about that,—but I can find nothing to say for it on general grounds.

After the jury in the Beecher-Tilton trial disagreed, and the case against Beecher had lapsed, Charles Anderson Dana said editorially in the New York *Sun,* "Henry Ward Beecher is an adulterer, a perjurer, and a fraud; and his great genius and his Christian pretenses only make his sins the more horrible and revolting." To me that piece of plain language sounds purely objective. On the one hand, it has not the accent of mere vituperation, it is thoroughly dignified; and on the other, it is not the language of a person who is mainly concerned with wangling somebody into believing something. When Mr. Jefferson wrote that one of his associates in Washington's cabinet was "a fool and a blabber," his words, taken in their context, make exactly the same impression of calm, disinterested and objective appraisal as if he had remarked that the man had black hair and brown eyes.

Or again, while we are about it, let us examine the most extreme example of this sort of thing that I have so far found in English literature, which is Kent's opinion of Oswald, in *King Lear:*

Kent. Fellow, I know thee.
Osw. What dost thou know me for?
Kent. A knave; a rascal; an eater of broken meats; a base, proud, shallow, beggarly, three-suited, hundred-pound, filthy, worsted-stocking knave; a lily-livered, action-taking, whoreson, glass-gazing, super-serviceable, finical rogue; one-trunk-inheriting slave; one that wouldst be a bawd, in way of good service, and art nothing but the composition of a knave, beggar, coward, pandar, and the son and heir of a mongrel bitch.

Now, considering Kent's character and conduct, as shown throughout the play, I doubt very much that those lines should be taken as merely so much indecent blackguarding. I appeal to Mr. Walter Hampden to say whether I am not right in thinking that an actor who ranted through them in the tone and accent of sheer violent diatribe would ruin his part. Frank Warrin cited those lines the other day, when he was telling me how much he would enjoy a revival of *Lear*, with our gifted friend Bill Parke cast for the part of Kent. He said, "Can't you hear Bill's voice growing quieter and quieter, colder and colder, deadlier and deadlier, all the way through that passage?" Angry as Kent is, and plain as his language is, his tone and manner must carry a strong suggestion of objectivity in order to keep fully up to the dramatist's conception of his rôle. Kent is not abusing Oswald; he is merely, as we say, "telling him."

IV

I repeat that I have no thought of weaving a web of implications to entangle Mr. Russell. I may say, however, how greatly I wish he would go at least some little way with me in the belief that, with the revival of free speech which he so ably urges, there should go a revival of plain language.

When we speak freely, let us speak plainly, for plain speech is wholesome; especially, plain speech about public affairs and public men. Mr. Justice McReynolds gave us a noble specimen of it in his dissenting opinion and his accompanying remarks on the gold-clause decision. Such language has not been heard from the Supreme

Bench since the days when John Marshall Harlan used to chew up about half a pound of plug tobacco, just "to get a good ready," and then turn loose on his affirming associates with a dissenting opinion that would burn a hole through a rawhide. Nothing like it, indeed, has been heard from any public man in America, as far as I know, since the death of William Jay Gaynor; and it bucked me up almost to the point of believing that there might be some sort of future for the country, after all.

That is the sort of talk we should be hearing on all sides of any and every public question, and with reference to every public man. I have long since given up reading political editorials and the "interpretations" of political reporters. I detest a flavoured stink; and the stench of propaganda that has been soaked in the musk and patchouli of indirection is peculiarly odious. If these interpreters set out, say, to deal with some public man of rank and responsibility who is on the other side of the political fence, they usually begin by buttering up his good intentions, fine gifts and excellent character, and then proceed to associate him with some flagrant piece of political rascality; thus by indirection making it appear that he is actually a knave and a dog. Really, one loses patience with this perpetual and exclusive concern with making people believe something, with "putting something over," rather than with plain objective statement. Even the editorial technique of Mr. Pott and Mr. Slurk had at least the merit of eschewing indirection.

It seems to me indeed that the association of plain language with free speech is a natural one; that legality alone is not enough to ensure free speech. Freedom of speech means more than mere freedom under law. It means freedom under a régime of candour and objectivity; freedom under a paramount concern with truth and clearness of statement, rather than a paramount concern with making one's statements acceptable to the whims and sentimentalisms of an enervated people.

This thought tempts me to go on and examine some specific infringements on the relation between freedom of speech and plainness of language; it brings Jeremy Bentham back to mind, with his chapter on what he calls "impostor-terms." But this essay is already too long, and I must end it here. If my reader's patience holds out, I may take the matter up again and carry it on from where I now leave it.

Brussels, July, 1935.

15

Impostor-Terms

IN THE last essay, I ended my observations on free speech and plain language at the point where the name of Jeremy Bentham came up in my mind. I suspect that Bentham is not much read nowadays, in this country at least, although it would seem that we Americans ought to have a soft spot in our hearts for him, because he built a first-class philosophical defense-mechanism for the only moral standard we ever had. According to Bentham, the way to tell right from wrong is by applying the test of utility. Whatever is useful is right. Also, in order to decide this matter of usefulness in cases where there appears to be as much weight on one side of the question as on the other, you apply Bentham's famous test of "the greatest good to the greatest number." If you can assure yourself that a given action will produce the greatest good to the greatest number, you need not have any further doubt about its moral character. One may remark in passing that this doctrine is a great life-saver for a statesman's conscience; the New Deal, for example, would seem to be based on a kind of degenerate Benthamism. The trouble is, of course, that one can never be sure about what will actually produce the greatest good to the greatest number. All sorts of unforeseen factors keep turning up to make a mess of things,—chiefly the "imponderabilia" which Prince de Bismarck held in such reverent dread,—so that often the thing we have gambled on to produce the greatest good to the greatest number turns out to be extremely bad all round, and we discover that we have been matching our wits against a job which only omniscience can handle.

Bentham must have been one of the most interesting beings that ever lived. He had immense ability, endless curiosity, untiring diligence and no humour whatever; and this is just the combination of qualities that would make the student of civilization seek him out and follow him delightedly up and down the earth to see where he would break out next. His lack of humour made him an utterly unpredictable person. No one could tell from day to day what fantastic idea he would seize on, or what he would do with it. For example, one of his innumerable odd contrivances was a scheme for building prisons in circular or semicircular form, so that one guard stationed at the centre could watch all the cells. He spent three or four years on this scheme, pestering the British Government about it until he actually got them to put some money in it for an experiment. He called his circular prison a panopticon. To be fair with him, however, he did not originate this idea, but borrowed it from his brother Samuel,—this sort of outlandish ingenuity seems to have run in the family,—who was in the textile business, and had conceived the notion of building a mill on the principle of the panopticon, which should require but a single foreman or superintendent to watch all the hands. My impression is that he actually built one, but I am not sure.

Jeremy Bentham, however, had plenty of ideas of his own. He was rich, and lived at his ease for eighty-four years, with nothing to do but jump from one thing that interested him to another—mainly things that no one else on earth would pause over—and write about them with the most deadly seriousness. For example, his devotion to the utilitarian principle led him to consider what use the dead might best be put to in behalf of the living, and this gave rise to a disquisition of considerable length. In further pursuit of this thought he also wrote a pamphlet of some thirty pages, called *Auto-Icon,* in which he showed how, by a process of embalming which apparently amounted to petrifaction, a man might become his own statue, thus doing away with the inaccuracies, conventions and trivialities of sculpture. Now, really, what an inestimable thing it would be to know a man with a mind like that, which at the same time was a great mind, a mind that in every respect except humour was of the first order, or nearly so! Bentham bequeathed his own body for dissection in the interest of science, as thereby promoting the greatest good to the greatest number. He also bequeathed his skeleton to University College, London, where, I understand, it is still kept according to his directions. I have never seen it, but I am told it is still there, seated in a chair in a commanding situation, and dressed in his best suit of clothes.

Nevertheless, anyone who takes Bentham for a man of pure vagary makes a great mistake. Nor is he to be passed over, as the fashion is nowadays, as no more than an uncommonly fantastic figure in a fantastic and out-moded period. In his writings on government and juris-prudence he is distinctly something to be reckoned with, and his influence has grown steadily throughout the cen-tury that has elapsed since his death in 1832. In many of his occasional and fragmentary writings also, Jeremy still has a good deal on the ball, as our phrase goes, even against the more scientific batting of these times. The boys do not knock him out of the box as handily as one might think they would. It is one of these odds-and-ends of Bentham's writing that occurred to me in connexion with my remarks on the use of plain language, and I shall now go on to speak of it.

Bentham left an unfinished work, or rather the ma-terials for one, on *Fallacies;* it is a mere set of notes. One section or chapter of this is devoted to a consideration of what he calls *impostor-terms.* He puts these in the gen-eral category of "fallacies of confusion," saying that their object is to perplex or confuse the hearer when discus-sion of their subject-matter can no longer be avoided. Thus, for example, it has long been a trick of politicians to speak of an opposing group or school as a *faction,* on account of the special implications of the word. Ben-tham's note on these fallacies, and particularly his note on the use of impostor-terms, should be carefully studied and prayerfully understood. If every American mem-orized Bentham's formulas and applied them steadily to the daily diet of impostor-terms with which the jargon of politics and journalism supplies him, it would do more to promote a revival of intellectual honesty than any other exercise that could be suggested.

In the first place, Bentham lays down the general rule

that impostor-terms are applied "chiefly to the defense of
things which under their proper name are manifestly
indefensible; for example, persecutors have no such word
as *persecution,* but *zeal.* It substitutes an object of appro-
bation for an object of censure." Then he goes on to observe that in the employment of impostor-terms two
things are required:

1. A fact or circumstance which, under its proper
name and seen in its true colours, would be an object of
censure, and which therefore it is necessary to disguise.

2. An appellative which the sophist employs to conceal what would be deemed offensive, or even to bespeak
a degree of favour for it by the aid of some happier
accessory.

To this may be added Bentham's further observation
on terms which have a question-begging character. The
object of their use, he says, is

to cause, by means of the artifice, that to be taken for
true which is not true. The proposition is not true and
can not be proved, and the person by whom the fallacy
is employed is conscious of its deceptive tendency.

By way of illustration, Bentham cites the use of terms
like *honour, glory, dignity,* to extenuate flagitious political projects. When, for example, politicians determine
on some freebooting enterprise, the regular thing is to
pretend that national honour and dignity are somehow
concerned, when in fact they are not concerned. Thus
our national honour was not concerned in the Mexican
War and the Spanish War, nor was British honour concerned in the Boer War; nor French honour in Morocco.
All these were purely imperialist undertakings, or, in

plain language, sheer brigandage. But brigandage, "under its proper name and seen in its true colours, would be an object of censure"; and therefore the politician is obliged to find some appellative "to conceal what would be deemed offensive, or even to bespeak a degree of favour for it." One finds it hard to believe that so sharp-set a person as M. Mussolini actually takes any stock in the notion that Italian honour and dignity are at all concerned in his enterprise against Homer's "blameless Ethiopians," with whom Zeus himself condescended to make holiday; yet he propagates that absurdity diligently.

II

The three foregoing canons which Bentham laid down constitute a complete formula for detecting and identifying impostor-terms, wherever found. I now propose that we take a few of the terms most commonly used by our publicists, economists, journalists and politicians, and apply Bentham's canons to them in order to see how they stand up under critical examination. I make this proposal as a sort of corollary to my little effort in behalf of free speech and plain language, because it appears to me that the right to speak freely and plainly carries the correlative obligation to speak correctly; and therefore the use of impostor-terms is ruled out as well on grounds of simple integrity as on those of a decent respect for the merits of our native tongue. We will first take four terms out of the current glossary of economics, and then two out of the current glossary of politics. Space will not permit me to cite any more, but they will be enough for the purpose; the reader can extend the list indefinitely at his own pleasure.

Individualism

This is a question-begging term; its object is "to cause, by means of the artifice, that to be taken for true which is not true." When, for instance, one of our "sophists," as Bentham calls them, declares that an era of economic individualism is at an end, his use of the term implies that such an era did at one time exist. This is a proposition which, as Bentham says, "is not true and can not be proved," for no such era ever existed. One set of sophists ascribes the merits of our progress to a policy of economic individualism (usually adding the word *rugged* to enhance the imposition), while another set ascribes its defects to the same policy; but both are alike employing a question-begging term in behalf of their several purposes.

A policy of economic individualism, rugged or otherwise, can not exist where the State makes any positive interventions upon the individual in his economic capacity. It can exist only where the State confines itself to purely negative interventions, such as punishing fraud, enforcing the obligations of contract, and the like. In this country the State has made positive interventions upon the individual from the beginning, in rapidly increasing number and variety. The instance that will perhaps most readily come to mind is furnished by the State's system of tariffs. Without regard to the specific merits or demerits of this system, one may observe that it constitutes an arbitrary and positive interference with the free self-direction of commerce and industry; such, indeed, being its express and recognized intention, as is shown by the eagerness with which tariffs are sought. There is great truth in the bitter remark of some Western Congressman, that the biggest hog-calling contest in the world begins when a Congressional committee forms on the steps of the Capitol, and cries, "Tariff, tariff, tariff!"

Other forms of positive intervention appear in concessions, land-grants, subsidies. All these have existed here from the beginning; and as far as one can see, the most that rugged economic individualism has done to distinguish itself was to run to the State to wangle the benefit of them, by hook or crook. One set of our sophists points to our railway-systems as monuments to the spirit of rugged individualism. The fact is, however, that precious few of our railways came into being as other than speculative enterprises, furthered by State intervention in the shape of land-grants and one-or-another form of subsidy.[1] Indeed, in their inception, our transcontinental companies were hardly to be called railway-companies, save by courtesy, since transportation was so purely incidental to their main business, which was that of land-jobbing and subsidy-hunting. A few years ago I saw the statement—I do not vouch for it, but it can not be far off the fact—that the current cash value of the State's inter-

[1] Our great coal-carriers and ore-carriers, built by "private enterprise," are no exception, because their existence is due to the State's primary intervention in granting monopoly-rights to the rental value of the coal-fields and ore-fields they tap. The "private enterprise" that in one way or another got the economic advantage of this State-created monopoly is certainly no very impressive exhibit of rugged individualism.

ventions in behalf of the Northern Pacific Railway would enable it to build four transcontinental lines, and, in addition, to build a fleet of steamships and maintain it in an around-the-world service. If this be rugged individualism, let future lexicographers make the most of it.

The sum of the matter is that when our sophists speak of economic individualism, whether by way of praise or blame, they are using an impostor-term. In either case it is a term applied, as Bentham says, to the defense of something which under its proper name is manifestly indefensible. We all know, for example, that the true reason for seeking a tariff is that it licenses the beneficiary to extort from the domestic consumer the difference between the price of his product in a competitive and a noncompetitive market; in other words, to rob him of that difference—and robbery, under its proper name, is manifestly indefensible. All the State's positive interventions for the distribution of economic advantage can be shown, by a similar process of analysis, to come to the same thing. Now, the point is that neither set of sophists who hawk the term *individualism* wishes those interventions to cease. The only difference between them is that one set wishes the incidence of those interventions shifted from one group or class of beneficiaries to another, while the other set does not. The very last thing that either set wishes, however, is that the State's distribution of economic advantage should be "seen in its true colours," and exhibited under its proper name. Therefore both sets of sophists agree in employing the same impostor-term, the one by way of commendation, and the other by way of disparagement.

Laissez-faire

When Colbert asked some merchants what they
thought the French State might best do to help business,
one of them replied, "Let us alone." This term, like
individualism, has been taken over into the vernacular
of journalists, publicists and politicians, who have made
up a question-begging character for it out of whole cloth.
No such régime ever existed in this country; American
business never followed a policy of *laissez-faire,* never
wished to follow it, never wished the State to let it alone.

On the contrary, it has sought State intervention at
every tack and turn of its affairs, often—in fact, quite
regularly—employing most disreputable measures to ob-
tain it. We all remember the cynical remark of one of
our representative industrialists, that it was cheaper to
buy legislatures than to buy voters. When the State made
some primary intervention to confer an economic advantage,—as in the case of our railways, for instance,—and its
beneficiaries got into a tangle with one another over the
use of it, the regular thing has been to run to the State
for another intervention to straighten the tangle out.
Then another tangle, another agonized plea to the State,
another intervention which piled complication upon
complication, particularity upon particularity,—the text
of the Senate's proposed banking bill, published on the
first of July, covered almost exactly four pages of the
Wall Street Journal!—and then the same sequences, with
ever-multiplying complications and ever-increasing particularity, repeated again and again.

Laissez-faire, indeed! It is one of the few amusing

things in our rather stodgy world that those who to-day are behaving most tremendously about collectivism and the Red menace are the very ones who have cajoled, bribed, flattered and bedeviled the State into taking each and every one of the successive steps that lead straight to collectivism—steps that must lead there, that can not possibly lead anywhere else, and can not possibly be retraced. Who hectored the State into the shipping business, and plumped for setting up the Shipping Board? Who pestered the State into setting up the Interstate Commerce Commission and the Federal Farm Board? Who got the State to go into the transportation business on our inland waterways? Who is always urging the State to "regulate" and "supervise" this, that and the other routine process of financial, industrial and commercial enterprise? Who took off his coat two years ago, rolled up his sleeves, and sweat blood hour after hour over helping the State construct the codes of the late lamented National Recovery Act? None but the same Peter Schlemihl who is now half out of his mind about the approaching spectre of collectivism, bureaucracy, pink Socialism, personal government and all the rest of it. One would almost think he might catch sight of this roaring anomaly sooner or later and enjoy a wholesome laugh at himself, but as yet he seems not to have done so.

Laissez-faire, however, is a useful impostor-term, serving the same purpose as *individualism.* Its use causes that to be taken for true which is not true, and the object of its use is to disguise that which, under its proper name and seen in its true colours, would be an object of censure—that is, the distribution of economic advantage by the State. Therefore, since both sets of sophists are equally interested in keeping up this disguise, both sets use this term as more or less synonymous with *individualism.*

Free Competition

The use of this term implies the existence of an economic régime which has never existed. The American enterpriser has always operated behind the screen of a tariff which he himself, in a burst of candour, has so well named "protective." He has never faced the world on terms set by free competition, but always on terms set by handicap. In the domestic market also, his terms of operation, especially in the so-called "basic" industries, such as agriculture, have largely been set by other modes of State intervention. The fact or circumstance thus indicated is usefully disguised by a question-begging term like *free competition* or *the competitive system,* and therefore both sets of sophists employ it. No such system exists in the United States, or has ever existed.

Capitalism

The implication of this term is that the use of capital is a distinguishing mark of our economic system, a characteristic by which it may be identified; and this is not the case. Use of the term therefore causes that to be taken for true which is not true. No economic system which is not capitalist ever existed anywhere in the world, or can be conceived of as existing. The extreme of collectivism is as purely capitalist as our present system or any other system; the difference being only that collectivism transfers the ownership and management of capital from private hands to the hands of the State. By definition, capital is that portion of wealth which is applied to the production of more wealth; and an economic system which does not contemplate this segregation and employment of capital is unimaginable.

The term seems to have been foisted into our economic glossary by collectivism, in the first instance, and it is therefore rather strange that those who most abhor collectivism should not be above using it, as they habitually do. The collectivist's idea of capital, as well as one can make it out, appears to be that capital is not capital until it is put to some predatory or oppressive use; somewhat as one might say that dynamite is not dynamite until it goes off. The term is useful, however, as a disguise for the actual characteristic mark of our system, which is the private monopoly of rental values in natural resources. "The monopolist system" would have a bad sound, and therefore the term *capitalist* is substituted, according to Bentham's second canon of impostor-terms.

III

One set of sophists—the set which seems of late to have rather the best of it in getting the public ear—often lump three of the foregoing impostor-terms together as a sort of blanket formula to serve their purpose of shifting the incidence of State intervention from one class of beneficiaries to another. They put it that "a policy of economic individualism, free competition and *laissez-faire*" is responsible for most of our society's economic ills. This is, of course, a mere multiplication of absurdity, but it deserves a moment's notice because our sophists usually take the condition of England in the early part of the last century as a horrible example of what this three-decker policy brings about when allowed to run unchecked. The story is so monstrous and shocking that their contention gains a great deal of *prima facie* plausibility which is nevertheless misleading; and therefore it is worth while to examine their assertions briefly, in order to see what precisely they amount to.

At that period, our sophists say, England's industry and commerce were operating under an unqualified policy of economic individualism, free competition and *laissez-faire*. This policy issued in the most appalling social conditions that can be imagined, the conditions which Dickens, Carlyle, Kingsley and Ruskin described so vividly in their impassioned preachments. It produced great hordes of miserable beings who lived in squalor and destitution, working in the mills and mines under a régime of starvation wages, killing hours, vicious industrial hazards. It harnessed children and women underground to cars loaded with coal or ore. It sent men to sea in coffin-ships officered by ruffians. It brought forth the huge and hideous industrial centres which William Cobbett called *Hell-holes*. It produced industrialists like Mr. Plugson of Undershot, Mr. Bounderby and Mr. Bottles. You ask what this policy will come to in America—well, there you see what it came to in England.

Just so. The story is a familiar one, we all know it, and we all agree that its horror and hideousness can not be overdrawn. There is, however, not one word of truth in our sophist's assertion that these horrors were due to "a policy of individualism, free competition, and *laissez-*

faire," for the very good reason that no such policy ever existed in England. They were due to State intervention. When the factory system came in, those hordes of miserable beings were already on hand in full force; they were there because State intervention had expropriated them from the land; [2] and they went into the factories for whatever Mr. Bounderby or Mr. Bottles chose to give them, because it was either that or else to beg, steal or starve.[3] Following this primary intervention, the State made one secondary intervention after another in a long series, all in behalf of Mr. Bounderby and Mr. Bottles. It is the acme of absurdity to pretend, as our sophists do, that Adam Smith's economics are the economics of individualism and free competition. They are nothing of the kind; they are the economics of landowners and mill-owners; and the incidence of State intervention invariably followed the line of direction that those economics set.

In such circumstances, the sane and logical thing, as some Englishmen indeed perceived, would be to do away with positive State intervention. Very few were interested in that way of approach to the problem, however. As in the case of our sophists, the only idea of reform that interested anybody was that of urging the State to go on multiplying its interventions still further, and merely shift their incidence of benefit from Mr. Bounderby to Stephen Blackpool, and from Mr. Bottles to Zephaniah

[2] Readers who are interested in this statement might look up the history of the Enclosures Acts and the Statute of Frauds.

[3] Even Marx was aware that economic exploitation is impossible until expropriation from the land has taken place. See his chapter on colonization.

Diggs.[4] This being the case, the three-in-one impostor-term became useful, and it accordingly went into currency for the purposes set forth in Bentham's second canon.

IV

Passing from economics to politics, we choose two terms in most common use.

Democracy, democratic

At the time when our political system was formed, these were terms of great opprobrium, as *communist, bolshevist,* are now. The writings of our earlier statesmen, even those who had a general leaning towards the liberal side, show that they understood it in this sense exclusively; as when Morris, Gerry, Madison, Randolph, speak of the "turbulence," "dangers," "excesses," of democracy. Those whom we now would call left-wing statesmen, like Samuel Adams and Thomas Paine, seldom use it. I do not at the moment recall a single instance where Mr. Jefferson applies it to a political system, though there may be some. The satirical literature of the period presents "democrats" as an order of beings almost subhuman, uniformly low, ignorant, vicious, and above all, venal.

Presently, however, when the "party-system" came into being, and the scuffle for office became intensified, the term rapidly gained respectability. This was a purely

[4] The virtues and excellences of Mr. Bottles are most sympathetically set forth in Matthew Arnold's *Friendship's Garland*. There too the reader will find an account of the "social problem" presented by the public activities and private character of Zephaniah Diggs.

natural development. The rationale of the party-system, as Mr. Jefferson said, is that "the nest of office being too small for them all to cuddle into at once, they divide into two parties, the Ins and the Outs." The former wish to stay in, and the latter wish to turn them out and get in; and therefore there is lively competition in buttering up "the sovereign people," and inflating their self-esteem. Hence, under this intensive cultivation, the term soon passed into the bud of respectability, and from that into the full bloom of honour and dignity. There is a certain grim humour in wondering how our earlier statesmen—for example, John Adams, Washington, Alexander Hamilton—would take it if they could hear some electioneering adventurer praise them for founding "our great and glorious democracy."

To show how far remote from anything like democracy our political system is, one need only cite the Judiciary Act of 1789, which established judicial control over legislation. It vested the supreme political authority in a small oligarchy. The members of this oligarchy are not elected; they are appointed; the people have no semblance of choice in the matter. They are, moreover, appointed for life, and are wholly irresponsible; their acts can not be brought under any kind of review.[5] Excellent as this system may be, it is manifestly a long way from democratic. The exigencies of practical politics, however, make it advisable to disguise this fact, or even, as Bentham says, "to bespeak a degree of favour for it by the

---

[5] Nullification by the Executive, which has taken place in two instances, merely changed *quoad hoc* the form of our political structure from an oligarchy into an autocracy, thus giving it even more of an undemocratic character.

aid of some happier accessory"; and therefore the terms *democracy, democratic,* have been pressed into service as impostor-terms.

Republic, republican

Republican political theory is based upon the right of individual self-expression in politics. When the Constitutional Convention met in 1787, its members were beset by a wholesome dread of what Locke called "a numerous democracy," and their main purpose was to devise a system which should have the appearance of recognizing this right of individual self-expression, without the reality. Madison defined this purpose with great clearness and candour. It was, he said, to safeguard the public welfare and private rights from the dangers of democracy,[6] and at the same time to retain "the spirit and form of popular government." Their task was the same, in short, as that which has confronted all modern pseudo-republican system-builders; it was the task of devising a system which should be formally republican, but not actually such. They accomplished this task by erecting that most ingenious mechanism of "checks and balances," with the practical workings of which we are all well acquainted. However meritorious such a political mechanism may be, its model is obviously imperial rather than republican; imperial, one might say, with the difference that professional politicians are put in the place and function of the prætorian guards. They meet

[6] His words are "the dangers of such a faction." He uses the question-begging term *faction* in precisely the way that we have noticed.

periodically, decide what is to be done, and by whom, and then submit their decisions *pro forma* to the voting public on election-day. This being the case, the reasons for using *republic, republican,* as impostor-terms are sufficiently clear.

So one might go on at length with minor impostor-terms in our political glossary, such as *sanctions, reparations, mandates,* and the like. I should especially enjoy making a few observations on the way our sophists have weaseled the term *liberal* into a cloak for the most illiberal of men and the most illiberal of policies. All our job-holders parade themselves as liberals nowadays, and their policies as liberal policies. But I have not space to comment on this, which is perhaps as well, for an appropriate comment would perhaps be more vigorous than edifying.

V

Thoreau would not read newspapers; he said that one fire was like another, one murder was like another, and "when you have once established a principle, what is the use of endlessly multiplying illustrations?" So the reader may feel that his excursion into Benthamism might have been considerably shortened, with no loss to speak of. This would be true, perhaps, but for the fact that impostor-terms, like counterfeit coins, are circulated chiefly by innocent persons who have not taken the trouble to examine them, and do not know their character. It was with this fact in mind that I could hardly bring myself either to cut down my list of examples or to take examples that are less striking and can be disposed of in fewer words.

The moral of all this, however,—if one may call it that,—can be set forth quite briefly. Mr. William F. Russell came out lately with a vigorous and excellent plea for free speech. I ventured to second it, adding a few words in praise of plain language. Now, the assertion of every right—sometimes perhaps unfortunately—implies the acceptance of a corresponding responsibility. If therefore we assert the right to free and plain speech, it would appear that we should also give some thought to the responsibility for clear and correct speech. As much as anything, if not more, it is the vast currency of impostor-terms—circulated for the most part, I repeat, in all innocence—that interferes with the perception of that responsibility; and my treatment of the subject has been made with the deliberate view of showing, as vividly as possible, how great and how unsuspected that interference may be.

Dinant, July, 1935.

16

The Gods' Lookout

NOT long ago I glanced at a book called *Natural Law in the Spiritual World,* which had a great vogue in its time, half a century ago. Having never read it, I had a moment's curiosity to find out why it was so popular. I did not get far with it, because I saw at once that it dealt mostly with "great matters which are too high for me," and, like the Psalmist, I was diffident about meddling with them. The title, however, served to precipitate a notion which had been vaguely in my mind for some time, that, whatever may be the case in the spiritual world, certain laws and principles have a wider application in the material world than they are commonly supposed to have. I had been thinking in particular of three laws that are officially recognized in economics, but I believe nowhere else, and it seemed to me that they operate about as regularly and powerfully outside this restricted sphere as they do inside it. The first of these is called the law of diminishing returns, the second is called Gresham's law, and the third one is so seldom cited that it has no pocket-title. I shall say a word about the first two now, and consider the third later.

The law of diminishing returns is fundamental to industry. It formulates the fact, which strikes one as curiously unnatural, that, when a business has reached a certain point of development, returns begin to decrease, and they keep on decreasing as further development proceeds. Thus I suppose, according to the logic of the deacon's one-hoss shay, it is theoretically possible for a business to be so big that it would not bring in any returns at all. I know nothing of such matters, having never been in business, but I am told on good authority that the law of diminishing returns is much more effective than the antitrust laws for protecting society against the oppression of industrial monopoly. The idea is that when a business becomes overgrown and returns decrease, small independent concerns can begin to compete profitably, eating in around the edges of the big concern, and meanwhile reaping the fruit of the big concern's labours in developing the market.

Gresham's law has to do with the nature of currency, and the common formula for it is that "bad money drives out good." That is to say, it is always the worst form of currency in circulation that fixes the value of all the others, and causes them presently to disappear. This law bears the name of Sir Thomas Gresham, an eminent English financier of the sixteenth century, who made observations on the law, but was not the first to formulate it. Gresham's law usually comes into play whenever a government undertakes to settle a bill for its misfeasances by the larcenous expedient of "managing" its currency; hence of late years this law has been very busy with the currency of many countries. In Germany, for example, shortly after the war, the flood of paper money sent all metallic money out of circulation in a hurry, because it was worth more as old metal than as currency. For the same reason, whenever a paper or silver token is no longer the same thing as a gold token, gold tokens disappear at once; and then, if a government resorts to highwaymanry and forcibly robs its subjects of whatever gold may be in their possession, as our government lately did, it can do quite nicely by itself.

The Belgian Government raided its currency after the war, cutting down the franc from twenty cents to three cents and less, and the mint began putting out an odd-looking sort of one-franc piece that seemed to be made of tin. A few days after this, a man gave me a pre-war silver franc as a curiosity; he had got it somewhere in change. I have never seen another. As far as I know, silver francs have not been demonetized or confiscated,—certainly they were not at that time,—but I doubt whether there were half a dozen of them in circulation in all Belgium a week after the tin franc appeared.

II

The term "natural law" is a pocket form of expression, handy enough, but inexact and easily lending itself to improper assumptions. As a matter of fact, what we call a natural law is nothing more than a registration of experience. If human experience of some natural phenomenon has been uniform, it sets up a correspondingly strong expectation that subsequent experience will be likewise uniform, and we call the formula for that experience a natural law, even though the term be a misnomer, strictly speaking, for we actually know of no "law" anywhere in the universe that guarantees the ful-

fillment of our expectation. It is always with this understanding—or it should always be—that one speaks of the
laws of optics, the law of gravitation, Huyghens's law,
and so on, as "natural laws"; and thus likewise when one
speaks of Gresham's law and the law of diminishing
returns.

Mr. James Truslow Adams and others have com-
mented on the social incidence of the law of diminishing
returns, so we need give only two or three illustrations
showing how this law works in the realm of æsthetics
and culture. There is a whimsical saying current among
music-lovers that the way really to enjoy the music of a
string quartette is to have the performers group themselves around your chair. This is no great exaggeration.
Let us suppose that a string quartette plays the *Kaiserquartett* to an audience of five qualified amateurs in a
music-room of ordinary size. The five get a distinct
æsthetic experience in a high degree, probably the highest of which they are capable. It is the nearest thing to a
sense of actual participation. Logically, if five get this,
forty should get it in the same degree, so next evening
they ask in as many amateurs as the room will hold comfortably, say thirty-five, the strings play the *Kaiserquartett* again, but the thirty-five do not have the same experience to the same degree, nor do the original five have
it. Next evening the strings play the *Kaiserquartett* to
three hundred qualified amateurs in a public hall, and
while all hands get something very interesting, pleasant,
delightful, nobody gets just *that*. It is simply not there
to be had; it is gone.

We all remember how our tourists used to plume
themselves on the nice little places they had found in

Europe, "where nobody ever goes," and we may remember, too, that we were sometimes tempted to put this kind of talk down to snobbishness. Far be it from me to suggest that snobbishness is not an inveterate trait in our nation, but I think that in this instance our tourists are entitled to a clean bill. I think instinct warned them that a great influx of qualified seekers after an æsthetic experience similar to theirs would carry their own experience over the margin of diminishing returns; and their instinct was sound, for that is precisely what it would do.

I spent a month last summer on an island in the Mediterranean, a small one, difficult of access, and almost uninhabited. It has great natural beauty, but no doubt other islands have as much. Its peculiar charm is in the sentimental associations created by an unbroken run of rich and fascinating history which reaches far back beyond the Christian era. Hence, from the time of Nostradamus and Rabelais down to the present, men of letters have sung this island's praises, poets and romancers have found in it an abundant source of inspiration. The few qualified persons who go there have an experience so rewarding that I know of none of the same kind to compare with it. Suppose now that other persons, persons well furnished with the rather special qualifications necessary for the purpose—suppose that they heard of this experience, assumed that because a few had it any number might have it, and began to flock thither in large droves: the æsthetic returns would promptly decrease, and not only would the many fail to get precisely this experience, but the few would no longer get it. Nobody would get it. Instances where this has actually occurred will suggest themselves at once, for they are many.

We may take one more illustration, this time recalling the old and sound definition of a university as a student sitting on one end of a log and Mark Hopkins on the other. One may assume that the student was a qualified person, for otherwise Mark Hopkins would not be sitting there; he would have got up and gone home. That student got a specific return, peculiar to just those circumstances. Suppose now that twenty qualified persons notice this, think it is a good thing, go in for it; well, they too get pretty much the same thing in the same degree, but probably not quite. Hopkins is still there, the log is still there, but the margin of diminishing returns is close at hand. Then a hundred come in, three hundred, five hundred, only to discover that the margin was crossed somewhere far back in the beginning of the stampede, and that nobody is getting anything like what the original student got, or even the next twenty.

In the foregoing illustrations I have been careful to premise that all the persons cited are qualified. The listeners to the concert, the visitors to the island, and Mark Hopkins's students, are all supposed to be qualified in intellect, character, temperament, and a certain degree of preparatory experience, to take in and assimilate whatever benefit the several occasions may offer. I do this to show what happens when the law of diminishing returns works "straight" and without any complications; in other words, to show what happens on the theory so commonly held, that if a few qualified persons get a certain benefit, any number of qualified persons may get the same benefit under the same circumstances.

If, now, we substitute the theory which is much more widely held, that if a few qualified persons get this benefit, anybody, qualified or unqualified, may get it, we may perceive at once, I think, that the margin of diminishing returns would move considerably forward; also that the more unqualified persons tend to predominate, the further forward it would move. Going back to our illustrations, the larger the proportion of unqualified persons among the concert-audience, the visitors, and the students, the sooner the law of diminishing returns would set in. This is a matter of such common experience that it needs no comment, so we will pass on to consider the appearance of a second "natural law" in the premises.

III

Suppose the concert-audience of three hundred or more were made up largely of casual and miscellaneous persons; the natural thing for the musicians to do would be to change their programme. They would not play the *Kaiserquartett;* they would play something that they thought would hit nearer to a common denominator of their audience's capacities. In fact, it occurs to me at the moment—I had not thought of it before—that I have never seen the *Kaiserquartett* on an American programme; which of course is by no means to say that it has never appeared on one. It is a mere commonplace that programme-making for a qualified audience is one thing, and that for a popular audience is quite another; and this is true because popular programme-making finds itself always striving against the iron force of the law that "bad money drives out good." One might doubt that Mr.

Kreisler, let us say, makes up his programmes out of the kind of thing that he would choose to listen to himself. Programme-making like Mr. Damrosch's, for example, does its best to slow down the operation of Gresham's law, but even Mr. Stock's, to name the best we have in the way of programme-making, shows that it can not be successfully withstood. The development of the gramophone and the radio has encouraged the notion that by keeping a great deal of poor music in circulation one creates a larger demand for good music and helps a taste for good music to prevail. But we are discovering that things do not go that way; and the reason is that a "natural law" is moving them in a direction exactly opposite.

The current repertory of the radio shows this, quite as the current repertory of the cinema shows the same law at work in the field of drama. The radio enables Mr. Damrosch to pick up eligible persons, one by one, all over the country, and offer them advantages which they would otherwise be unlikely to get. The gramophone performs a like service, and it is a very great one. But the stated repertories of both instruments are evidence of the continual tendency of an enormous volume of indifferent music to press upon Mr. Damrosch and crowd him out; they, like the repertory of the cinema, are an impressive study in the operation of Gresham's law. It is the worst music in circulation, and the worst motion-pictures, that fix the value of all the others, and continually tend to drive them out.

By way of example in another field, two or three recent experiences have made me wish that some competent person like my friend Mr. Duffus would undertake a study of literacy in the light of Gresham's law and the law of diminishing returns. Not long ago I looked over a library said to contain a copy of every book published in America down to the year 1800. It bore witness that in those days reading was a fairly serious business; I could find nothing resembling what we should call popular literature on the shelves. The inference was that literacy was not general, and that those who read did so for other purposes than mere pastime, purposes that were pretty strictly non-sensational; and there is every collateral evidence that such was the case.

Mr. Jefferson laid great stress on literacy as an indispensable asset to good citizenship and sound patriotism. He was all for having everybody become literate, and those who have examined his own library (it is preserved intact in the Library of Congress) may easily see why. *Mutatis mutandis,* if everybody read the kind of thing he did, and as he did, he would have been right. But in his laudable wish to make the benefits of literacy accessible to all, Mr. Jefferson did not see that he had the operation of two natural laws dead against him. He seems to have jumped to the conclusion that, because certain qualified persons got a definite benefit out of literacy, anybody could get the same benefit on the same terms; and here he collided with the law of diminishing returns. He seems also to have imagined that a general indiscriminate literacy would be compatible with keeping up something like the proportion that he saw existing between good literature and bad; and here the great and good old man ran hard aground on Gresham's law.

I spent some time last year in Portugal, where the status of literacy and the conditions of the book-market

are about what they were in Mr. Jefferson's America.
One saw very little "popular literature" on sale, but an
astonishingly large assortment of the better kind. I made
my observations at the right moment, apparently, because, like all good modern republicans, the Portuguese
have lately become infected with Mr. Jefferson's ideas
about literacy, and are trying to have everybody taught
to read and write; and it interested me to see that they
are setting about this quite in our own incurious, hand-
over-head fashion, without betraying the faintest notion
that anything like a natural law may be a factor in the
situation.

Doubtless what has happened elsewhere will happen
there. In the first place, the Portuguese are likely to discover that, while no illiterate person can read, it is a
mere *non distributio medii* to conclude that any literate
person can read. The fact is that relatively few literate
persons can read; the proportion appears to be quite
small. I do not mean to say that the majority are unable
to read intelligently; I mean that they are unable to read
at all—unable, that is, to gather from a printed paragraph anything like a correct idea of its content.[1] They
can pretty regularly make out the meaning of printed
matter which is addressed to mere sensation, like news-

[1] In the interest of accuracy, I submitted these statements to a
prominent educator who says that his experience fully bears them
out. He carried on experiments over a dozen years with college
freshmen—that is to say, with persons who were not only literate
but had gone so far as to pass their entrance examinations. He ex-
perimented in this way: selecting a paragraph of very simple but
non-sensational prose, he asked the freshmen to read it carefully;
then to read it carefully again; then to read it aloud to him; then
to write down in their own words the gist of what they had read.

matter, statistics, or perhaps an "informative" editorial or article, provided it be dosed out in very short sentences and three-line paragraphs; but this is not reading, and the ability to do it but barely implies the exercise of any faculty that could be called distinctively human. One can almost imagine an intelligent anthropoid trained to do it about as well and to about as good purpose; in fact, I once heard of a horse that was trained to do it in a small way. Reading, as distinguished from this kind of proficiency, implies a use of the reflective faculty, and not many persons have this faculty. According to the newspapers, Mr. Butler, the president of Columbia University, was complaining the other day that the practice of reflective thought had pretty well ceased among us. There is much to be said on this topic, but it is enough to remark here that literacy will not do duty for the power of reflective thought where such does not exist, nor does a state of literacy presuppose its existence.

To cite a rather comical illustration of this truth, a clerical friend lately told me of the troubles that a candidate for confirmation was having with the Nicene Creed. This candidate was a man of more than middle age, completely literate, and of considerable prominence and wealth. The article that he balked at, curiously, was non-

Hardly anyone could do it. He made the interesting remark that the reflective faculty is more easily stirred by speech than by print, because the communication of ideas by hearing is an older racial practice; their communication by sight is something comparatively new, to which the race's capacities are not as yet well adjusted. Therefore, he said, the indiscriminate spread of literacy puts into people's hands an instrument which very few can use, but which everyone supposes himself fully able to use; and this, obviously, is mischievous.

theological and non-metaphysical; it was the one which sets forth that the Saviour "was crucified also for us under Pontius Pilate." He wanted to know why they crucified Pontius Pilate. He knew who Pilate was, and what his rôle was in the great drama, but he had never before heard anything about Pilate's being crucified, and he wondered why the circumstance should be brought in here as one of those things which a Christian should know and believe to his soul's health.

A person of any literary experience, even the slightest, sees such instances time and again, not usually so bizarre perhaps, but essentially quite the same—instances which show beyond peradventure that the persons concerned simply can not read. When confronted with a paragraph requiring the most moderate exercise of reflective thought, they are helpless; and no equipment of sheer literacy can possibly make them less helpless. I have published so little and in such desultory fashion that I can claim nothing for my own experience with the public; yet I regularly get letters from persons who have manifestly gone as far with my writings as literacy will carry them, but who are as manifestly unable to make out correctly the content of English prose as simple and direct as the prose I am writing now.

As for the operation of Gresham's law, one need say little; it is so easily discerned that a glance at the nearest news-stand will show it well enough. The average literate person being devoid of reflective power but capable of sensation, his literacy creates a demand for a large volume of printed matter addressed to sensation; and this form of literature, being the worst in circulation, fixes the value of all the rest and tends to drive it out. In this country, for example, it has been interesting to see the reluctant and gradual submission of some of our few "serious" publications to this inevitable fixing of value. They have brought their aim continually closer to the aim of journalism, addressing themselves more and more to sensation, less and less to reflection, until now their policy favours almost exclusively the kind of thing one would naturally look for in an enterprising Sunday newspaper. Only the other day I came across a market-letter put out by a firm of literary agents, and I observed with interest that "the serious essay, travel, foreign-affairs type of article is unlikely to find a good market, unless by a well-known name."

I had occasion lately to look up something that one of our "quality" magazines published in 1874, and as I went through the two bound volumes I noticed the relative space they gave to material addressed to the power of reflective thought. For curiosity I made a comparison with last year's issues of the same magazine; and I can not suggest a more convincing exercise for any person who doubts the validity of Gresham's law in the premises, nor can I suggest a more substantial basis for generalization.

Gresham's law has, in fact, done far more than revolutionize publishing; it has set up a brand-new business. In the face of this fact, which seems none too well understood, we see publishers and authors occasionally showing something of the splendid intrepidity that one admires in the leader of a forlorn hope, and one thinks of them as perhaps the most public-spirited of all created beings. A little while ago my friend Mr. van Loon, for example, who is a very learned man, brought out a superb book, quite the kind of book that he himself would be glad to read; one need say no more for it than that. He and his publisher must both have known that they could not turn a penny by it; if it paid for itself it would be lucky. The full force of Gresham's law was pressing them instead to put their time and money into another of Mr. Van Loon's ingenious and attractive vulgarizations of history, which would be "sure fire" with a large literate public; yet they went on—went on in the teeth of the fact that under Gresham's law a "good book" must be a book as much as possible like another book that has sold a great number of copies.

What I have been driving at in all this is the suggestion that if we must reëxamine our social theories we should do so with an eye to natural law. Everyone seems a little uneasy about these theories at the moment, and many of our leading publicists say that they must be overhauled; well, if that be so, the practical thing would be to keep on the lee side of natural law while we do it. We have been a little careless about this hitherto, and the consequences are suggestive. Our idea of mass-education, for example, does vast credit to our intentions; like perpetual motion, the thing would be fine if it would work, but the mischief of it is to keep it from colliding with natural law. As results stand now, a graduating class of two, three or five hundred persons is practically nothing but a tableau-display of what the law of diminishing returns can do when it tries. Again, the promotion of mass-literacy is a noble experiment, but apparently there is no way to accommodate our idea of it to the insidious action of Gresham's law. With regard to these and all other aspects of our equalitarian social theory,

my only aim is the humble one of suggesting that we
bear in mind the disregard that nature has for unintelligent good intentions, and the vixenish severity with
which she treats them.

IV

Finally, since various aspects of political theory are
much to the fore just now, I suggest that we follow the
same procedure with regard to them. Our ideas about
the function of government may be very praiseworthy,
very creditable, but surely the first thing is to find out
whether natural law is with them or against them; and
it is in this connexion that I cite the third law which I
mentioned at the outset. This law is fundamental to
economics, though for some reason our professional
economists seldom say much about it; its formula is, *Man
tends always to satisfy his needs and desires with the
least possible exertion.* Not, it must be understood, that
he always *does* so satisfy them, for other considerations—
principle, convention, fear, superstition or what not—may
supervene; but he always *tends* to satisfy them with the
least possible exertion, and, in the absence of a stronger
motive, will always do so.

A candid examination will show, I think, that this law
is also fundamental to any serious study of politics. So
long as the State stands as an impersonal mechanism
which can confer an economic advantage at the mere
touch of a button, men will seek by all sorts of ways to
get at the button, because law-made property is acquired
with less exertion than labour-made property. It is
easier to push the button and get some form of State-
created monopoly like a land-title, a tariff, concession or

franchise, and pocket the proceeds, than it is to accumulate the same amount by work. Thus a political theory that admits any positive intervention by the State upon the individual has always this natural law to reckon with.

At the time our government was set up, a century and a half ago, some political thinkers, notably Franklin, had perceived the incidence of this law. Their idea was that it should be no function of the State to intervene upon society's economic life in a positive way, but only negatively as occasion required, to punish fraud and to safeguard the general régime of contract.[2] Aside from this, the State's only function should be that of safeguarding the lives and liberties of its citizens.

Contemporary British liberalism had the same idea; it advocated a rigid policy of State abstention. Liberalism's career was remarkable in presenting a most instructive object-lesson to those who study it in the light of natural law. Its programme missed one point, admitted one exception; and the consequences of this imperfection forced liberalism in the end to turn squarely around on its basic principle, and become godfather to the most elaborate series of positive interventions ever conceived in England.

This imperfect policy of non-intervention, or *laissez-faire*, led straight to a most hideous and dreadful eco-

[2] Franklin wrote, "Perhaps in general it would be better if government meddled no farther with trade than to protect it and let it take its course. Most of the statutes or acts, edicts, *arrêts* and placarts of parliaments, princes and States, for regulating, directing or restraining of trade, have, we think, been either political blunders or jobs obtained by artful men for private advantage, under pretense of public good." *Works*, Vol. II, p. 401.

nomic exploitation; starvation wages, slum-dwelling, killing hours, pauperism, coffin-ships, child-labour—nothing
like it had ever been seen in modern times. Mr. Gradgrind, Mr. Bottles and Mr. Plugson of Undershot
worked their will unhindered with a fine code of liberal-
ist social philosophy behind them, and the mess they
made shortly stank in the nostrils of all Christendom.
People began to say, perhaps naturally, if this is what
State abstention comes to, let us have some State intervention.

But the State *had* intervened; that was the whole
trouble. The State had established one monopoly,—the
landlord's monopoly of economic rent,—thereby shutting
off great hordes of people from free access to the only
source of human subsistence, and driving them into the
factories to work for whatever Mr. Gradgrind and Mr.
Bottles chose to give them. The land of England, while
by no means nearly all *actually* occupied, was all *legally*
occupied; and this State-created monopoly enabled landlords to satisfy their needs and desires with little exertion or none, but it also removed the land from competition with industry in the labour-market, thus creating a huge, constant and exigent labour-surplus.

Franklin saw this clearly; he used Turgôt's language
almost word for word to show that the "labour-problem,"
qua labour-problem, really does not exist—it is purely a
problem of State intervention, State-created monopoly.
He said:

Manufactures are founded in poverty. It is the number
of poor without land in a country, and who must work
for others at low wages or starve, that enables under-
takers [i.e., enterprisers] to carry on a manufacture. . . .

But no man who can have a piece of land of his own, sufficient by his labour to subsist his family in plenty, is poor enough to be a manufacturer and work for a master.

But liberalism did not see this, never saw it; and the consequence was that in the end it was forced by political necessity to sponsor an ever-lengthening, ever-widening programme of regulations, supervisions, exemptions, subsidies, pensions—every measure of positive State interference, almost, that one could think of.

When the State has granted one privilege, its character as a purveyor of privilege is permanently established, and natural law does not permit it to stop with the creation of one privilege, but forces it to go on creating others. Once admit a single positive intervention "to help business," as our euphemism goes, and one class or group after another will accumulate political power in order to command further interventions; and these interventions will persist in force and frequency until they culminate in a policy of pure Statism—a policy which in turn culminates in the decay and disappearance of the society that invokes it.

Such is the grim testimony borne by the history of six civilizations, now vanished, to the validity of the law that *man tends always to satisfy his needs and desires with the least possible exertion*. We ought to be quite clear about this, as a matter of understanding the course of our present governmental policy. Some of us incline to regard the New Deal as something out of the run of our national history and unrelated to it, whereas it is exactly what the run of our history must inevitably have led up to.

One need only shift a switch in the New York Central's yard some three inches to determine whether a train shall go to Boston or to Chicago. We shifted the switch a hundred and fifty years ago, and set the national train going toward the Chicago of hundred-per-cent Statism, with our old friend natural law furnishing abundant steam. The New Deal means merely that we are now somewhere near South Bend, Indiana, and going strong; and if anyone knows how to reverse that train and head it toward Boston without an awful catastrophe, he is just the man that a good many of us would like to see.

The American State at the outset took over the British principle of giving landlords a monopoly of economic rent. That shifted the switch; it established the State's character as a purveyor of privilege. Then financial speculators sought a privilege, and Hamilton, with his "corrupt squadron in Congress," as Mr. Jefferson called them, arranged it. Then bankers, then industrialists; Hamilton also arranged that. Then, as the century went on, innumerable industrial subgroups, and subclasses of special interest, were heard from, and were accommodated. Then farmers, artisans, ex-soldiers, promoters of public utilities, began to accumulate political power with a view to privilege. Now, since the advent of universal suffrage, we are seeing the curious spectacle of the "unemployed" automatically transformed into the strongest kind of pressure-group; their numerical strength and consequent voting-power compelled Mr. Roosevelt to embrace the extraordinary doctrine that the State owes its citizens a living—an expedient little noticed at the time, I believe, but profoundly interesting to the student of historical continuity.

Moreover, as we saw in the case of Mr. Bottles and Mr. Plugson of Undershot, when the State confers a privilege, natural law impels the beneficiary to work it for all it is worth; and therefore the State must at once initiate a whole series of positive interventions to safeguard, control and regulate that privilege. A steady grist of "social" legislation must be ground; bureaus, boards and commissions must be set up, each with its elaborate mechanism; and thus bureaucracy comes into being. As the distribution of privilege goes on, the spawning of these regulative and supervisory agencies also goes on; and the result is a continuous enhancement of State power and a progressive weakening of social power, until, as in Rome after the Antonines, social power is quite extinguished—the individual lives, moves, and has his being only for the governmental machine, and society exists only in the service of the State. Meanwhile, at every step in this process, natural law is pushing interested persons, groups and factions on to get clandestine control of these supervisory agencies and use them for their own advantage; and thus a rapid general corruption sets in, for which no cure has ever yet been found, and from which no recovery has ever yet been made.

V

In a sense, no doubt, it seems officious to write a paper that squints toward a vindication of natural law, because natural law is quite competent and handy at vindicating itself; it needs no help, and has no notion of being any man's debtor. Tiberius Cæsar said in his strong commonsense way that "offenses against the gods are the gods' lookout," and perhaps it would be as well, certainly less thankless, if one should leave in their hands such little matters as those I have been discussing. Indeed, one must do that finally, for one can not hope that criticism based on nothing more pretentious than the plain natural truth of things will be much regarded; so probably as much or as little would be gained by doing it in the first instance.

Yet, in another view, it may be worth while to point out to simple-minded persons like myself, who are perhaps a little confused by the outpourings of publicists and the din of eager innovators, that natural law still exists and is still a respectable force. I have read many words about social reconstruction, industrial reconstruction, political reconstruction; in fact, as I write this paper I am inspired by the latest efforts in the great new enterprise of "economic planning." All these, in their innocent disregard of natural law, remind me of a piece of music I once saw, written for a cornetist. The music was good, but the composer had not put in any rests for the cornetist to take breath; well, as soon as one saw that, one knew that further examination of the piece was pointless. So, in what the journalists call "these hectic days," a suggestion that natural law is still at work, and that there is really not much that one can do about it, may be somewhat of a time-saver and trouble-saver to minds of the simpler sort, like my own; and to such, and such only, I offer it.

New York, February, 1934

17

The Path to the River

NORMALLY, one turns into it at about my age; or perhaps I should say, one discovers that one has turned into it, that one is off the main road. The point of departure must have been most inconspicuous; I did not notice it. All I recall noticing is that of a sudden I began to miss many familiar sights and sounds of traffic. The sensation was odd; it was somewhat like the sensation in one's ears when a locust stops chirring. It brought a certain pleasant ease, a feeling of liberation and expansion of spirit, leading up to an untroubled interest in the rich and quiet beauty of my new surroundings.

The path is winding; one can only guess how long it is, for one can not see its end from any point short of its last turn, apparently. Its declivity, so far, is very gentle; one hardly feels it. One has few companions, latterly almost none, and one is content with that. One or two are willing to go the whole way with me, which troubles me a little, and I hope they will not insist. They are young, and taking this journey just for company would break the continuity of their lives, and be but a tedious business, besides. Then, too, since they will some day be taking it on their own, why should they force themselves to take it twice?

My most astonishing realization is that I have lost a great lot of luggage. I can not imagine what has become of it. I thought I was still carrying almost all I started out with, but as I stop to count it up, a great deal of it is gone. Evidently one begins life like a person on his first trip to Europe, by loading up with things that one has no use for, and that get themselves left behind un-noticed, here and there. I discover that my interest in many matters which I thought were important, and would still say, off-hand, were important, no longer ex-ists; interest in many occupations, theories, opinions; re-lationships, public and private; desires, habits, pleasures, even pastimes. I can still play good billiards, for instance, and if anyone asked me, I should reply unthinkingly that I enjoy the game; and then it would occur to me that I have not played for months running into years, and that I no longer care—not really—if I never play again. As an item of luggage, billiards has gone by the board, though I do not know when or how; and many matters of apparently greater importance have gone like-wise. Other orders of interest, however, remain intact and, for all I can see, as fresh as ever—I think indeed much fresher, though this may be an illusion. At all events, it is only with these that I feel any longer a gen-uine concern.

Awareness that this process of unconscious sifting and selection has been going on is presumably final evidence that one is off the main road and well on the path to the river. It is called, rather patronizingly, "the acquiescence of age"; but may not that mean no more than an acquiescence in matters which have in the long run proven themselves hardly worth troubling one's head about? "The fashion of this world passeth away," said Goethe, "and I would fain occupy myself with the things that are abiding." If that be the acquiescence of age, make the most of it.

One in my position is expected, I believe, to have a special interest in questions about what, if anything, takes place on the other side of the river, and whether we are likely to have any hand in it. Do we indeed cross the river or do we melt away forever in its depths? I have never had any curiosity about these matters, nor have I any now. Such thought as I have given them has been unaffected, so far as I am aware (and I can not be responsible for what the Freudians might find going on in my *Unbewusstsein*) by any feeling of personal concern. Perhaps this absence of curiosity and concern may go some way towards giving my thoughts a passing interest for others who are likewise incurious and unconcerned, and I, therefore, write them down.

II

As a very small boy with a lively imagination and a budding sense of humour, I used to entertain myself at great length with speculations on what the human world would be like if we all lost our bodies. I made it out as on the whole a rather attractive picture, except that eating had to be counted out; this seemed an appalling calamity. It was more than balanced, however, by other considerations which were all to the good, such as the doing away with clothes and houses and, above all, the abolition of work. Work was inseparably related to food, clothes and shelter; and if there were no need for these, nobody would have to do any work, which suited me admirably.

There appeared to be no difficulty about imagining a distinct human personality existing apart from physical properties, or pervading them, as magnetism—whatever that is—pervades iron. In fact, the most nearly real world I knew, the only one about which I could approach anything like certainty in my own mind, was the world of consciousness. I got at its phenomena directly and was sure of them. I was not so sure of the phenomena of my physical environment, for I got at these indirectly through sense-perception, and my senses were always letting me down in one way or another; I was always having to true up their findings by experience, mostly disappointing, as in the case of plaster-of-Paris fruit or the apparent soundness of tree-limbs. Again, a sense of the most intimate phenomena of consciousness —those associated with music, for instance—was quite incommunicable by physical means; yet I saw that it was somehow communicated to other persons, to my father and mother and certain cronies, for they made responses so appropriate as to leave no doubt.

So sense-perception impressed me early, if vaguely, as a rather poor and fallible interpreter of my environment, and as having little to do with establishing my most interesting approximations to certainty. As I grew older and understood better what stringent limitations our dependence on sense-perception does really impose on us, I began to wonder how our actual present environment would appear if one could get oneself in immediate contact with it, and be no longer dependent on the very incomplete and special reports of five extremely imperfect and special faculties, or "senses"; one so imperfect, indeed, as to be almost useless, and another not much more valuable.

Thus it came about that when at the age of twenty or so I read the observations of Professor Huxley and others on the subject of consciousness, they seemed simple and clear, and not in the least surprising. "The transition from the physics of the brain to the facts of consciousness," said Romanes, "is unthinkable." Just so did it impress Huxley, as not only inexplicable but actually unthinkable. Consciousness exists, and we know it only as existing in association with that which has the properties of matter and force; yet it is clearly not matter or force or any conceivable modification of either; and an interpretation of it in terms of matter and force is simply beyond the power of thought.

By way of illustrating this as simply as possible, Professor Huxley cites the sense of red colour. I am now writing by the aid of a lamp done in red lacquer; I look at it and see that it is red. Trace the whole process of this perception; suppose, says Huxley, that you could watch all the light-waves, nervous reactions, molecular motion in the brain, possible electrical discharges, "as if they were billiard-balls"; at the end you would be as far from the ensuing fact of consciousness, "the feel of redness," as you were at the outset. The phenomena of consciousness can be to some extent controlled by mechanical means or by some appropriate chemical agent like bhang or alcohol, but this throws no light on the nature of consciousness itself. A colour-blind person's testimony

about my lamp might not agree with mine, but the content of his consciousness, whatever it may be, is still as
unaccountable in terms of matter and force as mine is.

At high noon one day on a crowded street in Berlin,
a man behind me hooked his umbrella into my collar,
after the manner of Mr. Squeers; and while he was hand-
over-handing me in, I recognized him as an old acquaintance who had also recognized me. Just what was it that
we recognized? There was not a particle left of the
physical structure that either of us had seen before; we
had not met in fifteen years, and our former bodies were
all worn out and gone. A resemblance persisted, one may
say, and he recognized that. True, no doubt, in the first
instance; but he also immediately recognized *me;* and
in my turn, instantly getting by the accidents of clothes
and physique, I also recognized *him.* One may say, again,
that our "personalities" overlived these physical changes,
and recognized each other. Very well, but just what is
personality, and how does it contrive to do all this over-
living, and where do matter and force come in? If personality can overlive three, four or half-a-dozen bodies
and get along so handsomely without them, might it not
manage, on a pinch, to get along without any?

In other words, since we know consciousness only in
association with matter and force, must we regard that
association as intrinsic and essential? Can consciousness
persist dissociated from them, either independently as
bare "personality," or in association with some unknown
quantity which has not their properties? If someone
says flatly that it can not, we must ask him how he knows
that. If he says it can, we must ask the same question.
The conditions of inquiry being what they are, if he can

give a competent answer either way, all we can say is that he is just the man whom a great many people would like to see.

III

Such was the conclusion reached by the best science of the last century, and I have not heard that latter-day science has brought forward anything to invalidate or modify it. One may, therefore, I think, be excused from taking interest in any attempts to reach a "scientific proof" that personality survives death, because these attempts must rest on evidence of the senses; and in the premises, this order of evidence, as we have seen, is inadmissible. For example, if a person says to me, "You will never see me again after I die," it is open to me to reply, "Possibly; but since I never yet saw you and do not see you now, why should I expect to see you then? I see a body and some clothes, but the body is not the same one that I saw a week ago or that I shall see a week hence. I never saw *you,* never shall and never can."

Or, on the other hand, suppose he says, "I can prove objectively that I shall be alive after death," I might reply, "Why, bless you, you can't even prove objectively that you are alive now." Nor can he. Or, suppose he puts it thus, "Personality survives death; and to prove it, I will cause bells to be rung, furniture to be moved around, photographs to be taken, and messages to be written, all by invisible agencies. I will even cause a disembodied spirit to invade my own physical organism and control it, and give you assurance by word of my mouth." I might reply, "Yes, that is all very fine, very good, but it may not prove what you say it does. It may prove only that you are an uncommonly smart man. Moreover, if I admit your evidence, I can admit it only *in limine;* that is, admitting that the disembodied spirit is there and is alive, what does that prove about a future state for you, me, Tom, Dick or Harry? Nothing. If the spirit says it does prove something, who knows but the spirit may be wrong? The assumption that it must be right is clearly gratuitous." The *Santissimo Salvatore* spoke with immense philosophical profundity and soundness when He said that "if they hear not Moses and the prophets, neither will they be persuaded though one rose from the dead." If any conviction on this matter is to be reached, its reasonableness must be established by an entirely different method of approach.

This, apparently, is as it should be. Prince Alfonso of Castile is said to have remarked that if he had been present at the creation of the world he would have suggested some valuable improvements. If man were never to progress beyond the first stages of development, we too might suggest some; we might suggest a world in which there should be no pain, sorrow, labour, bereavement, disappointment, hardship. The trouble is that without these any progress in human development is unimaginable; nobody could ever get on. If there were no such thing as pain, if nothing hurt, the race would not last six months; if there were no sorrow or hardship, it could not elaborate any more character than a jellyfish—and so on. When one thinks these matters through to their logical end, taking careful account of everything, one finds it impossible to imagine human development going on as satisfactorily in any other circumstances than those we are in.

Hence it is probably no bad thing that man is held

down pretty closely to the consideration of one world at a time. Suppose it were otherwise; suppose that by some miracle he were able to get what we call scientific proof that he would, or that he would not, live after death,— cogent, irrefutable proof,—it is easy to imagine the utterly enervating preoccupations that would ensue upon him in either case. One can not say whether they would be more debilitating and retarding in the one case or in the other. The flavour of such preoccupations that one gets from the history of mediæval Christianity is enough to intimate the irreparable misfortune that would be brought upon a world possessed by certainty on this point. It is a great advantage to us that by the ordinary standards of analysis we can know no more than we do; that conviction alone is admissible in the premises, and that the reasonableness of conviction, whether affirmative or negative, can be made out only by an order of evidence which is distinctly subjective.

For my own part, I have an extremely strong conviction that human personality overlives death; so strong and apparently so reasonable that I have long ceased to question it. This is not the same thing as saying I believe that my own personality will survive death, for I can not say that; in fact, I doubt it. I have an instinctive feeling that it will, but when I examine the basis available for rationalizing that feeling, I find it too slight to command confidence. These statements are not inconsistent, as I shall presently show.

IV

There are certain orders or categories of human activity which are useful and indispensable, to which, nevertheless, one can not attach the idea of persistence. As I saw in my childhood's fancies, there is an insurmountable incongruity in such an association; natural truth is all against it. These are what St. Paul calls the ἐπίγεια. The King James Version gives the translation, "earthly things"; that is to say, lines of activity which meet purely physical demands, and which can not be conceived of as going on after these demands have ceased. For example, one can not possibly imagine oneself manufacturing motor-cars "to all eternity," as our phrase goes, or selling bonds, or running a bank. Death would automatically dissociate us from innumerable pursuits such as these, and we can perceive at once that it must do so.

On the other hand, there are categories of activity with respect to which an association with persistence is at least imaginable. Natural truth, if not flatly affirming this association, is at least not flatly against it. In the light of natural truth there is no absolute, violent, even ludicrous incongruity in the suggestion, such as instantly appears when we attempt to contemplate the idea of persistence in the other categories just mentioned. For example, when the Greek mathematician said that God "geometrizes continually," his conception strikes us as not precisely unimaginable or precisely ridiculous. Natural truth goes along with it far enough at least to intimate that despite philology, geometry is not quite one of the ἐπίγεια. It has a differentiating quality. As much may be said of the Aristotelian ποίησις, and of the exercise of certain virtues and affections. Even the clear and lucid perception of the later Greeks saw here no actual collision with natural truth. The last words of Socrates, both to his friends and to his judges, the elegiac lines on

Plato's young and gifted successor, the Master of the Portico, show conviction open either way; natural truth asserts no jurisdiction. It is only in the association of persistence with the practice of love [1] that we first see natural truth legitimized in the parentage of a profound conviction. Heliodorus and Diogeneia, the devoted lovers, died within the same hour; and their friend Apollonides declares that death is no bar to their felicity, but that they are now "as happy lying in the same tomb as they were when lying in the same bed."

As I have already said, I could not possibly prove, even to myself, by the accepted standards of scientific analysis, that I am alive at this moment. *Cogito ergo sum* takes one but a precious little way, as has often been shown. Yet I know I am alive, I have an unshakable conviction about it, built up in this way: In the realm of the ἐπίγεια there are certain disciplines, mostly very rigorous, such as the discipline of hard physical work, the discipline of business and its competitions, the various disciplines prescribed by the social order. Engagement with any of these is attended by a keen sense of *life,* and the closer the engagement the more abounding and exalted the sense becomes; and this sense gives rise to strong conviction and supports it. Our vernacular has terms that reflect this experience. A hard set of tennis, for instance, makes one feel "all alive," and so does a fast bout at commercial competition, or leading a forlorn hope in an attack on sales-resistance. Thus too do we speak of the "live man" or the one who is "alive on his job."

[1] Ἀγάπη; στοργή hardly covers it; certainly not ἔρως.

Conviction on this point, then, appears to be pretty strictly the fruit of experience. Now, leaving the ἐπίγεια and going over into the categories where natural truth is not so peremptory about its findings, one meets with a precise parallel to all this. Here, too, are certain disciplines; the discipline of pure mathematics (to touch again the matter already spoken of), the discipline of the ποίησις, the discipline peculiar to the successful practice of certain virtues and affections, such as the affection of love.[2] Here, too, the occupation with these disciplines is attended by a strong sense of *life,* but life of a different order, corresponding to the order of experience that excites this sense. Here, too, the more one does with these disciplines, the harder one works at them, the stronger this sense becomes; and when it becomes strong enough it leads to conviction—sometimes, as in my own case, impersonal. I am sure as one can be of anything in this highly uncertain world that *some* will survive death, but my own practice of these disciplines has been too weak-willed and fitful to give me any assurance beyond this; it does not assure me that I shall be among them.

The point is that in both sets of categories alike the sense of life and the conviction proceeding from it are matters of experience alone. Conviction is conditioned by experience; it is practically impossible to entertain a conviction that experience does not to some degree back up. Hence it is not to be wondered at that a conviction of the persistence of personality is relatively uncommon at the present time. Both in the realm of thought and action the general tendency is towards an

[2] Ἀγάπη again.

exclusive preoccupation with the ἐπίγεια; take the ἐπίγεια away, and practically the whole of our experience disappears with it; there is nothing left with which we can associate the idea of persistence. It is impossible to make conviction transcend experience; hence the effort to relate persistence to the only kind of life that we have ever experienced results merely in the consciousness of a wholly inadmissible anomaly.

The fifteenth chapter of the First Epistle to the Corinthians is one of the few passages of Scripture that remain at all generally well known; we hear it read at funerals. We may have remarked how impatiently and perfunctorily St. Paul runs off his arguments for persistence, or as he calls it, "immortality," and that in the midst of his arguments he drops in the apparently irrelevant quotation from Menander, that "evil communications corrupt good manners." There is no irrelevance here, however; the quotation conveys the whole point of what he has to say. The civilization of Corinth, like our own, was wholly made up of mundanities; and the gist of the passage is as if he had said, "Here are your arguments, but I might about as well save my breath. You can not take them in, not because they are unsound, but on account of your evil communications; you can not transcend your own experience. The only kind of life you know anything about is not worth being immortal, and you can not help being aware of it."

One may not overpress the point, of course, yet it is worth remarking how persistently the Biblical writers relate the idea of *life* to the practice of special disciplines in the second set of categories that we have been noticing. One such discipline "tendeth to *life*"; in the practice of it "is *life,* and in the pathway thereof there is no death." Another discipline, vividly personified, declares that "whoso findeth me findeth *life.*" Of another it is said, again, that whoso followeth it "findeth *life.*" Of another, that its admonitions "are *life* to those that find them." The great exponent of these disciplines is said to have come that they "might have *life.*" His precepts go forth, "and they that hear *shall live.*" A concordance will show the almost unfailing regularity with which this association occurs; and while, I repeat, too much may not be made of it, one may observe in it, as far as it goes, an interesting correspondence with the suggestions of experience.

V

Unquestionably, too, as one studies the order of nature, one gets certain intimations of purpose. One must speak of these with great caution, for theologians and poets alike have monstrously exaggerated their evidential value. Nevertheless, they are not, I think, to be flatly disregarded; natural truth invests them with a plausibility that is doubtless slight and vague, but is yet sufficiently definite to keep them in view. Nature appears to be very wasteful and to "make for righteousness" by very roundabout ways; yet on closer inspection her most conspicuous wastes turn out to be made in behalf of some highly interesting economies. The most one may say, perhaps, is that under her régime nothing is going to be saved, finally, that is not worth saving. Whether all that is worth saving will be saved is, of course, another question. Still another question is, how far our present estimate of what is and what is not worth saving will be found in the long run to accord with her inscrutable economy.

For my own part, I could not hold it as any count against the order of nature if my own personality did not survive death. On the other hand, my intimations of purpose in nature, vague as they may be, are distinctly affronted by the suggestion that certain other personalities do not survive death. If Socrates, Marcus Aurelius, Dante, Cervantes, Shakespeare and Rabelais do not survive death, then, as all my intimations lead me to see it, the order of nature is a most inglorious fizzle. My intimations bear the same testimony, too, in behalf of equally eminent practitioners, such as we have all seen and revered, who have passed their days in humbler stations and whose eminence, therefore, remains unknown to the world at large.

I see no reason why the great majority of mankind should survive death, because experience and the intimations of purpose in nature alike present the idea of persistence as an achievement, as a matter of diligent and progressive adaptation to environment; and here, too, the analogy with our physical life seems close and orderly. Von Humboldt says that no one could pass from Siberia into Senegal without losing consciousness; one could not expect to survive a sudden change into an environment wholly alien to one's adaptations. To all appearances, then, in respect of adaptation to any other than a purely secular environment, the vast majority are so dead while they live that one may suppose they stay dead when they die. It is quite conceivable that a person's body might outlive his faculty for adaptation; in other words, that his soul—if for convenience one may so designate that faculty—may die before his body does. Quite conceivably his soul might die without his knowing it. Quite conceivably, too, on the other hand, he might have enough vitality of faculty to stand the actual transition into an alien environment, but not enough to enable the process of adaptation to go on; somewhat like a consumptive who has been too dilatory about measures which, taken in time, would enable him to rebuild himself after moving into a favourable climate.

It is thus, then, that I view the matter; and as I have said, as far as I am aware, I view it without prejudice, and certainly with no sense of personal concern. Experience, the intimations of purpose in nature, and the largest available understanding of nature's economies, all, I think, suggest this view as at least permissible; the view that—

> the energy of life may be
> Kept on after the grave, but not begun;
> And he who flagged not in the earthly strife,
> From strength to strength advancing—only he,
> His soul well-knit, and all his battles won,
> Mounts, *and that hardly,* to eternal life.

VI

My adventures on the main road were uncommonly many and diversified. I sought them with ardent curiosity, turned them inside out, and got all kinds of profit from them, except money and fame. Yet I can think of none that I would wish to repeat, nor do I ever find myself looking back upon any of them with any sentiment except that of thankfulness that almost all of them were good. They were good, I have had them, I am sincerely thankful for them, but now that their time is past, I seldom think of them at all, and never desirously or with regret. Nor am I ever tempted to throw any inquiring glances forward into the future, not even upon the fact of death. One rehearses for it so many thousand times on going to bed at night that one is unlikely to get stage-fright over the full-dress performance. The most beautiful figure in all human history, meditating in his en-campment "among the Quadi, at the Granua," told him-self with hard common sense that "he who fears death either fears the loss of sensation or a different kind of sensation. But if thou shalt have no sensation, neither wilt thou feel any harm; and if thou shalt acquire an-other kind of sensation, thou wilt be a different kind of living being, and thou wilt not cease to live."

Among the many keen interests of the present there are one or two little undertakings that for my own satis-faction I should like to complete, or at least to carry farther forward. I hope the path will remain peaceful and easy enough to permit me to work at them while I am still able to work. But I am not aware of any anxiety even about this, for these conditions are not in my con-trol, and if they went against me I could find no reason to complain. My state of mind with reference to them, as far as I know it, is that of one who regards himself as

. . . a citizen of this great state, the world: what differ-ence does it make to thee whether for five years or three? . . . Where is the hardship, then, if no tyrant or unjust judge sends thee away from the state, but nature who brought thee into it? The same as if a prætor who has employed an actor dismisses him from the stage: "But I have not finished the five acts, but only three of them."

Thou sayest well, but in life the three acts are the whole drama; for what shall be a complete drama is determined by him who was once the cause of its composition, and now of its dissolution; but thou art the cause of neither. Depart then satisfied, for he also who releases thee is satisfied.

Brussels, February, 1932

—